The Will of a
Wildflower

PEGI ROBINSON

1st WORLD
PUBLISHING

Copyright © 2017 Pegi Robinson

Published by 1st World Publishing
P.O. Box 2211, Fairfield, Iowa 52556
tel: 641-209-5000 • fax: 866-440-5234
web: www.1stworldpublishing.com

First Edition

LCCN: 2017915211
Softcover ISBN: 978-1-4218-3790-1
Hardcover ISBN: 978-1-4218-3791-8
eBook ISBN: 978-1-4218-3792-5

This material has been written and published for educational purposes to enhance one's well-being. In regard to health issues, the information is not intended as a substitute for appropriate care and advice from health professionals, nor does it equate to the assumption of medical or any other form of liability on the part of the publisher or author. The publisher and author shall have neither liability nor responsibility to any person or entity with respect to loss, damages, or injury claimed to be caused directly or indirectly by any information in this book.

Children change after a near-death experience, even though they can't process any of it. We return with gifts we don't even know we have—until we use them.

The Will of a Wildflower is my spiritual journey through this life. Everyone has a unique story. This one is mine. What I learned—once I stopped avoiding the past and bravely turned around and faced it—amazes me every single day.

Contents

THE WILL OF A WILDFLOWER POEMS

PART ONE

CHAPTER 1
MY CHILDHOOD

My earliest memory: I am sitting in a crib talking to God. I tell Him there's been a mistake. I was sent to the wrong family. I don't know these people. They are strange, and they don't like me.

I just sit there, waiting to be switched to my correct family. I'm sure the problem will be solved. But nothing happens. No explanation. No reassurance. No rescue.

Silence is my answer.

I am on my own.

My mom quit school to marry my dad when she was seventeen. They called their first child "Junior." While Dad was at work, Mom sometimes would walk down the street to the local tavern. She said she didn't drink—she just wanted someone to talk to. It was raining one day as she pushed Junior home in a stroller from the tavern. Mom's oldest sister Diane saw them, and she confronted Mom. Junior had been sick, and Mom had taken him out in the rain without a jacket. Out of concern for the baby, Diane called and told our grandma.

Mom was at a neighbor's house when Grandma arrived and found Junior home alone. Grandma called Dad at work and told him to take Mom and the sick baby to the hospital, where Junior died a few days later. He was nine months old. A gravestone and a black-and-white 8 x 10 photo hanging on Mom's living room wall are all that's left to prove that Junior existed.

My parents had four more children—Molly, Sam, Tonya, and Jack. Just after Mom turned twenty-seven, she became pregnant with me. She was determined to have an abortion. Her hands cracked and bled from hanging laundry out on the clothesline, and she couldn't take it anymore. Dad bought her a clothes dryer to convince her to have me, and he "got fixed" after I was born.

Mom said I was a pretty baby, born with a full head of thick black hair. She named me Peggy, after her friend. I was born on Lord Street in Marietta, Ohio, in 1961.

When I was three, we moved to a tiny five-room, three-bedroom house that sat close to the road in Constitution, Ohio. Grandpa and Grandma had lived there, but they grew tired of life in the country and moved back to town. My parents were buying the house from them on land contract. The property was once part of the Underground Railroad, but that was long before my time.

A train station sat at the bottom of our hill. After it closed, my uncle opened a store in the building, which was later torn down. A nearby pond is still there and is now a popular family fishing spot. I don't think anyone used it but us back then.

According to Mom, our grandma was half American Indian and her grandmother was an Indian squaw. She said Grandma didn't want anyone to know, because in Grandma's day "being Indian was the same as being black."

Us kids looked like our mom—light olive skin, dark brown eyes, and dark brown hair. Dad said we were "members of the Blackfoot Tribe" because we were always suntanned and ran around bare-footed. Our parents tried to keep our shoes good for school and church.

A church bus driver, a neighbor, or our grandma always made sure we went to church so Mom could "enjoy a little peace and quiet" at home. I used to pray that our parents would go to church with us, especially if a special event was planned. Tired of my nagging, Mom said, "Your grandmother crammed religion down my throat for years. I've had enough of it to last me a lifetime." Another time, she told me Dad was an atheist.

Our school clothes were mostly a box of hand-me-downs from our older cousins. I also wore my older sisters' hand-me-downs, including knee socks and underwear. I used rubber bands to hold up my socks because I was tiny for my age, and Tonya was chubby.

I didn't care that we were poor. I didn't even know we *were* poor until Tonya pointed it out to me one day, saying, "Look at how they dress, and then look at us. Look at their house, and then look at ours. See what they eat, and then look at what we eat."

That's when I realized she was right. We were poor, but I still didn't mind. I thought we were a happy family—and, besides, Mom told us rich people were mean and selfish.

Molly was the oldest, but it wasn't long before I was assigned to keep an eye on her. Mom would say, "There goes Molly, carrying her suitcase down the train tracks. She's headed for town again. Go get her." I was the only one Molly would listen to. Sometimes while we were driving down the road, Mom would yell, "Grab her!" because Molly had opened the car door and started to step out as we were speeding down the highway. Whoever sat closest to her had to pull her back in and shut the door. Molly never seemed to be afraid, but when I grabbed her, the sight of moving pavement under her foot scared me enough for both of us.

Tonya was a tomboy, a bully, and Dad's favorite. Dad laughed at everything she said and did. He ignored the rest of us—unless we were in trouble. Tonya claimed I was Mom's favorite and picked on me because of it. During the day, she hated me. But at night when we shared the bottom bunk, she was nice to me. That's how I learned unconditional love.

My oldest brother, Sam, was mean. He usually played by himself in the woods. I think he tried to avoid Dad as much as possible so he didn't get in trouble. My brother Jack was Tonya's puppet—he did everything Tonya told him to do, which usually involved picking on me or ignoring me.

Dad worked and Mom was a housewife. We were a typical 1960s Appalachian Ohio family. I loved being a kid. I loved my family deeply—especially Mom.

Although we were poor, Dad somehow managed to buy a brand-new console color TV. We also received a lot of nice presents for Christmas. For Easter, we received baskets of candy, and we three girls each got a new dress and an Easter bonnet for church. We watched fireworks and made homemade ice cream on the Fourth of July, and sometimes we played softball as a family. Dad would take us fishing, swimming, and for a Sunday drive in the country. My favorite memory of Dad is sitting beside him on the front seat, watching him whistle as he drove.

Sometimes we went to the drive-in, and once in a while, we got a root beer float at the A&W. It came in a frosted glass mug. Adults got a big one, and kids got a small one. A waitress delivered it on a tray that attached to the driver's window.

One day, we each got our very own Kentucky Fried Chicken dinner in a box. As our parents passed them to us in the backseat, I said, "Wow! I didn't know we were rich!"

At Halloween, we searched through old clothes to create costumes. We went trick-or-treating in town, and Tonya and I were in awe of the beautiful big homes there. I would stare at the beautiful entryways and staircases as long as I could before I was pulled away to the next house.

All our aunts, uncles, cousins and grandparents lived nearby in the same county. No one visited our home very often, but we visited our grandparents regularly, and each of us could sometimes spend the night with our favorite cousin.

Sam, Tonya and Jack called me "Spoiled Brat," "Mommy's Little Baby," and "Tag Along." They wanted nothing to do with me—other than to pick on me. I think my mom spoiled me because I was small and dainty, while Tonya was boyish and Molly was mentally disabled. It was nice to feel special, but it came with a price. I was hated by Sam, Tonya, Jack, and Dad for it—everyone but Molly, who was "in her own little world." She was always nice to me.

My only defense against the bigger kids was to scream for Mom. I learned to scream so loudly the older kids would run, covering their ears. I took pride in that. I loved to see them run away from me. I felt I had some control. I was tired of being picked on all the time.

One day when I was five, I played in my room with my Barbie dolls. Mom walked in, wiped her neck with a dishtowel, and fanned herself. "It's too hot," she said. "Let's go swimming." I jumped up quickly and changed into my bathing suit. Jack did the same. Tonya was the only other kid at home that day.

Mom told Jack and me to go on ahead, and she and Tonya would be down after bit. Jack bolted out the back door, and I ran after him. I couldn't keep up. He was already at the far end of the pond diving in by the time I reached the shallow part.

I couldn't swim like the older kids—I could only dog paddle. I carefully eased myself into the water as Jack swam laps to the center of the pond and back again. I used my feet to feel around the bottom, since there were sudden drop-offs that were dangerous. If I slid into a deep section, I'd be in over my head.

I couldn't believe Mom had let us go swimming without Dad being there. We always went as a family. I also wondered why she let Jack and I go alone. It was fun to have that much freedom, but it was also a little strange. I noticed a board floating near me—which felt like I'd just received a present!

Us kids often played in a nearby dump looking for treasures—it was like we were shopping. We were always excited to bring things home to play with. Mom always told us, "Take that right back where you got it from!" So, it was natural for me to wonder if that board could work as a raft.

I laid my belly across the board and it worked perfectly! I headed straight for the center of the pond. When I got there, I yelled out to Jack, "Look at me!"

Jack swam towards me. When he got close, I knew I'd made a horrible mistake. Jack always took toys from me.

Before I could get out the words, "No, don't!" Jack grabbed my board, jumped on it, and returned to doing his laps.

Terror consumed me. I splashed and screamed. I was in way over my head, and I didn't have a clue how to swim. I tried to keep my head above water, but it was no use. I'd had no business going out in deep water. I should have learned to swim—or at least tread water—or float.

My eyes were above water only a few seconds before I sank. I thrashed under the water, but I couldn't get my head back up. I sank down deeper and deeper, tumbling and turning and gulping water. I screamed until I couldn't scream any more, and then I cried. I was surrounded by muddy brown water. I couldn't tell which way was up or down or sideways. I didn't know if I was heading for precious oxygen or the muddy floor of the pond. I didn't know what to do. I was lost.

It was lonely, being where nobody can see you, where no one knows you need help. I thought about Mom and Tonya still at the house. I could see them in my mind. They were in the kitchen, getting ready to come down. I saw them clearly—like I was there watching them. I felt connected to them, like I was tapping into their emotions. I had looked up to them as my protectors, yet they were unaware I was drowning. They were calm as they concentrated on finding things in the kitchen to bring to the pond.

My gulping turned to choking, then to horrific pain in my throat. I thought my throat would burst. I was terrified.

Then everything stopped. It was like I'd been sleeping and just awakened. Everything had changed. I was calm and still and quiet. I was no longer choking or crying. I thought my parents must have lied to me, since they'd always said to be careful so you don't drown. But I wasn't drowning—I was just fine. I didn't hurt and I could breathe. I was no longer scared. I couldn't wait to tell the other kids about this. We can so breathe under water! There is no such thing as drowning!

The muddy water turned a bright, shiny, transparent green. It was no longer scary down there. I could see everything. It was beautiful! I dropped down even deeper, but it was okay. I was nudged by fish swimming right past me. As they bumped into me, my body drifted off to the side. They kept banging into me. I watched with amazement as I saw their eyes, mouths, fins, and tails move right in front of my face. I wondered why they weren't afraid of me now. When we fished with Dad, sometimes we tried to catch fish with our bare hands. They always got away because they were afraid of us. Why weren't they afraid of me now?

A vivid memory surfaced—I could see myself, a year or so earlier, staring into our goldfish bowl. I wondered why the fish weren't afraid of the little treasure chest at the bottom. I decided the fish knew the chest wasn't alive, so it wasn't a threat to them.

And now I understood. The fish in the pond weren't afraid of me because they knew something I didn't—I wasn't alive.

I didn't want to be known as the dead girl at the bottom of this pond. That would make people feel weird about fishing and swimming there, and this was a fun place. I didn't want to ruin it for everyone. I also didn't want my family to think of me being left down there. I imagined them always saying, "That's were Peg is."

Then I began to rise to the top of the water. That's when I noticed I was no longer in my body. I had left my body behind, and now I was my thoughts and my vision. My thoughts were the only thing I heard, and they were so clear now. I heard nothing else—only my thoughts.

It wasn't just my hearing that changed. My vision was different too. I could see under the water and over the water at the same time. It was like when you look at a fish tank. You are outside it looking in, and you can see above the water and under it at the same time.

I somehow knew I had a choice—to stay under the water or to go above. I was bored with under, so I chose above. It seemed like things happened now just by thinking about them.

Above the water's surface was a sunny summer day full of vibrant color. I wanted to go up higher, above the pond, but I was afraid of heights. I realized how silly that was. Still, I wanted to take it slow, since this was all new to me.

I rose slowly until I got as far as the tree tops, which I figured was high enough for now. I could go higher later. I stayed directly above the center of the pond, above where my body floated below. I couldn't see me, but I still felt like me. I had changed and I was adjusting to it.

I looked down at the ground at the entrance of the pond near the road. I had walked down there so many times before, but I'd only seen the surroundings at eye-level for my height. I felt special now, being able to see from up high like I was hovering in a helicopter. I looked straight across at our road as it bent up around the top of the hill. Tree tops were behind me. Railroad tracks led towards town to my right, and the highway was in front of me. I saw over the highway clear to the Ohio River. Seeing the world from this height, I knew I must have been a ghost. And the only thing I knew about ghosts was what I'd seen on TV.

Later, I looked down again and noticed Mom and Tonya were at the pond now. They sat on a bedsheet, rubbing lotion on themselves at the entrance of the pond. They faced the pond but looked at each other as they talked. I couldn't hear them, but I sensed their conversation. It was intimate, mature and female.

They still hadn't noticed I was missing. They still didn't know I drowned.

I was envious of Tonya, being able to talk to Mom like that. I wasn't yet old enough to have that sort of discussion, and now I never would. I was angry that they weren't even looking for me. The anger melted away and I looked around again. And there, down on my left, was Jack. On my board! He didn't need my board, but he had taken it away from me and I had drowned without it! Anger rose up in me until it turned to rage. I had never felt emotions that intense before. They were strong, and they would sweep in like a wave, growing in intensity. Then they would quickly roll away, leaving me with insight.

I judged my family and saw they did not love me. It wasn't fair! Something informed me that children were sent to earth to be loved. That's why God sends them here. But no one loved me. I was sad for a moment, then that swept away too. I thought about my situation and what to do now. There were benefits to being a ghost. I no longer had to listen to my parents or worry about getting into trouble. Since I could hover over the pond, I figured I could fly too. I could go wherever I wanted.

I looked around. Which way should I go?

I imagined old people-ghosts talking around a table in an empty house. I imagined myself walking in and asking if they knew where any kid-ghosts were. I saw this as if it were happening. I then thought about all the graveyards in town, and I thought maybe I could find kid-ghosts to play with there. I imagined that I searched in town for signs of others like me. Kids die sometimes too, I thought. I just had, and yet I was still here.

I was about to leave to do these things, yet, in thinking about them, I felt like I'd already done them. It felt like I was in several places at once, yet I never moved from the pond.

Then, for the first time since I'd died, I heard something other than my thoughts. An adult female voice spoke in the air in front of me a short distance away. "Don't go yet," she said. "If they find you soon, you might go back."

I was annoyed that someone was still going to tell me what I could and couldn't do. Find me? That wasn't going to happen. They haven't even noticed I was gone yet. I couldn't even see me down there, so how would they find me?

And go back? What was she talking about, go back? I was already dead. You can't just go back. That isn't how death works.

Still, she told me to wait. I figured I would, but it wasn't going to do any good. I would wait awhile, and then I would leave. I didn't have to listen to anyone anymore.

The next thing I knew, I was dangling over my brother Jack's right shoulder. He was carrying me back to the house. Mom and Tonya walked in front of him, to the right, looking straight ahead and whispering.

I looked down at the pavement. Water poured out of my mouth and nose like a garden hose. It tasted terrible! The water ran down Jack's bare back. He was mad that he had to carry me, and even madder that I was now barfing on him. Jack called out to Mom, "Can I put her down now?"

Mom and Tonya swung around. Mom grabbed her chest and gave a deep sigh of relief.

I was alive. I had come back to life while Jack carried my dead body back to the house.

Mom nodded to answer Jack's question, then she and Tonya turned around and continued walking up the hill to our house. I could still feel their conversation and emotions. Tonya looked at

Mom, listening to her, as if she were Mom's best friend. Mom had been worried she would get in trouble for letting me drown. They were going to keep my drowning a secret and pretend that it had never happened.

Jack set me down and ran to the house. He had complete disregard for me. He didn't care that he caused me to drown, nor that I was now alive. He just wanted to get home.

I now stood alone in front of the train tracks in the middle of the road, feeling like a drowned rat. I was sick as a dog from the pond water still in my belly. I was weak and could hardly stand. I felt so alone. I needed my family, but they were only concerned about themselves.

Then I remembered what I had just learned. My family didn't love me, it wasn't fair, and I was just about to go exploring.

I had a choice now—I saw an alternative to this life. I could go up the hill to that family who didn't love me, or I could walk back to the pond and get in. That old feeling that I'd been sent to the wrong family returned.

I knew drowning hurts and it was very scary, but I wouldn't fight it this time. Soon I could be flying. I came so close to being free, but here I was, still trapped in this hopeless, loveless situation. They would wonder how I ended up back in the pond. It would be a mystery.

An angel appeared before me, hovering slightly above the road. When I'd been dead, it was her voice I'd heard. Now I could see her too. She was made of white light in the shape of a young woman in a flowing white gown of light. "No," she said softly. "Don't."

"Why not?" I asked. "You know they don't love me."

She didn't deny it. She told me I would have love someday.

"When?" I asked.

"When you have your own family, you'll have lots of love."

"Promise?"

"Yes, I promise," she said in her soft voice. "But it won't be for a while yet."

I knew she was about to leave, so I asked her where I'd find that love. She looked to her right, raised her right arm, keeping it straight, and pointed her finger towards town.

Then she was gone.

Still sick and weak, I walked sadly on up the hill and went home. I felt very alone. Even though no one else loved me, I had to love myself. I had to become my own mother.

I went to my room, put on my nightgown, and went to bed. I had to take care of myself now. I couldn't depend on anyone else. I reached down and picked out a children's book and flipped through the pages. I saw the familiar picture of the house made from a boot. "The old woman who lived in a shoe, had so many children, she didn't know what to do."

I turned the page to a picture of the inside of the old woman's house. Beds were lined up neatly in a row like an orphanage.

The angel promised I would have a lot of love someday when I had my own family. Now I wanted to have a large family. I wanted so many kids I wouldn't know what to do with them all. In my heart, I was now a future mother. I fell asleep, warm and safe in my bed, filled with hope and knowledge of my future.

For a while after the drowning, strange things happened to me. I went to my Sunday School class, which was just up the road from our house. The teacher said to pick out a coloring page from a shelf and sit down. I found a coloring sheet of Jesus and the children. This is it! *This is the one!*

The picture showed Jesus sitting on a big rock with one child on His lap and several other children standing beside Him on His left, like they were all waiting their turn. The picture became alive and real. As I colored, I sang "Jesus Loves Me" over and over, growing louder and louder.

Then I saw myself standing in front of Jesus, waiting for my turn. I was in Heaven, I was going to sit on Jesus's lap next, and I couldn't wait! I wanted to push the other kid off, but I knew that wasn't nice. I had to be good. Yet, I was so impatient. I could feel how much He loved the children. I felt His sweet, tender love. I soaked it up like I was bathing in sunshine. I was so happy.

Something informed me that he loved children of every color. I felt that very strongly, even though it wasn't on the page. It was an insight. As I sang the words "Jesus loves me, this I know, for the Bible tells me so. Little ones to him belong, they are weak but he is strong," the more excited I got and the louder I sang. I was in the classroom, yet I was also in the air and I was in Heaven.

The whole class complained to the teacher, asking her to make me stop, saying I was too loud. I looked over at one little boy my age with a crew cut. He held his hands over his ears so tight that his elbows were stuck straight out. He squeezed his head hard as he pleaded with her to make me stop.

The teacher looked at me, smiled, and said, "No. Leave her be. She is full of the Spirit."

CHAPTER 2

THE WILDFLOWER

Not long after my drowning, Dad took us all to a nearby lake to go fishing. This was my first time being around water since I had drowned. I didn't want to bother the fish—I was bored with fishing now. I wanted to go exploring.

As I wondered off, Mom motioned Jack to go with me. "Keep an eye on her," she whispered through her cupped hand.

Apparently, I couldn't be trusted alone around water now.

Jack followed me into the woods along the lake, complaining that he had to babysit me now. He said it wasn't his fault that I had drowned.

Tonya caught up with Jack to see what was going on. He complained to her about me always getting him into trouble.

They went off in another direction, leaving me alone. I found a clearing and looked around. It was boring and ugly—nothing to look at. There were old dead leaves, cracked dry mud, rotten logs, and sticks. Yet I wanted to find something beautiful. So I just stood there. I didn't want to go anywhere else, but I didn't know why.

Then I noticed a beautiful wildflower growing out from under a rock. I sat down and stared at it. How did it grow with that rock on top of it? How was that even possible? Yet, there it was, all alone. It just seemed so happy to have made it, to have survived. It danced in the wind, rejoicing, not caring where it was, where it came from, or that it was alone.

My thoughts grew clear and the outside world became quiet,

like it had when I'd drowned. A vivid memory came to me. I remembered my mom, her two sisters, and my grandma sitting outside one day. They were discussing their favorite flowers. One by one, they each proudly announced a fancy, hard to grow or expensive flower-shop flower. I thought of the girls in my class who wore pretty dresses, their long, curled hair decorated with bows and ribbons, and wearing fancy socks and shoes. I envied them. Dad always made us girls get pixy haircuts, and I was poor and plain.

Then I gained insight. It was explained to me that I was like this wildflower, and those girls were like those fancy flowers that needed special care to grow. But I didn't need all that stuff to survive, because I had something they didn't have—a strong will. Like the wildflower, I was growing up in a harsh environment. I was given a promise that I would survive too. Someday, I would be strong and free like that wildflower, and I would dance in the wind and celebrate my victory. I had a long, hard road ahead of me, but because of it, I would have a strength inside of me that those girls would never know.

And there was one more thing. Like that wildflower, I would also grow up to be beautiful.

I was so excited to learn about my future! I went to the lake and picked as many wildflowers as I could find. I knew, no matter what anyone else thought, they were all beautiful!

As we got in the car to go home, Mom yelled at me to throw those "weeds" out. I did. But I grinned all the way home squished in the backseat, knowing I had a secret.

Nobody knew it yet, but I was not a weed. I was a flower, and someday I would be strong *and* beautiful!

One day I woke up from a nap while the other kids were all at school, and three people stood beside my bed. They were dressed like they were from a hundred years ago. There were two women, one old and one young, and a tall man in the middle. I had a feeling they were wife, husband and daughter. The women both wore long dresses with full-length aprons. Their hair was pulled back tight. The man wore faded bib overalls and a long-sleeve dress shirt. They just stood there, not moving, looking down at me like they knew me.

They looked sad, as if they were mourning my death. I figured they must be seeing someone else when they looked at me, because I didn't know them.

I closed my eyes, hoping they would disappear, but they didn't. I had a feeling they were ghosts, but they looked real. Finally, I closed my eyes tight and said I wouldn't open them again until they were gone. Finally, when I opened my eyes, they were gone.

I got up and found Mom in the kitchen, cooking. I asked her who those people were in my room. She said no one was there but us. I described them to her and assured her they were there. She said the only people she knew who looked like that were the ones who lived up the hill from us a few houses, but they had moved. They had dressed like that. They didn't believe in running water or electricity.

When Tonya got home from school, I bugged her until she agreed to go to that house with me. We peeked in the windows, and the house was empty. We went inside and saw a water pump between the living room and kitchen area. I didn't believe in ghosts—I had forgotten about when I was a ghost when I drowned—so, to me, they had to be real people.

Then one night after I went to bed, I had to get up to pee. I wasn't allowed to get up after we were put to bed. I knocked on the bathroom door. Dad was mad because I was up and had disturbed him. He slammed his newspaper shut so loudly that I jumped. He came out of the bathroom and told me I had to sit there all night and not get up—and I wasn't going to tattle about it to my mother either.

I sat there all night and was bored. My butt felt like it was cut from the rim of the toilet seat. I held my arms down straight to lift myself and get some relief, but I never got up. I looked around at everything there was to look at in the bathroom. I stared at the small window along the ceiling above the toilet. I wished I could go outside and catch lightning bugs. I wished very hard, even though I knew it wasn't possible. Then I sat there and watched a ghost come out of my right side. It crawled up the wall on its elbows and knees right beside me, then it went right through the glass of the window and was gone.

I didn't understand. Was that me, a part of me, or someone else? I feared someone would see "me" out there, and I would get blamed for what "it" did.

What was it doing out there? I struggled to make sense out of what had just happened. If it were me, I would be catching lightning bugs, but what if it were in the neighbor's house playing with that girl's toys? Or maybe it was flying over the river or down the highway. It was free, but I was still sitting on the toilet.

I waited for it to come back. It never did. I was afraid Mom would walk in and notice it was gone. But the more I thought about it, I realized she wouldn't notice anything. After all, I was still there.

I wondered how I could just wish something—or just think about it—and then it would happen, no matter how impossible. I didn't understand at all. Tonya was the one with the "vivid imagination," not me. I always tried to tell the truth. I hated lies. Yet these things were happening.

I never told anyone about these experiences and dismissed them as soon as they were over. What made perfect sense to a limitless soul, made no sense to my childish mind.

Finally, morning came. When I heard Mom getting pans out to start breakfast, I ran as fast as I could to my room so she couldn't ask any questions. As I ran, I heard her say, "My, you're up early."

Things soon went back to normal. My "normal" was Sam always trying to touch me, and I was sick of having to watch out for his hands. I had to be quick and swat his hands away.

One day, we came back from a Sunday drive. Molly and Sam had stayed home alone. Molly greeted me in the boys' room. She smiled. "Peggy, you are going to be an aunt. Sam and I pretended we were a married couple, and I'm going to have Sam's baby."

My advanced insight kicked in. I knew Sam had raped her. I use the word *rape* because Molly was as innocent as a kitten. She couldn't understand what was happening, and Sam knew it.

Later, Mom told us that Dad had molested Molly, and he had

gone to counseling for it. I was socially awkward, very shy, and had trouble putting my feelings into words, yet, I felt outrage over my big sister being harmed when no one else seemed to care.

I think I was around six when Dad had a party at our house. His brothers and their teenaged sons played cards in our living room. Later, I grew tired and went to bed. I had my nightgown on and walked into the room we three girls shared. I didn't bother to turn on the light—I just went straight to bed.

After I crawled in, I realized a man sat there. He picked me up and put me on his lap. It was my uncle. He slipped his fingers inside my underwear and said, "This is what a little girl feels like."

My eyes adjusted to the dark. There was a circle of men standing in my room. My uncle passed me to the man on his left, and around the circle I went, being passed like I was an object for show and tell. Every one of them slid their fingers in for a quick feel—all but one. He said no, he wasn't doing it, but he still passed me to the next man on his left.

Some leaned against the wall, some sat on our dresser.

I had been so tired and it happened so quickly, I barely had time to understand enough to react. By the time I had been passed to the last man standing in front of our bedroom door, I thought only of escaping. A man blocked the door, but I shoved his legs out of the way.

I think I ran out the door, but I can't remember anything else until later that night.

We were all in the car that night and Dad was driving. Tonya was up front in the middle and Mom was in the front passenger seat. I was squished in the backseat behind Dad, sitting by Jack. Sam and Molly took up the rest of the backseat. I was crying.

Jack said, "There's something wrong with Peg. She won't stop crying."

Mom turned to look, as did Tonya. "What's wrong?" she asked.

I told her I didn't want to go to our uncle's house, and why.

Mom yelled at Dad about his family being sick, and how his dad and brothers molested his sisters. When we got to my uncle's house, Dad went inside. Mom had told him to go beat the shit out of them. The kids all laughed and told stories about what they imagined was happening in there. Apparently, we had watched too many Westerns.

When Dad didn't come back, the stories turned dark. What if Dad was hurt? Anger and blame turned on me. It was my fault if Dad got hurt. It was because of me.

Finally, Dad came out and told us we all could go in now. "They are going to apologize." I hoped they were all bloody with black eyes.

As we walked in, they were lined up on either side of the long hallway. They were not hurt at all. They were all laughing. They shook our hands, welcoming us in as they passed through to the kitchen in the back. I darted off to the left, through the living room and then the dining room and back, like a mouse trying to escape a trap. I then darted up the stairs on the right of the hall and into a bedroom. There was a closet with an attic door. I hid in there. I heard Jack come up to play with our younger cousins. I opened the door and told him where I was. I made him promise to come get me when it was time to go. I didn't want be left there when my family went home.

Another time, Jack and I were playing in the woods across the railroad tracks, near a gas well. We found an old Jeep and jumped in. Jack was pretending to drive while I sat in the front passenger seat. He said to pretend we were on a date and he had just picked me up. I went along with it and asked where he was taking us. We were having fun and not doing anything wrong.

Sam came along and jumped in the backseat and pulled me back there with him. He was angry and said he would show me what people do on a date.

I screamed and fought to get away from him. Jack told him to leave me alone. We were just playing. Sam tried to make it sound like we were being dirty because we used the word "date." He tried to justify his actions by blaming us.

Just then Tonya rode by on her bike and yelled that she was going to tell on us. She pedaled home as fast as she could, laughing all the way. She reminded me of the wicked witch on *The Wizard of Oz.*

Sam and Jack ran after her. I ran too, but I was too small to catch up. I was the last to get there, so I knew my story would never be believed. Dad always believed Tonya anyway, since she was his favorite. I knew the boys would come up with a story to tell Dad too.

When I got to the house, Dad already had the kitchen chair in our bedroom and his belt out for the whipping. He called me in. He said Tonya already told him what had happened, but he wanted to hear my side of it. Dad had a certain way of whipping us. He whipped us from oldest to youngest, starting with the oldest and working his way down to me. He repeated this procedure until someone told the truth—or, at least, something he believed. I was anticipating him whipping us until he was given "the truth." He had already talked to the other kids—now was my turn. The other kids must have been in the kitchen, because I didn't see them when I walked in the front door.

I didn't know how to tell the truth about what had happened. I couldn't talk "dirty." I wanted to tell Dad about how Sam always tried to touch me, and how someone needed to make him stop, but I didn't have words for any of that. So, I came up with a lie—one that would put a stop to Sam trying to do stuff to me for good. I knew the incident in the Jeep could've been worse if Tonya hadn't come along when she had. Who knew what Sam planned to do next? Not after what he'd done to Molly.

So, when Dad asked, "What were you doing out there? Tonya said she saw something."

I replied, "Sam called it *fuck*."

Dad's eyes bulged and he yelled for Sam.

Sam went in our room, and it sounded like Dad beat him half to death.

The worst belting we ever got from Dad was on Christmas day. Dad wanted to know who tore an arm off Tonya's doll. Nobody would admit doing it. Dad lined us up and belted us for what felt like eternity. We just wanted to go to our grandparents' for Christmas, like we always did after we opened presents. But we couldn't go until someone told the truth. Mom said Tonya likely did it herself, just to see the other kids get in trouble, since she sat on the couch beside Mom, laughing at us getting whipped.

So then Dad told Tonya to get up there in line too, and the line began again.

Finally, Sam lied and said, "Fine! I did it!"

We knew Sam hadn't done it. He just said he did to put an end to the beating. Tonya didn't even like dolls. She and Jack broke my toys every Christmas right in front of me, and Dad never did anything about it. Jack played with dolls, so I wondered if he did it. Years later, Jack admitted he had. But on this Christmas, Dad beat Sam worse than ever and shamed him for making us all get whipped.

It's funny how some things stand out in your mind forever while other things are forgotten. I was hit by a car and knocked out when I was little. I woke up in the hospital and was fine. We had been at Sam's baseball game, and I was busy making sand castles in the parking lot. Jack told me a car was coming and he ran out of the way. I thought he was just trying to steal my sand. I only have a faint memory of it. All I remember is guarding my sand one minute and being rushed into the hospital on a stretcher the next, with my grandma yelling at the paramedics to hurry up.

Tonya was always trying to scare me with ghost stories, and would take me to a large abandoned house down the road and try to convince me it was haunted. Just like I always had to protect myself from Sam's sneaky hands, I had to protect myself from Tonya's lies and pranks. One day Tonya got me, though.

Our family went somewhere without Tonya and me—possibly because I always got carsick. Even though I was very skinny and small for my age, my belly stuck out like the starving kids I saw on TV from Africa. Anyway, Tonya had to stay home and watch me. As Tonya and I stood on the front porch watching our family leave, a white van went up the hill. Tonya grabbed me and pulled me inside and quickly closed all the doors and pulled the curtains.

"Didn't you see that van on the news?" she asked.

I said, "No."

She said the police were looking for that van, because it was full of people who went around killing kids when their parents left. She peeked out of the curtain and said we had to hide in the hall closet. They had seen our parents leave and they had seen us on the porch, and now they were coming for us.

We sat in the closet hiding for the longest time. She said she heard them come in, and now they were in the kitchen, now they were in the living room. They knew we were there and they wouldn't stop until they found us. She told me about other kids they murdered.

I was scared, but she said I couldn't cry or they would hear me.

She said they would look in the closet next, so we had to hurry and run to our bedroom and shut the door fast. This was a life-or-death move. They could grab us and kill us. We ran and got in our bedroom. Now I was even more scared. We were out of our safety net. She said we had to prepare to die.

We got on our hands and knees and begged God not to let us suffer. She said I had to tell God that I was ready to die. I was still on my knees praying into my tightly held hands and crying when suddenly Tonya jumped up, ran to the bedroom window, pulled back our bedroom curtain, and cheerfully announced, "Mom and Dad are home!"

She opened the bedroom door and ran to the back door to greet them.

Yet, I tried to never tell on her so she would like me.

This began my policy of not just fearing lies, but hating them, as well as trying to never be made a fool of again by them. I saw the pain that lies can cause and despised people who hurt others with lies. Sometimes I became the tattletale they accused me of being because I was determined to stand up for the truth.

One day when I was in the fifth grade, I discovered that my best friend Stacy had quit speaking to me. Girls in our class huddled around her and asked what was wrong. She told them, but wouldn't tell me. It broke my heart to see her crying and not be able to help her. Her family and mine had recently become friends. Her parents, Don and Kathy, were now friends with my parents. Sam was friends with their oldest son, and he was dating their oldest daughter, who became friends with Tonya. I was friends with Stacy, and her little brother played with Jack.

I always had a hard time making friends, since I wasn't smart and I was immature. I was happy to finally have a best friend in my class. Our classmates stopped picking on me after Stacy became my friend. I had been allowed to go to her house several times to have tea parties.

Stacy had told me how she missed her dad because he was a truck driver and rarely home.

So now I kept asking Stacy to please tell me what was wrong.

The other girls patted and rubbed her back.

Finally, Stacy blurted out, "My dad isn't my dad anymore! He's *your* dad now because your mom is a whore!"

I was shocked—and speechless. I didn't want her dad. I didn't understand what was happening. But I stayed away from her after that. The other girls kept babying her and glaring at me. The boys then got in on the drama too, to impress the girls. Everyone in my class hated me. The girls kept pulling Stacy away from me. I have heard that nothing bonds people together like hate does, and this was a perfect example of that. This was the most unified I'd ever seen our class.

By lunch time, it was unbearable. I hid behind the big curtain on the stage. Some boys found me and went and got more boys. They kept running up to me, kicking me, spitting on me, and calling me names. They came at me with fists drawn and making threats.

After lunch, I was too afraid to walk back to class. I stayed hidden on the stage. Someone found me and took me to the office. They called my mom and told her to come get me—they said it wasn't safe for me there.

I stayed home from school for a few days. Then Mom told me I didn't have to worry, we were moving. I didn't have to go back there.

I was trying to watch Captain Kangaroo in our living room when Don, Stacy's dad, walked right in our house and stood in front of the TV. He kissed Mom for a long time, then he turned to me, smiled, and said, "I am your dad now."

Inside, I heard myself scream, "My mom *is* a whore!"

I didn't want Don for a dad—I already had a dad!

CHAPTER 3

AFTER OUR PARENTS DIVORCED

We moved from the country back to Marietta, Ohio. I was in the middle of the fifth grade. At my old school, girls still had to wear dresses to school and a uniform in the all-girls gym class. At my new school, everyone wore blue jeans, and boys and girls took gym together. I felt like I was caught in a time warp because I didn't have blue jeans.

On my first day of school, I wore a dress and Tonya's baggy underwear. It was summersault day in gym class. We were told to line up. As we reached the gym teacher, we were to do a summersault.

"I can't," I said. "I have a dress on."

The teacher was a man, and he replied, "It won't be anything I haven't seen before!"

The whole class broke out in laughter. As I did the summersault, I was laughed at again. I never went back to gym.

When I got by with skipping gym, I started skipping school. Nobody ever noticed. I passed grades five and six with hardly ever attending. My grades were bad, but nobody cared. I went to the office once and confessed, but they just ignored me.

Not long after we moved to town, Mom left with Don. Dad moved in with his girlfriend and her two girls, Darlene and Barb, who were around Tonya's age. Dad pulled into the alley behind our house one day and made us go out and meet our new stepsisters.

Mom moved back home, but went on the road a lot with Don. I was now usually the only one home. Mom gave Tonya money and food stamps to take care of me, but Tonya spent it all on herself and her friends while she was at their houses.

Sam was having sex with a neighbor girl, Karen, who lived alone and babysat her little brother while their dad worked away. Sam and Jack stayed there. That family always had a lot of food.

I wasn't allowed to go there because I was a "tattletale." They drank and smoked, and I caught Jack doing stuff to Karen's little brother in their attic. I decided it was probably for the best that I didn't know what they were doing there anyway.

Later, Sam and Jack were accused of raping my younger cousin, so they weren't allowed back at my grandma's house anymore. My younger cousins were like little brothers to me. I cried when our grandma's neighbor told me about it. I felt like it was my fault for not being there to protect him. I worried I wouldn't be allowed to play with them now because of what my brothers had done. My little cousins loved me and looked up to me, and I liked being like a big sister to them. I wondered if maybe this wouldn't have happened if I would've told on my brothers more. These were things I still couldn't discuss with anyone, even if there was anyone to listen. I just didn't have the words.

Then Don moved in.

One day, Don's wife Kathy showed up. She drove down our street and ran right into the back of Mom's car. She got out, and she and Mom got in a fistfight in our front yard. Mom tried to dig Kathy's car keys into Kathy's wrist. I went inside and told Tonya, who just laughed, so I called the police. Kathy took her four kids and left town. I don't think Don ever saw them again.

Don was a violent alcoholic who picked on Molly. Molly was working, but Mom took her paychecks, so she finally moved in with Dad, then she got married to Daryl.

One day, Molly and Daryl came to get her stuff while Mom was gone, but Mom arrived home and caught them in the front yard. I was watching them from the front porch. Mom threw a bed rail at Daryl's head like a spear. I yelled for him to watch out just in time, or Mom would've killed Daryl.

Molly and Daryl lived right up our street, but Mom didn't allow me to go see her. When I found out they had a baby, I went anyway. Molly was living in a storage building and said she wasn't allowed in the house to see her baby. Her mother-in-law had taken Molly to Columbus and had tests done. They said Molly had a chemical imbalance, and it was Mom's fault. Molly said she thought it was Dad's fault, because he was the one who molested her.

I took Molly to a neighbor's house and had her call her case worker and tell them she was living in a storage building and not permitted to see her baby. They came and got her. I told Mom, thinking she would feel sorry for her and help her. But she was still too mad at Molly for moving in with Dad.

One day I was home alone taking a Mr. Bubble Bath and playing in the bubbles with my Barbie dolls. Sam barged in and demanded that I get out of the tub and lie down on the floor. I refused. I covered myself up with a towel and screamed at him to get out. Sam insisted and wouldn't leave. I stood in a puddle of water with bubbles on the floor, still demanding that he get out. It was a shouting match, me saying, "Get out!" and him telling me to "Lie down!" He said if I didn't do what he said, he would lie and tell Mom that I "screwed all the neighbor boys."

I said I'd rather have a whipping than what he was going to do to me. I told him to go screw the fat girl next door—I already knew he was doing that anyway. He glared at me awhile, speechless. He knew I would tell. He left.

One other day, he came in the house again when I was alone. I was at the foot of the stairs, so I was cornered between Mom's bedroom and the living room. He shoved into my face a Polaroid picture of our mother naked. He said to look at it, and said he took the picture of her himself. I kept turning my head and tried to get it out of my face. He said he'd had sex with her, and so had his friend Brian.

I called him a liar and said Don must have taken it and Sam had found it under their mattress, and he'd better put it back. He kept laughing and tormenting me with it. He insisted he was telling the truth.

I was eleven and still very small for my age. Sam was sixteen and the size of a full-grown man now.

Later, I saw him holding something over Mom's head and laughing since she couldn't reach it. She slapped him and yelled at him to give it to her. Sam just laughed. Sam had the upper hand now because he was bigger than Mom, Dad was gone, and Don wasn't there that night. I knew there was some sort of blackmail going on. Mom had lost control of Sam.

One night, just as it was getting dark out, my cousin Sandy and I were walking to her house on the West Side. A car pulled up beside us and stopped. They started to say something to us, so we walked over to the passenger side window. There were two men, hippies, and the one in the passenger seat opened the glove box, pulled out a pistol, and told us to get in.

We ran to Sandy's house and told her parents. They called my parents and the police. Tonya came to see what was going on. Tonya said we were lying and tried to make us say we were lying. She told everyone we admitted to making it up, but we hadn't made it up. Tonya was afraid we would get attention, and that was something reserved only for her.

Unfortunately, they believed Tonya.

The police never came.

One night a friend's older sister, Sarah, knocked on our door. She said men were chasing her and tried to rape and kill her. She asked if she could come in. Don said she couldn't, even when I told him what she'd said. He said if I let her in, he would beat my ass. She pleaded for help.

She looked terrified. I hid her under my bed until morning, then she snuck out and went home, after thanking me.

Tonya saw Sarah leaving and told on me that next morning. As Don beat me on our living room floor for it, I cried for my mom to help me. Mom pretended to yawn as she read a magazine. She giggled and refused to look my way. That is an image I will never forget. Don was her "little baby" now, not me.

Even though I was hungry when nobody was home, I found

ways to entertain myself. One day I decided to build a Barbie hotel. I walked several blocks to the Super America gas station to get boxes. It took many trips on a hot summer day, but I finally had enough. I used a staple gun to attach them all together. It took up half of my side of the bedroom wall. I used crayons and pens to draw curtains and wallpaper on the sides, and carpet on the bottom.

People always said I was too old to still be playing with dolls, but now that I was old enough to make Barbie clothes and a hotel, it seemed like a waste to stop. I also heard that once you're done with dolls, you start liking boys. I wanted to stay as young as I could, for as long as I could. I would swing at the school playground at night, singing for hours at the top of my lungs. I knew I sounded terrible, but I didn't care because I enjoyed the freedom I felt flying up to the night sky. I wasn't the type of kid who tried to fit in. I tried to find my own path.

I have one memory that does not belong to me. It never happened to me. I am a little girl, maybe ten or eleven. I'm wearing a fancy dress with white silk gloves and fancy shoes and socks. My hair is longer, dark, and curled. I am waiting with my parents, who adore me and seem to be very wealthy, to get in a helicopter.

My father is my world and very handsome. He is wearing a suit. We are holding on to our hats as we wait for the wind from the blades to die down. Then we get inside the helicopter. The pilot and a copilot wear dress shirts and slacks, with hats over tight haircuts. They are all so nice to me and give me attention. They try to ease my fear of flying. We start to fly, and the memory ends.

I asked my mother about this, and she assured me it wasn't me. I know it didn't happen to me, yet it stays in my memory as though it did. Maybe in a different lifetime, I wondered. Maybe I was so loved before, that I needed to come back to go through life unloved this time. So much in life can't be explained.

I have always had a deep longing for a kind, handsome father. I never felt that my dad was my real dad. He had false teeth and would flip them in and out of his mouth to gross me out. I used to listen to Jim Reeves' albums over and over all day, wishing he were my dad. His voice sounded so kind, mature and loving.

One day, as we were headed to Grandma and Grandpa's house, I noticed a bunch of kids playing outside on the corner of the street. I jumped out of my seat and watched them. *That's my family!* I strongly felt that I had run and played in that yard before. It was a big family of poor kids. I had no idea why I felt I belonged to them and not the family I was with in the car, but the feeling was so strong, familiar and undeniable, that I can't just dismiss it. I longed for a family in the past that I couldn't remember. That's all I knew for sure.

Sometimes I stood in front of Grandma and Grandpa's house, looking at houses and feeling I'd been in them before. I felt as though I should be able to just walk right in and look around, but I knew we weren't allowed to do that. Yet, I would stand there on the sidewalk just remembering, like I had done that before and I should be able to do it again. I felt I should be able to just float in and out of houses like a ghost and it would be fine. It made no sense. I felt caught between two worlds, one of another time and one of now.

So I just stood still on the sidewalk, confused.

Finally, I made a friend again, Kimberly. When it was time for her to go in and eat, her mom would send me home because I'd ask for food. When I came back, her mom would ask what I ate. I always said, "Tomato soup and grilled cheese," because that's what I wished I'd had. But there was nothing at my house to eat once the Wonder bread and Miracle Whip were gone. Kimberly's mom said she didn't believe me because I always said the same thing. I overheard her tell someone one day, "I don't think they're feeding her."

When Kimberly moved, I was lost. I rarely had a friend, so when I did, they meant everything to me. So, without her, I was very lonely. It was summer, so there was no free school lunch. My mom was gone all the time with Don. If a visit with Dad wasn't set up, we had to walk across town to see if he was home. He never liked me much before, but now he wanted nothing to do with me. He said I was a "mommy's girl," and he knew I would side with her. The divorce really was the "divorce from Hell."

Our parents and step-parents hated each other. Everything revolved around being on one side or the other. I was walking down the street one day, feeling very low, lower than ever before. I was hungry, even hungrier than before. I missed Kimberly, I missed our little house in the country, and I missed my family. I then noticed a big family of kids playing softball like we used to. They saw me watching and asked if I wanted to play.

We only played a little while before they were called in to come eat. I started to leave, but they invited me to stay for dinner. I accepted! We walked into their two-story brick home, and there was a large dining room table beautifully set. At that moment, I saw who I wanted to be like when I was a mother. The house smelled good, and I could feel the love in it. The kids were of every shade of brown. A large brown woman came out from the kitchen to look at me when the kids asked if I could eat with them.

She smiled and said, "Sure, as long as she asks her parents' permission first."

I ran home beaming. I wanted to belong to that family. I didn't know what to do if my mom wasn't home to ask. They were everything I wanted in life. When I got home, I asked Mom if I could have dinner with them. She asked who, so I told her where they lived. Don told me no, and if he ever caught me near that street where those "niggers" lived, he would bust my ass so hard I'd never sit down. He bragged that the beatings he'd given me before would be nothing compared to what he would do. I ran to my room to cry my eyes out. My strong will kicked in.

Don always had a farmer's tan—dark face and arms but white everywhere else. I thought about how stupid he looked, especially for someone who judged anyone else for skin color. I made a promise to myself that day that my kids would never use that "N" word, and they would never be prejudiced. Teaching prejudice is something horrible parents do to their kids. Jesus loves all the children in the world, "red, yellow, black or white, they are precious in his sight." If they had ever gone to church, they would know that.

I wished someday I could have a big house and a lot of kids—of every shade! The mother at the house became my role model.

One day in sixth grade health class, I could barely pay attention. I looked out the window, daydreaming. I was so behind I didn't even bother anymore. But on this day, I heard something my health teacher said. I couldn't get over it. He told us how sometimes old people in nursing homes and babies in orphanages die by willing themselves to do so. It was called "failure to thrive."

Mr. Cooper said sometimes when nursing home patients' families stop coming to see them, they don't want to live anymore, so they lie down and die. Nurses don't have time to sit and hold babies in orphanages. Even though the babies are perfectly healthy, they can lose the will to live because nobody loves them. He talked about how love is needed to survive, just like food and water.

I wanted to jump out of my chair, stand on top of my desk, and yell that we had to do something about this, and do it right now. I looked around at the kids in my class, but they looked as bored as ever. I couldn't believe we lived in a country that would sit back and accept this! I didn't want to wait until I was older. I hoped to find a way to do something before then. I thought my head would explode, yet I knew I was just a kid, and kids can't change the world.

CHAPTER 4

AFTER MOM AND DON GOT MARRIED

Mom and Don told us we were moving to the country near Coal Run, Ohio, and would transfer to Fort Frye Junior/Senior High School when summer was over.

One night, I came home after dark. All the lights were off in the house except for in the kitchen. I slowly walked back to see who was there. Sam, Tonya, and Jack stood there, not saying a word. Tonya held a big bag of rat poison in one hand, and a tablespoon in the other, about to scoop some out.

"What's going on?" I asked.

"We're going to poison Don's coffee. Now that you found out, you have to be in on it too or we can't do it," Sam said.

I did a double-take to see if he was serious. He was. They all were. I shook my head no.

"Don and Mom are taking a nap. When they get up, Don will fill his coffee thermos, then drive his semi. He'll get sick, wreck the truck, and nobody will ever know," Sam continued.

"No," I said. I saw a semi accident in which the cab was on fire. A lot of people could get hurt. I shook my head again. "No. Mom loves him, and I won't do that to her."

Sam tried to convince me, saying that he and Tonya and Jack didn't want to move back to the country. "We've had freedom for two years. Nobody cared what we did. Now Don thinks he's going to be our boss and tell us what to do." He brought up examples of times Don had beat us.

Again, I said, "No."

"Well, I ain't leaving my school and my friends. I ain't moving again," Sam said. "They moved us once already when they got divorced, and they ain't moving us again. I like Marietta. I'm not moving back to the country. I'll move in with Dad."

My answer was still no.

Sam sneered at me. "From here on out, whatever happens to us kids because of Don is your fault. We could've ended the torment today."

I was fine with Sam leaving. In fact, I was glad.

Tonya smiled as she gently folded the rat poison bag closed and quietly put it back under the kitchen sink. She put the tablespoon back in the drawer.

Not long after that, before we moved, I walked across the train bridge to the West Side to visit my cousin. As soon as I crossed the bridge over the Muskingum River, I ran into Tonya. She told me to go with her—she wanted to tell me something. I didn't want to go with her, but she kept insisting. She wouldn't tell me what it was about until we got to where she was taking me.

I finally went along. She led me back over the train bridge. When we reached the middle, where the pier is, Tonya told me to jump. I refused. She said she'd done it, and didn't I want to do everything she did? I knew she was using my love for her to try to kill me. She said she would do anything if her friends called her a chicken. I told her she could call me anything she wanted, I wasn't doing it.

I walked away, feeling pain in my heart, knowing my sister wanted me to die. And, no doubt, she would act shocked when she learned of my tragic death. As if she weren't involved.

She feared I would tell on them for trying to poison Don. I had given up telling a long time ago. No one cared, so I didn't bother.

We moved to a house in the country near Coal Run. I started junior high school. Don abused us kids, concentrating on the oldest to the youngest. First, he raged on Molly until she moved out. Then Sam was the victim-of-choice, and he moved out. When Don started in on Tonya, I knew it was a matter of time before she left too. She was still Dad's favorite, and she had become more like a sister to our new step-sisters, Darlene and Barb, than she ever was to me. But still, I didn't want to lose her. I loved Tonya more than anyone now, even though I knew she didn't care about me. It was just the way life was. I couldn't stop loving someone, no matter what they did to me.

One night after we moved again, Don started in on Tonya. He had a belt in his hand. "Get upstairs!" he commanded.

I jumped up in Don's face like a protective dog snapping at him. I demanded he leave her alone.

Don ignored me, pushing me out of the way, all the way up the stairs. Don shoved Tonya into our bedroom and slammed the door in my face.

I swung it open and jumped between them as Don tried to beat Tonya with his belt. "Leave my sister alone!" I screamed.

Don finally gave up and walked out.

As soon as he did, Tonya said, "I'm not staying here."

She opened our second-story bedroom window and climbed out onto the TV antenna. Thunder roared and lightning lit up the sky. Rain poured down.

I was afraid she would be struck by lightning. But she didn't hesitate, so I followed her.

I knew she was leaving. I loved her the way a child loves her mother—unconditionally. I thought I couldn't live without her. We had shared a bed until I was ten. After that, we still shared a bedroom. I always wanted to do what she did.

I followed her to our neighbor's house. Brenda was my age, but she was mature, so she was friends with Tonya, not me. Brenda had three older brothers, and I think Tonya liked one of them, which was why Don was mad at her.

Tonya called Dad and asked him to come get her. He said he would be there as soon as he could. While we waited, we made prank calls to people. "Is your refrigerator running? You better go catch it!" Stuff like that. We even called a random number in the phonebook and I acted like I was having an affair with the woman's husband. The woman believed I was a grown woman and took me seriously. I confessed I was just a kid and it was a joke, but she wouldn't believe me. She yelled at her husband.

Tonya was a bad influence. I realized what we were doing was wrong, but Tonya just thought it was funny. I felt horrible remorse in my gut, but Tonya was excited. I called the woman back and, finally, she believed it was a joke. She and her husband gave me a well-deserved lecture.

When Dad came, Tonya and I went to his car while he knocked on Mom's door. Mom was surprised that Tonya was out there—she thought she was in bed. When Dad returned to his car, he saw me. "I know why Tonya is here," he said, "but why are you?"

I didn't know what to say.

He said I could spend the night, but that was it.

His rejection stung. I returned home the next day, and Tonya stayed with Dad.

Sam wrote a letter to the judge about Mom, reporting some of the bad stuff that went on. Mom said it was lies. She let Dad have custody of Sam to avoid further investigation.

Mom and Don got married, and Mom became pregnant. Soon the court said Tonya had to come home, because Mom wouldn't allow Dad to have her. We moved to Beverly, Ohio. Tonya started dating a Catholic, and Don hated Catholics, so Tonya ran away to live with Dad again—for good this time. Mom hired a lawyer and brought up Dad's sexual abuse of Mom's youngest sister, Tammy.

Dad had raped Aunt Tammy for years. It started when he met Mom. Aunt Tammy was nine years younger than Mom, and Dad abused her while she was still a child.

My aunt had never talked much to anyone about his abuse. When she confessed it to Mom's lawyer in his office, she said Mom looked away and ignored her like she hadn't heard a thing. This hurt my aunt, and she never got over it. She had looked up to my Mom the way I looked up to Tonya. Mom was supposed to be her protector.

My mom has two sisters and two brothers who were very kind. I sometimes wished I had been born to one of them instead of to my parents.

Trying to turn me against my dad, Mom told me a story about my dad molesting Aunt Diane's twins. Mom walked in and caught Dad with his penis shoved through the rails of their baby bed, trying to make the babies think it was a bottle. I told Aunt Tammy, and she said, "Your mom better hope Diane never finds out about it. Diane will kill her."

A girl I knew from junior high ended up marrying my older cousin, one of Aunt Diane's sons. At a party, she made him apologize to me for touching me when I was a baby. He said he liked to pet me because I was so pretty.

I was so uncomfortable that I laughed it off, saying, "Oh, is that why I love my hair being brushed so much?"

They looked at each other as if to say, "No, that isn't what we mean." They were so serious.

But I wasn't ready to hear any more about abuse at the time. Some things I just didn't want to know. At that time, it was too overwhelming. My family's abuse was enough to deal with, without adding more to it.

I liked the small town of Beverly when we moved there. I could walk anywhere, like I had in Marietta. In Marietta, I could walk to the YMCA and the public pools to go swimming. I taught myself to be a good swimmer and how to dive off the high dive. Poor kids got a free pass to pools, which I appreciated. In Beverly, the pool wasn't far—it was by the high school, which was close to our house, so I walked to school too. Across the street from us was the public library. I no longer had to depend on the book mobile for books like I did in the country. Up the street was a Baptist church. Tonya, Jack, and I were all baptized there, and we walked there every Sunday for church and youth group activities.

I also walked to the local nursing home and volunteered as a Candy Striper. I was very proud in my white nursing outfit with red stripes. I also babysat sixty hours a week for a young couple up the alley. I made fifty cents an hour. I saved all of my money, minus enough for a Three Musketeers Bar, a Payday Candy Bar, a pink Hostess Snowball and a bag of Funyuns once every two weeks.

Tonya shoplifted, so she had a lot of nice clothes. When the summer was over, I proudly walked to the local Ben Franklin store and bought my school clothes for eighth grade. They weren't stylish like Tonya's, but I didn't care much about that. I was just proud because I paid for them myself.

I volunteered to sell poppies for the American Legion and won a prize for selling the most. I was then allowed to waitress at their banquets. All I wanted for my fourteenth birthday was a bible. I still have it. It reminds me of what a good kid I was then.

One day my friend Jill and I were walking down our street when a car pulled up. Jill said she knew the men, so we got in. I didn't think anything of it. They drove us just across the bridge to Waterford. At the end of the bridge, they turned right and drove down through a field to the river where they had a camper. Jill started making out with one of the men in the car, so the other one took me in the camper. I refused to go in. He made me think it was so I didn't have to watch Jill and that man make out, but once inside he tried messing with me. I jumped up and ran all the way home.

Later Jill took me to a house, and once inside, a man asked if I were a virgin. I lied and said I wasn't because they were making fun of me for being one. He led me to his bedroom door and told me to prove it to him. Instead, I ran out of his house and ran home.

My mom and Don had a baby when I was fourteen. They named him Kyle. I was so happy to no longer be the youngest. When they brought him home from the hospital, Don said we weren't allowed in his room, which was the living room. Don said Jack and I would hurt him, because we would be jealous of him, and hate him because he belonged to Don. That was one of the meanest things I think Don could have said about us kids. We were told to not even look at Kyle.

In junior high, I started taking every Home Economics class offered. I knew whatever I would grow up to be, I would be a mom too. I wanted to be the best mom I could. Learning to do that well felt like the most important thing I could do for my future. I also refused to take any study halls. I had heard that if you had enough credits, you could graduate at the end of your junior year. I didn't care about grades—all I cared about was credits. I joined the Future Homemakers of America Club.

I was developing my sewing skills and learning how to use a sewing machine. Both of my grandmothers were excellent seamstresses, but they wouldn't teach me how to sew. Our school did a fundraiser by making stuffed black terrier dogs to sell. I enjoyed it so much that I hated to see the fundraiser end.

I stopped hanging out with Jill, and Rhonda became my best friend. She had a big family, and they lived just down the street from us. They could all sing well. I sounded terrible, but I enjoyed singing with them. Cassette players were popular then, and me and my friends would record so we could play back to hear what we sounded like.

Other than an evil stepdad, I was enjoying my childhood again. We lived in a beautiful two-story home, I had plenty of friends, and there was always plenty to do.

Then we were told we were moving again. Each town and each school was a different culture. Each one made me feel like a different person.

CHAPTER 5

HIGH SCHOOL

I had just finished junior high and moved down the hall to the senior high school when we moved again. I started Warren High School after we moved to Layman, Ohio.

I went to the fair one night and ran into Tonya. She took me to a party, and I got drunk. She dropped me off in time for Mom and Don to pick me up. I had wet my pants as I sat waiting for them on a street curb, but I didn't know it at first. Mom and Don didn't notice anything until I threw up all over them in the front seat of the truck. That night I sat in the tub and cried and yelled at Mom for divorcing Dad and for our family being split apart. It was the first time I cussed in front of her. She stood there and watched me but walked out without saying a word. She couldn't handle the truth. Nothing I said mattered, and that made me feel worse than if I hadn't said anything at all. To finally tell someone how you feel, just to find out they don't even care, is reason to never tell anything again.

I wondered why they let me sleep in so late the next day, until I was told to clean up the truck. They had left the windows up so my vomit would bake in the hot sun. Don thought it was funny. I admit, I did too. It was clever. It was nice to get a punishment that made sense for a change. Don thought my getting drunk was funny because he was a drunk.

After only a few months at Layman, we moved to Bartlett, Ohio, which was still in the Warren school district. Kids I once knew from Warren Elementary went there. They said I was pretty now and wanted to be my friend. They told me who was who, and told me who to stay away from and why. I didn't forget how they treated me over Don's daughter back in the fifth grade. I thought I would be better off to hang out with the "bad" kids, because they didn't judge anyone. Anything you were or wanted to do was fine with them. They seemed to be more real and honest, and accepted you for who you were rather than try to get you to conform into something you weren't. I wasn't into snobs, studying or sports. I was into freedom. I looked more like a teenager now than a child. I thought I was a hippie.

I told my new friends we would buy a school bus and paint it purple, then paint flowers all over it and tour the country together, selling crafts. We picked out nicknames. I picked "Wildflower."

I missed Tonya, so trying to be a bad ass was my way of honoring her memory. It was salt in Don's wound for causing her to leave. I resented growing up without her—even if it angered her when I copied her. She had threatened to quit Flag Corps at Fort Frye if I joined too, so I helped work on floats instead. Tonya complained that people called me *pretty*, but only called her *cute*. She made fun of my small breasts and seemed to find fault with everything about me. She was a thief and a bad influence on me, yet I felt lost without her.

After we moved again, Don told our neighbors that I was a whore. A nineteen-year-old woman next door was friends with Don. I tried to be her friend too. She and I went looking for churches, but never found any she liked. She insisted I was not a virgin because Don had told her "all about" me. She said she wasn't stupid—she would never believe me.

One day, we were in front of the diner beside her house when bikers pulled up and said hello as they headed into the diner. Don ran out of our house and whipped my butt all the way home.

The bikers told Don to leave me alone. I was humiliated. Don accused me of having sex with them and started the whore routine up again. I wanted to run away but was afraid, so I hid in the tall weeds in a field behind our house. I heard them searching for me. When I finally came out, the nineteen-year-old shamed me horribly for it. I was the most immature kid in the entire world, according to her.

I didn't know how to act anymore. I have no idea why Don thought I was a whore. Jack had sex with a friend of mine who spent the night with me. I woke up the next morning, and she was in his room instead of mine. Nobody called him a whore.

I had a big upstairs bedroom all to myself, which I loved. I spent one afternoon trying on clothes and dancing around my room. I was pretending I was a model, an actress and a singer, like I had when I was little. I was in my own little world. I hadn't noticed that it had gotten dark or that I had forgotten to close my curtains until I went across the street to visit a friend. There were several men, young and old, sitting in lawn chairs facing our house. They looked like they were waiting for a parade to start. As I walked past them, they said, "That was a hell of a show you put on!"

I wanted to die! It seemed to support the lies Don told about me!

Jack and I had to go on weekend visits to see Dad now. I was disappointed that Tonya no longer lived with Dad. She'd graduated and moved out. I slept in her bedroom during our visits. That made me miss her even more. I touched the things she left behind and cried like I was mourning her death. My dad and Tonya said they saw a ghost walking around the house, so they put crosses above every doorway to keep "her" out. I thought that was completely stupid, but I was afraid to voice my opinion. I just rolled my eyes when dad talked about seeing her again.

The fighting got worse between our parents. Finally, I said I didn't want to go see Dad because of the hell they put us through, talking bad about each other all of the time. Mom had me say that in court, and I no longer had to visit Dad. Mom and Don convinced me to tell my dad off over the phone. I refused to do so for a long time before giving in one night. I later regretted how I treated Dad. I was too young to understand. In our family, nothing was sacred. Everyone just spouted off any dumb thing at anyone they wanted to. We weren't taught morals or how to act. We were just put down all the time. I tried hard to stay good, but acting cool was becoming more important. It put protective walls around me.

I worked during the summer in the JTPA program, so I bought my school clothes again, only now I could afford stylish ones—and I now knew what I liked. Since the divorce, I'd been allowed to grow my hair long. Mom said the pixy haircuts were Dad's idea, so I convinced her to stop making me get them. I felt better about myself on the outside, but Don was slowly killing my insides.

One night when I was fifteen, I spent the night with Tonya. Now that she had graduated high school, she was a "house sitter" for a stock car driver who had a trailer in the country. I was thrilled to hang out with her and our stepsister Barb, and be treated as an equal. We ran around in a car with guys and drank and smoked pot.

We went back to the trailer, and, since her boss was away at a race, Tonya had a big party. She went with some friends into her bedroom and shut the door. I had a feeling they were doing harder drugs and she didn't want me to tell. I got bored, and my buzz was wearing off. It was a beautiful summer night, so I headed outside for a walk.

On the way out, I asked Joel, Barb's brother-in-law, if he wanted to go. All the men at the kitchen table stopped talking and looked at me. They started laughing like I'd made a pass at Joel. Barb's husband Jerry, Joel's older brother, stared a hole through me. It gave me a creepy feeling as Joel and I walked outside.

We walked down the long driveway, just enjoying our youth and the freedom of summer. We were talking about popular songs, and I mentioned "The Streak." I started to unzip my shirt as I joked about going streaking right then, but I quickly zipped it back up.

Joel laughed and told me no. I was fifteen years old, and he was a few years older than me. I was a little too relaxed—still a little high. We changed the subject and continued walking.

I saw Jerry crouching behind a bush along the driveway. He jumped out at me like a wild cat and dragged me off to the dark field next to the trailer. He threw me down on the ground and got on top of me.

"Jerry, what are you doing, man?" Joel yelled.

Jerry told him to hold my feet down. Joel refused, and told Jerry to stop. Jerry kept trying to keep me down, and, eventually, Joel started to help him. I kicked and hit them. I screamed as loud as I could and told them to stop. I used cuss words that had never came out of my mouth before.

Then Jerry lowered his pants and tried to enter me. I squirmed to avoid it. I was exhausted, but I kept fighting and screaming. It was going to happen despite my efforts. I had four hands all over my chest and fingers jabbing inside me. Now Joel held me down so tight I couldn't move. I turned my head to the left because I couldn't bear to watch.

My cussing and loud screams turned to tears of defeat running down my face and onto the wet grass against my cheek.

A large man stepped out onto the front porch of the trailer and lit a cigarette. It was "Bear," a friend of Tonya's. I didn't think I had enough energy to scream one more time, I was so tired from the struggle. But I screamed anyway.

"Help!" I kept yelling until my air left me.

Bear walked towards us—walked, not ran—and that made me mad. If you hear a girl screaming for help, why wouldn't you run as fast as you could?

As he approached, he just stood there. "Jerry, what are you doing, man?" he asked.

I screamed, "What the hell does it look like he's doing? Get him off me!"

Jerry told Bear to leave him alone. "She wants it!"

I screamed, "Do I fucking look like I want it?" I feared I'd made a big mistake by having Bear come. What if he joined in, too, like Joel had? I was sure Joel was going to rape me next. What if this big man raped me too?

Bear made them let me get up. I ran to the trailer. They followed, walking slowly behind me. I ran in and yelled at everyone to get Tonya. I had narrowly avoided Jerry entering me, so I announced, "Jerry and Joel tried to rape me. "

Someone went in Tonya's bedroom to get her. She didn't come out at first. I screamed for someone to call the police.

Someone said they may have to call a squad for Tonya. They thought she had overdosed.

Finally, she came out, smiling. I knew her—she had been faking an overdose. Everyone was more concerned about her tricks than about what had happened to me.

While waiting for Tonya, Jerry and Joel came in and sat across from me in the trailer's living room. I was furious that I had to look at their faces after what they had just done to me. Bear kept telling me to sit there and shut up.

Jerry started yelling back at me, but I was like a wild animal now, wanting to attack them both. Bear told Jerry to shut up too.

Someone told everyone it was time to leave. Tonya went outside to see her friends off. I went out and told her what happened. She smiled and said she knew, they had told her, and for me to just go back inside. She was" dealing with it."

I kept looking outside and pacing the floors. I wanted to go to a neighbor's house and tell them to call the police, but I was afraid to go outside. I didn't know who was still out there. Tonya was acting way too calm and sneaky.

When Tonya came in, Barb was close behind, carrying their newborn baby. This was the first time I'd seen the baby. Jerry ducked behind Barb and came in with them.

I screamed for him to get the hell out, but they continued in and went straight back to the master bedroom. I couldn't fly into Jerry like I wanted because he was hiding behind Barb, who was holding their baby. I wasn't about to do anything violent around a baby.

Tonya told me sweetly in a fake voice to calm down, they were spending the night. Nobody would bother me—Barb was with Jerry now. And Tonya would be right there in her room, between us down the hall. She said that if Jerry came out of the room, she would hear him. She told me to sleep on the couch and we would talk about it the morning—just like she had told me earlier to get back inside and we would talk about it when she came back in. But there was no talking being done. It was bullshit! I wanted it dealt with right then. I didn't want him there.

I woke up the next morning. Tonya, Barb and Jerry were in the kitchen, talking. I heard Tonya tell them, as plain as day, to not worry about it, she would take care of it. She would convince me that I dreamed the whole thing.

I lay there, stunned, crushed and lost. Barb and Jerry left with their baby. When Tonya's boss came home, it was almost time for lunch. He said he was taking Tonya and me to the steak house in town. As soon as we got our plates from the buffet and sat down, I told him everything.

He looked at Tonya.

She giggled and said, "Oh, she has been rambling on all morning about that. I think she dreamed it."

He said he believed me because I told on myself too—what I had done wrong, stuff I could get in trouble for. He asked her why I would do that if I were just trying to get someone else in trouble?

Tonya avoided the conversation. After we were done eating, it was time for me to go home.

This had been the first time I'd been allowed to see Tonya in a long time. If I told Mom what had happened, I wouldn't be allowed to see her again. Tonya would tell everyone I was a liar and to stay away from me. She and her friends would just say it never happened. It would be my word against all of them. Still, I wished someone would take me to report my "almost being raped" to the police.

Tonya planned to join the Army. She wanted to be an Army tank mechanic, and I didn't want to mess things up for her. I loved her deeply and wanted her to like me. I never told anyone else what had happened. Just like everything else that happened to me, I figured no one would care and no one would do anything about it anyway. Somehow, I was always the whore and everything would end up bad for me.

I was on a downward spiral, becoming more withdrawn and un-trusting. I think my sexual paranoia began earlier, because when we lived in town, an old man who lived across from our house made me cautious. He was nice—he would give me change and tell me to go buy a bag of candy. He said he saw what went on at our house and it wasn't right. He invited me to come in and eat with him and his wife several times, but I never once saw a wife. My instincts told me not to go in his house or I would never be seen from again. Looking back, I think that was odd. We didn't hear much about kidnappings in the seventies. There always seemed to be a small whispering voice in my ear, telling me to be careful when I was around men.

When we were younger and lived in the country, Tonya and I walked to the store several miles away. An old man pulled over and offered us a ride. He told us he would buy us candy once we got to the store, if we would just get in the car. He wouldn't take no for an answer. He got out of his car and opened his trunk. Tonya and I took off and ran back home and told Mom.

Sam would come to our house and insist on getting me down on the floor and tickle my ribs hard. I didn't want his hands anywhere near me. I couldn't stand him. He would get mad and say he was just playing with me. He didn't care that I was fifteen and too old to be tickled, or that it hurt. He had never tickled me when I was younger, so why now when I was a teenager?

Sam always had a nervous laugh when he was up to no good—I hated his laugh. He had been married, divorced and was in and out of the Army. I resented that he was still trying to touch me and pretending he never did anything wrong.

My grandma was at our house doing dishes one day. She looked out the kitchen window and saw Sam having sex with someone in the elementary school playground. She started referring to Sam as an animal. I was glad someone finally saw him for what he was. Mom would never confront him.

We moved to Stockport, Ohio. Tonya showed up one night and asked Mom if I could double date with her and her boyfriend Mark. She introduced me to Mike, Mark's friend. Mike and I liked each other right away. He had black hair and brown eyes, and was a little chubby. He was so nice to me. He was very non-threatening. I was a sophomore and he was a senior. He was in carpentry at the vocational school. I could tell him anything.

He lived with his parents in town. He came from a good home. He had a job and a new truck with a camper top on the bed. We went out every single Friday night at six p.m. It wasn't long before we were in love and planning on getting married after I graduated high school. I was so hungry for love that I fell as deeply as anyone ever could. Mike adored me and was always a gentleman. He was very protective of me. Mom said we could get married as long as I graduated first. I was very happy.

My birthday is two days after Valentine's Day, so the weekend before my sixteenth birthday, I met his family at a nice restaurant to announce our engagement. After our date the next weekend, he brought me home, and he still hadn't given me my ring as promised. I began to pout. He handed me a big heart-shaped box of chocolates for Valentine's Day. I said I didn't want it. He opened it and told me to pick a piece.

I refused, saying I was going home. I didn't know how he could be so cruel as to just forget my ring. If he had changed his mind, he could've told me. Maybe his parents objected to our marriage after they met me. I was so nervous around decent-acting people, I hadn't been able to eat in front of them.

Mike smiled and said, "Pick that one," pointing to a candy in the center of the heart. Suddenly I knew my ring was under there! I grabbed the chocolate, and there was my ring! That was the happiest I had ever been. We rushed into my mom's trailer to show my mom.

Mom was happy for us. It was just like in the movies. Then Don walked in, called Mike a "round-headed kid," and said we weren't getting married because we were "still wet behind the ears." Don told Mike to leave and never come back. I was afraid Don would hit Mike, so I told Mike to leave. Mike didn't want to, but Don said we had to break up. I wasn't allowed to see Mike again.

I lost my will to live. I would sit in my room and listen to music and cry. Sad songs became my addiction. "Whenever I want you, all I have to do is dream, dream, dream," and "Love hurts" were my drugs of choice. I would wait for Mike every Friday night at six p.m., knowing he wasn't allowed to come. I couldn't help the longing.

I sat in the bathtub and held a razor blade to my wrist—followed by self-loathing for being a coward. I got a hand full of pills from kids at school several times, and waited until bedtime to take them all. I had no idea what they were. I didn't care. Every time I woke up alive again after taking them, I was mad.

Late one night while out running around, I broke down and asked my best friend Judy to call Mike from a payphone at a gas station in Barlow. I wasn't allowed to call him. His dad answered, and Judy told him she needed to talk to Mike, it was "an emergency." She said he laughed and said, "I'm sure it is." I knew it was no use.

As Judy was on the phone, I walked over and stood in the middle of a lane on Route 339. I watched calmly as semi headlights grew closer. I prayed it would hurry. I was fully welcoming it to take my life instantly.

Suddenly, out of nowhere, Judy ran out and grabbed me as the horn honked. She saved my life, but I wasn't happy about it. She was furious with me and said she didn't want anything to do with me anymore. Neither did I. It is one thing to live a life without love. It is quite another to have a wonderful love and not be allowed to have it. What you once had, you now can never live without. No one takes teenage love seriously, but it is the deepest love—and the worst kind of pain. My love for Mike ached constantly, knowing I could never see him again.

Sometimes, just when you think things can't get any worse, they do. Don was getting more abusive. His drunken rages were getting worse. He now was constantly threatening to kill me. Every day, I was afraid that day would be the day he would finally kill me.

Oddly, it took my mind off suicide. I became determined to live to spite him. Don would beat me and I would withdrawal into a place where I felt nothing. I didn't like to be humiliated by him. I would talk to myself while being abused. "Go ahead, big man, beat on a little girl. Wow, aren't you tough." I perfected it to a fine art. It was my way of lying to myself in order to keep control. I thought I was developing a skill. What I was doing was allowing him to get by with beating on me and making me live in fear of him.

CHAPTER 6

RUNNING AWAY

One night we had the snowstorm of the century. Don came home drunk and started in on me. We were watching *Star Trek*, and my little brother Kyle tripped on his blanket and fell on his butt. Don said it was my fault. Jack took up for me for once, telling Don I hadn't done anything wrong.

Don threatened Jack. Then Don forced Mom and Kyle to go with him through that storm to get a pack of cigarettes. He had just gotten home. Why didn't he get them on his way? He just liked scaring people and being a dumb ass.

I hadn't run away before because I feared Don would start in on my mom and Kyle if I wasn't there. But after Mom was dumb enough to take Kyle out on those roads, I said to hell with it. I was fooling myself thinking I could stop Don from doing anything.

After they left, I walked through knee-deep snow for several hours to get to a friend's house to use his phone. I called Dad and asked how he was doing. He was cold towards me. I couldn't get up the nerve to ask to live with him. I had to walk back. I was stupid to try to run away on such a night. But I believed Mom and Kyle would be killed on the road and wasn't thinking straight.

When I got home, they were back. I ran to my room and barricaded my bedroom door so Don couldn't come in after me, like I had done so many times before. They assumed I hadn't gone far due to the heavy snow. Don only pounded on my door a little while before giving up.

Linda, a friend from the school bus, noticed my bruises and told me I needed to get out of there before Don killed me. I told her I wanted to go live with my dad. She told me to meet her cousin at five that night and her cousin would take me. She said he went to the vocational school and studied carpentry. She said he usually drove himself to school, which was why I didn't know him. He would be on the school bus that afternoon and she would point him out to me. After she pointed to him, we went to the back of the bus. His name was "Bug," then Linda laughed and said, "He likes you."

I got upset and made her promise that he knew this was *not* a date. I just needed a ride to Seventh Street in Marietta, to my Dad's, and that was *all*. She agreed she would tell him. I told her I wasn't over Mike, and I was too messed up right then to date anyone. She reassured me it was okay.

That night, Bug picked me up and we headed to Marietta. We were driving along when a police car went by. Bug said the cop was looking for me so he couldn't take me now. I told him Mom hadn't even had time to know I was missing yet. I asked him to just drop me off in Marietta somewhere and I would walk to my dad's if he was worried about being caught.

He refused. He said he had to wait until dark now before he could take me, so no one would see him. He said he wasn't getting into trouble because of me.

It didn't matter what I said, he wouldn't listen to me at all. He drove me to a lake in Athens County somewhere and wanted to "party." I told him I needed to get to my dad's house before it was late, and I needed to get there not smelling of alcohol and pot. I needed to go to my dad's *now*. I needed my dad to take my reasons for wanting to live with him seriously. I didn't want him to see me as a wild child looking for an excuse not to go home. I knew my dad didn't want me anyway, and going with the odors of alcohol and pot on me was not going to help matters.

Bug got mad and said nobody would ever find me in that lake.

I knew I was in trouble. Linda was the only one who knew who I was with, and she would cover for her cousin if something happened to me. They were a big family and they all stuck together.

I had heard rumors that they were always in trouble with the law. Plus, they were black and I was white. Linda and her girl cousins talked on the bus, saying people were prejudiced against them. They would stand up and start yelling how they were "not in the fields anymore." Someone wrote something racial on the girl's bathroom wall, and they were mad at every white person for it. I knew they would stick together if one were responsible for a missing white girl.

I refused to "party" with him. He drove to a bar in Athens. He ordered a drink and told me to drink it. I refused. He said he was going to the bathroom, and when he came out, we were leaving, and I was not to talk to anyone. He said he would go to jail if he was caught with me, and it would be my fault. He said he was trying to help me, when nobody else would.

As soon as he went to the bathroom, I went over to some guys who were playing pinball and tapped one on the shoulder. He ignored me, so his buddy nudged him and told him I wanted to talk to him. I told them there was a man in the bathroom who promised to take me to my dad's, but now he wouldn't do it. I told them I was afraid of him and I needed to get away. I needed a ride to Marietta. I had run away. I didn't care if they called the police, I just needed help.

Just then Bug walked out and they asked me, "Is that him?"

I said yes.

They got in a shoving match and started arguing. Bug told them to get away from me, I was "his." The guys told Bug, "She don't want to be with you, man!"

Bug grabbed me by the arm and drug me out of the bar, yelling, "See what you did now!" He drove me back to the lake.

This time I gave in. I drank and smoked pot with him—just enough to make him calm down and think this was a date. I knew my life was in danger if I didn't give him what he wanted. He just wanted a date. There was no way he was taking me to my dad's. I just had to focus on surviving the night. I had to accept that I couldn't go to my dad's yet.

He never made me sit by him or anything, so I thought I would be okay.

I wouldn't speak to him the rest of the night, though. I was done begging to go to my dad's. I had nothing left to say.

He was happy now that I had smoked and drank with him. He drove to the country somewhere and pulled into a two-story white farmhouse with a long driveway. The house set back down the driveway on the left, but he stopped at a shed at the start of the driveway on the right. He got out and broke a padlock off the door, then came back to his truck and grabbed me by the arm and led me into the shed.

It was a small tool shed. There were tools hanging on the walls and all over the floor. A cot was on the right. He began building a fire in a wood burner. I feared if I ran to the house there could be men there who might hurt me worse. I assumed this belonged to some of his family. I kept thinking back to that night at Tonya's trailer. I knew I couldn't scream or fight. He could kill me. I kept thinking about how mad he was earlier and how he'd said nobody would find me in that lake. I recalled how sometimes I had to let Don think he was winning. I was hoping Bug would stay calm now. But my gut said he was going to rape me.

And if he did, odds were, he would kill me if I made him mad. I lay on the cot, tightly facing the wall, hoping he would leave me alone.

My hope was shattered when I heard him say, "I hope you don't think I'm going to sleep on the floor."

Once he was done with the fire, I would be raped, and I would not be able to resist, or he would get mad again.

I planned to use what I learned when Don beat me. I would use my strong will of blocking him out of my mind so he wouldn't win. I hated the thought of not fighting and letting him win. He would take my body, but he wouldn't touch my soul because I wouldn't feel it. I refused.

I began to pray. I knew my family didn't love me, but they would really hate me now for what *I* had done. Don had everyone believing I was a whore. Don hated black people, so now he would have the proof that he wanted. Everyone thought girls who had sex with black men were the dirtiest kind of whore. My dad would hate me. My grandparents would find out, and they would hate me.

I wanted out of this shed and away from this creep, but I was stuck. I prayed hard that I was not even here, not even on this earth. Nobody on this earth loved me. I wished I was not even in this world.

Bug walked over to the cot and reached to touch me. I withdrew deep inside.

Suddenly I was floating in space in the black night sky among the bright twinkling stars. It was not a vision. It was not a dream, nor a wish, nor a hallucination. I was fully clothed in space looking down at earth.

Earth was so far away, it was the size of a globe I'd seen at school, so however far away from earth that would be, that's how far from earth I was. My long hair gently blew around me. The sweetest warm gentle wind brushed my arms and face, like I was at the beach at night.

I gazed down at the blue earth and was amazed at how heavy and huge it must be, yet it was gently hovering in space weightless, just like me. Other than the warm, gentle breeze, it was still and quiet.

I appreciated God for sparing me from the rape and answering my prayer. I was safe. It was a miracle. As soon as I began to fear I wouldn't be able to get back, I returned to my physical body. The rape was over. I had not been there at all. I had not experienced anything in my physical being the entire time I was in space.

That time when I was little and my soul went out the bathroom window but my body and mind stayed behind was strange. This time, my soul left with my mind and a spiritual body. I had no connection to this world or my earthly body while I was gone. I saw my body with me in space, and felt the breeze and warmth and weightlessness. Yet, I knew my physical body below was being raped. I did not see or feel or hear anything from this world while I was in outer space.

When I returned to this world, Bug said, "Wow! I want a wife like you some day!" I assumed that he meant easy.

I could sleep, knowing he wasn't going to get mad now, and focus on getting to my dad's in the morning. But I was puzzled by what had just happened. How did it happen? Had I developed a gift? A skill? Could I leave earth just by wishing to? I chalked it up to being a prayer that was answered. I put it out of my mind because I never wanted to remember this night again. I was too ashamed because I didn't fight back. Yet he didn't get my dignity. I had never known anyone to experience something like that. I was sure no one ever had, and no one would ever believe me. Bug may have done something to my body, but my soul was spared. I knew it was not my will that saved me. It was God's will. He lifted me up and saved me.

The next morning, Bug took me to a woman's house. I didn't know if she were his mother or grandmother, or who she was. He introduced me as his girlfriend. I could tell she knew better. She said, "You better get that little girl home. Her mother is looking for her."

I told her I needed to call my dad. Linda's boyfriend Mike took us in his car to Chester Hill to a phone.

As we entered Chester Hill, Bug said, "You better hide. They don't like white people here." He made me duck my head onto the backseat. I felt discriminated against, something I would never have done to them. Bug had treated me like I was less than human, and I no longer trusted Linda. This was starting to feel like it was planned to hurt me for some reason. I worked with their cousin "K" cleaning schools in the summer. I was friendly with everyone. I hadn't done anything to them. I was confused about everything. Bug didn't want anyone to know that he "helped" me run away.

I called my dad and asked him if I could live with him. He said he didn't have custody, so I had to call the police and ask them to bring me to his house. I called the police. They said to be at Bartlett Elementary and they would pick me up and take me to my dad's. I went there and waited. Jack pulled in and said he had orders to take me home. He kept trying to grab my arm, but I pulled away from him.

"Jack," I said, "you know Don will kill me."

"I have my orders." Jack had enlisted in the Marines and acted like a soldier there to capture the enemy.

I jerked his hand off my arm and screamed, "You are not in the military yet! You are not a soldier!"

Jack was yanking me to his car when Linda's Mike pulled in. He and Bug jumped out, grabbed me away from Jack, and took off with me in Mike's car. I was pleading with them to take me back. I had to wait for the police. I didn't know who were the bad guys and who were the good guys.

Mike drove like he was headed back to Chester Hill. We passed the cops, so I rolled down my window and flagged them down. Mike pulled over, let me out, and took off.

The cops put me in the backseat of their cruiser. Just then, Mom and Don pulled in. We were at the Y in the road that led to our trailer in Stockport.

The cops went over to talk to Don. Mom came to the cruiser and nicely asked me to roll down the window. She was faking the niceness, of course. But I couldn't roll down the window. I was in a police cruiser.

Mom pulled on the door handle, beat on the window by my head, then started pounding on the back glass. She was acting like a wild animal. She beat on the trunk, then climbed on the trunk and beat on the top of the roof! I couldn't believe how she acted.

The cops ran over, jumped in and drove off. They talked to each other. I interrupted and asked if they were taking me to my dad's. I sounded like a broken record. That was all I'd been asking for. They said no, they were called by my mom to find me and take me home. They said if my dad wanted custody, he had to file for it.

They said Don had told them he was going to kill me when he got me home. When they had told Don he didn't mean that, Don assured them it was his right because I was his "daughter."

"That guy is nuts!" one of the officers said.

Welcome to my world.

They drove me to the backside of Marietta Memorial Hospital and asked if I'd had "sex." They said, "We can do this the easy way or the hard way," and if I didn't tell them, they would take me into the hospital and hold me down while the doctor forced an exam.

So, I admitted I'd had "sex." Again, I was confused about who were the good guys and who were the bad guys.

They took me to Children's Services. They stayed while case-workers asked me questions. I told them about how I tried to get away, and that the men at the bar in Athens could verify it. They took me to a detention center, "The Open Door Home." I was told if I ran away from there, they would send me to reform school.

A girl there got mad when she heard I was being sent to a foster home. She said they only let the "pretty ones" go to foster homes. "Your own parents didn't want you. The people in foster homes only want you to rape you. That's why they only take the pretty ones. I'm not pretty, so I don't get to go." She had been there a long time.

After several days at the Open Door, a children's services worker took me to a foster home. I followed her in the door, remembering what the girl had said, then bolted back to the worker's car. The worker came back out and said I didn't have to go if I didn't want to. She never asked my reasons. She never asked me why I ran away from my mom's house. Nobody asked me anything.

I kept hearing that I had a court date coming up, but nobody ever said when or why. A staff member at the Open Door said Bug was charged with statutory rape. They said there was a restraining order so if he came near me, he would go to jail.

One day, while at the Open Door, I was told I had visitors outside. I walked out to see who it was. It was Linda, her Mike and Bug!

I told them to leave and never come back. I said, "He raped me. He was only supposed to take me to my dad's!"

Linda said, "He knows, but he's sorry, and he doesn't want to go to jail." She handed me ugly turquoise jewelry—a ring, a bracelet and a necklace. She said it was from Bug. Bug and Mike stood there, not saying a word, as Linda apologized for Bug and begged me to not tell on him. I took the jewelry and walked back in the Open Door.

I informed the staff that there was a restraining order saying Bug wasn't allowed around me, so they shouldn't have let him see me. I showed them the jewelry he gave me. They said nobody told them. Nothing was done about it.

Mom called to talk to me. She said Don promised to be good if I came home. Sam came to visit me and put me down for having sex with a "nigger." I told him he was just jealous because I wouldn't have sex with him, and told him to get out and never come back.

Molly came to visit and said I was going to have a black baby. Why didn't I want a white one that looked like me?

Dad came once. He said Tonya told him that I only wanted to live with him so I could see my boyfriend. He said I was not allowed to see him at his house. Of course, I didn't have a boyfriend.

I let everyone think whatever they wanted.

The day my court date arrived, I walked in believing everyone thought I was the worst person in the world. I felt like a criminal—yet, my only crime was not wanting to die by the hands of Don

Dad sat in the courtroom on the left side. Aunt Diane, Mom's oldest sister, sat by herself behind Dad. I wondered why she was there. No way was I talking about anything personal in front of her. There were people there I didn't even know. Mom was there, but Don wasn't. I wondered why Don wasn't in trouble.

The judge started the proceedings. He turned to Dad. "Do you want her?"

Dad stood up, said, "No," and sat back down.

That hurt. After everything I'd gone through to try to live with him. Dad didn't explain or turn to look at me. Something inside me died the instant he said "no" so coldly.

Something else came alive instead.

The judge told me to take the stand. How humiliating. As I walked between the rows of judging faces, I felt guilty of an invisible crime. I saw visions of innocent people in the past who were also not guilty, yet were punished just the same. I was among them. Like a pirate walking the plank on a ship, I looked down at the wood floor as I went. I saw visions of a black man about to be hung from a tree. I was like a murderer going to the guillotine, or a witch about to be burnt at the stake. I was guilty by hearsay. Righteousness judged by sinners.

Something inside told me, "You're weak, so I'm taking over

now." This "something" came up with a plan. "Go home. Don will kill you, but at least he'll go to prison and Dad will be sorry. Mom will lose her precious baby Don, but at least Kyle will grow up safe." I didn't have the guts to kill myself, but this way, everyone won. Humiliation turned to pride in only a few steps.

I was told to raise my right hand and swear to tell the truth. The judge asked me why I ran away. I remembered what Dad had said, so I used that. No one there could handle the truth, and I didn't have the words to tell it. So, I looked straight at the judge. "Because I can't get by with anything," I said in a flat tone with a stern, emotionless face. I was cold as ice. It was over. I had just given myself the death penalty.

The judge ordered me back to my mother's custody. Nails were put in my coffin.

The probation officer met with Mom and me briefly before I went home. She said she had to go over the rules of my probation. If I broke even one rule, I would go to reform school until I was eighteen, where I'd live with murderers and rapists. She said the judge wanted her to ask me one more time why I ran away. In all his years as a judge, he'd never heard a reply like that before.

Really! You ask me this now? my insides screamed. My mom sat right there. I was not discussing it in front of her. Someone could have asked me before today, and in private, and I would have talked all day. I had sat in the Open Door for weeks. I'd thought about spilling the beans, but then, I'd already come up with a plan. That was more than anyone else had done.

So, I looked at the probation officer and said, "That's my answer." I thought it was bullshit that I had to do everything they said now or go to jail, but no one else was in trouble for all the things they'd done to me. I had been raped, I had been beaten, I had been tormented. But I was the one in trouble. I couldn't wait to go home and die.

Yet, the probation officer's question made me reconsider my decision. Still, it was too late now to do the brave thing—I had to do the stupid thing.

I went home, but Don didn't start in on me. That wasn't going to get me killed. I had a plan, and I wasn't waiting around until he felt like it. I was in control.

Still, I regretted not speaking up when I'd had a chance.

To prove my point, my murder had to be soon. I was not about to go back to that weak little girl who was always afraid Don would kill her. I had to provoke Don to kill me. I remembered Mom told me once that Don would kill anyone who called him a son-of-a-bitch. She'd told me to throw the jewelry Bug gave me away. If Don saw it, he would kill me. He would kill me eventually anyway, so I was just choosing when, not him. I should be allowed that much.

I went in my room, put on that ugly jewelry from Bug, got my hidden pack of cigarettes out of my sock drawer, and walked into the kitchen. I put my feet up on the table, lit my cigarette, took a long drag, and blew it high in the air. Mom and Don were in the living room watching TV. They looked confused, as if they couldn't believe their eyes. They got up and walked into the kitchen. I looked at Don and smugly said, "What the hell are you looking at, you son-of-a-bitch?"

They both lunged towards me. I ran to my room. I wanted to die on my own bed. I envisioned the police coming and finding my bloody dead body and carting Don off to prison as Mom pleaded with them to not take her lover. But they both hit me and fought like sissies. I fought back, just to keep it going. They stopped and walked out. They realized I wanted them to kill me. Therefore, they wouldn't do it.

I yelled for them to come back and finish me off. This was my only plan. I didn't have another one.

Mom told Don that I just wanted to get him in trouble.

So, they had Jack beat me for them. Jack called me a skank and a whore on the bus home every single night. One night, I got off the bus and had almost reached the porch when he came up from behind me and knocked me out cold. I woke up in the yard, and it was almost completely dark. I had to have been out for several hours. Mom was home, and it hurt that she didn't care if I were dead or alive.

When I got up, I felt like I was in a trance.

I walked in the kitchen and got a butcher knife out of the drawer and headed back to Jack's room. I felt like I was in a dream. He was doing his homework at his desk, his back to me. He didn't know I was there. I could do it.

Except, I couldn't. I woke up from my trance and turned to take the knife back to the drawer. Jack heard me and ran after me. He knocked me out again in the hallway, the butcher knife in his hand.

I woke up the next morning in my bed. Jack laughed at me all week, bragging that Mom told him, "Pick that thing up off the floor. I'm tired of stepping over it."

He grinned. "See, even Mom doesn't give a shit about you."

I told my science teacher because I kept seeing double. He said I should go to the hospital because I had a concussion.

I laughed about it, because that's what my family did—they laughed about it.

When I returned to school after running away, I felt like the worst kid that ever lived. Mom said we were moving at the end of the school year, this time out of the county. I planned to never make friends again and to hate everyone after we moved.

I walked out of the smoking area and into the lunch room. A hot meal sounded better than smoking for a change. There was a guy standing in the crowded doorway talking to his friends. I couldn't stop watching him, and I didn't know why. I felt like something out of my control was making me notice his personality. Everything got still and quiet, and my thoughts became loud and clear. I asked someone his name, and they replied, "Jimmy." He wasn't my type at all. But every time I saw him, I was forced to take notice. The more I asked around and watched him, the more I realized what a good kid he was. Several of his friends came up to tell him something, and he listened intently, then always laughed. His friends patted him on the back, or shook his hand, before walking away, like they thanked him for his friendship. I admired that.

He was a farm boy, football player, wrestler, and in charge of Future Farmers of America. He reminded me of "Potsie" on *Happy*

Days. He wasn't the cool kid—he was the nice kid. I rarely ate school lunch, but now I did, just to watch him.

School was almost over for the year. As I walked sadly down the hall at school one day, a voice spoke to me. It told me that when I was a better person, Jimmy and I would meet again and we'd be together someday. But I had to go and become a better person first. It felt like it was pre-arranged. It was sort of like when the angel talked to me when I hovered over the pond. Although I couldn't remember that angel or drowning at that time, the communication felt familiar and comforting. It was so clear.

Someone came up to me and asked if I'd seen the shirt I'd made in the trophy case. They said that while I was gone, my shirt was sent to a competition, and I'd won first place. I walked over to the trophy case. The shirt I'd made hung there among all the team sport trophies. As I looked at the shirt, I noticed how it was art. It had an American Indian and an Egyptian flare to it. I couldn't afford expensive material, so I used muslin and zig zag trim on all the edges. It had triangle cuts at the sleeves, waist and neck. I think they liked my creativity and simplicity. This was a reminder of the girl I used to be. I glimpsed the beauty of who I was inside, and I felt proud of who I was again. I was getting back my identity.

CHAPTER 7

ENTERING THE TWILIGHT ZONE

As we drove into Peyton Plains, Ohio, I felt like we had just entered the Twilight Zone—like we had stepped back in time about twenty years. I had no idea how right I was to feel that way. Teenagers wore bell bottoms and rode old-fashioned bikes to the Dairy Queen to get an ice cream cone. These kids were too good, whereas I was too cool, too bad, and too damaged. I would never fit in at the small-town school. At a big school, you can disappear into the crowd. Here, I would stick out like a sore thumb.

I started the new High School at the beginning of my junior year. The hallway parted as I walked down the hall. I wore straight leg Levi's and Peach Converse tennis shoes. I had long dark brown hair parted in the middle. I walked with confidence and a stone face. I was not making friends here. My heart broke every time I had to leave my friends, and I wasn't doing it any more.

They called me a "city slut." The girls there had been dating the same guy since grade school and were worried I would take their boyfriends.

The head football player broke up with his head cheerleader girlfriend to ask me out. I was not impressed with jocks, even though he was the cutest boy in the whole school. He had blond, curly hair and an easy smile. The drama began with me the cause of it all. I knew that sometimes you just had to go with the rumors—they were unstoppable anyway.

I went out with him a couple of times. We were headed to the movies one night, and he kept asking me to hand him a beer. I grew irritated because he never offered me one, so finally I asked him why.

"I never knew a girl who drank beer before!" he said.

Yeah, the Twilight Zone.

We went to the mall and watched *Saturday Night Fever*. All he talked about was himself, his perfect reputation, and sports. I had a wall up. I wasn't going to like him. I told him to date someone else. Nobody was hurting me again.

I only wanted a date to get me out of the house. I went out with anyone who asked me, but only once. I didn't care what they looked like or if they were popular or not. I was an "Equal Opportunity Dater." I let them know I was not getting serious with anyone, and they weren't going to get anything in return. One of the ugliest guys in school lied and said I put out after I went out with him, so I stopped mercy dating.

Jack graduated and went into the Marines. I had hooked him up with my friend Sis and they got married. When he came home on leave, his abuse became unbearable. He would follow me around, calling me a dirty whore and any cuss words he knew. He always said he could smell me from clear across the room. I took long, steaming showers twice a day because of it.

One weekend, Jack brought a friend home on leave, and the guy tried to rape me. He just ran over and threw me to the floor and yelled in my face "You better fuck down bitch!" I pushed him off me and he apologized. He said Jack had a picture of me on his locker and promised a piece to anyone who drove him home. He said he wasn't even friends with Jack—he didn't even like him. He begged me not to tell, because he'd be in trouble with the Marines and with his fiancée. I didn't let him know nobody would care if I did tell. I let him worry.

One day, Mom and Don said they were going to call the probation officer and see if she would come get me. I hadn't done one single thing wrong—nothing. Don told Jack to "guard" me while they were gone. Jack told me to sit at the table and not move. I sat there. He said I moved. Molly was there, and she told Jack to leave me alone. Jack grabbed me and threw me to the floor and pinned me down, causing a bowl of popcorn to go flying all over the place. He said it was my fault for not obeying his order.

Mom and Don walked in. Don saw what was going on, and decided it was my fault. He said, "I can't stand the sight of her anymore!" He came towards me.

This was it. I always wondered how it would happen and when. Now as I stood up, I imagined myself pushed out the picture window behind me and landing on the driveway two stories below. I could see the cuts and blood all over my face and body.

I knelt to make it harder for Don to push me out. I grabbed ahold of the carpet fibers and braced myself.

The next thing I knew, I was waking up. I was still holding onto those fibers. Time had passed, because my family was sitting comfortably in the living room watching TV like they were interested in a program, and had been for a while. The dining room was opened to the living room, so I could see them clearly. That also meant they could see me.

Molly sat with them, facing the dining room. She saw that I was awake and moving. She sat up so she could see better over the back of the couch, and me on the floor. She blurted out, "I thought Don was going to kill you!" She started protesting my mistreatment, which was a bad thing to do right then. She said it wasn't right, I hadn't done anything wrong. She rambled on, and kept repeating that she thought Don was going to kill me.

I appreciated her concern, but I wished she would shut up because I was afraid that once they saw I was alive, they would come finish me off. They seemed to be pretty involved in whatever was on TV at the moment. I studied their faces as I stayed crouched in front of the dining room window trying to predict their next move, trying to not make them mad by being conscious. I didn't know what to do next. I woke up alive, but for how long?

Then I saw Mom, Don and Jack glance at each other like guilty criminals who feared they were finally caught. I watched every line of expression on their faces and twitches of their eyes close-up, even though I was across the room. I felt their emotions. They wanted to pretend nothing happened. They feared I would tell something, but I couldn't remember anything. I couldn't figure out what had happened to me. Whatever it was, their secret was safe. It was swept from my memory forever.

The next day, I tried calling my probation officer in Marietta. I was at a gas station pay phone in Peyton Plains. I kept getting a recording, and I didn't have enough money to keep calling. I told the operator that my family was going to kill me and I needed to talk to my probation officer. She kept telling me to add more money. I cried into the phone, "I don't have any more money! They are going to kill me!" It was useless. I had to turn around and walk back home.

One day, I was pushing Kyle on the swings behind the grade school as I usually did. We walked on home, and when I got there, Mom screamed at me that I was going to run off with Bug. She said Don had seen his truck in town, and why else would he be there?

I told Mom she could see me and Kyle from the window, so she knew exactly where I was, who I was with, and what I was doing. She said Don came home, told her, and took off after Bug to kill him. She informed me that they had contacted the Klu Klux Klan to have Bug killed anyway. "If Don gets hurt because of you," she said, "you don't have to worry about Don killing you anymore. I will kill you myself with my bare hands!"

I sat on my bed all evening, waiting for Mom to come in and kill me. I wasn't going to resist. I wondered how she would do it. I played it over in my mind. It was such an odd feeling to love someone so much as you waited for them to kill you. I just waited and waited, sitting straight up and not moving. Morning came, and it was never talked about again.

One day, Mom drove me to the probation officer's office in Pomeroy and told them to send me away somewhere. Because we were in a new county now, I no longer had my old probation officer. They asked Mom if I'd done anything wrong. She said no, I was just crazy. They asked her if she'd tried getting me in counseling. She said, "No, she wouldn't go." They asked if she'd asked me to go. She said no.

They asked me if I would go to counseling. I said yes. They asked if I would go right now. I said yes. They walked me down the street to a counselor. I talked to him and told him what my problem was—I was still in love with Mike. I couldn't stop thinking about him.

He asked me to describe myself. I said I was too skinny, my hair was bushy, I was ugly, and I was stupid.

He smiled sweetly at me and said, "That's not what I see at all."

I actually smiled and blushed a little.

"Your mother says you're jealous of Kyle, and she's afraid you might hurt him."

Tears burned my eyes. Out of all the lies they ever told about me, that one hurt the most. "Everyone loves Kyle."

"Is that why you're jealous of him?" the counselor asked.

"No. No, no, no. I love him too. Everyone thinks Kyle is my child because he's always with me. I take care of him all the time— Mom doesn't."

"Do you resent taking care of him?"

"No. I love taking care of him. I love having a baby brother. I would never hurt him, and she knows it. She has no right saying that about me!"

"Would you like to come to group counseling with teens your age?"

"I would love that," I answered.

He told me to keep a journal when I felt low and bring it with me when I returned. I agreed. I had never had anyone speak to me so kindly before, and I loved it.

I wrote in the journal and couldn't wait for the appointment with the group. But Mom would never let me go. I kept reminding her when there was a group meeting, and she ignored me.

This started my love of counseling. The junior high kids were starting to look up to me. They talked to me about their problems, so I counseled them. I helped everyone. Before I knew it, I was running a mini counseling center in the halls of the school.

The junior high guidance counselor approached me one day and joked that I was taking away all his business. Kids were telling their friends to go to me and not him.

I went to his office one day and asked him if he thought I'd be able to go to college. He said no—college was for smart kids and rich kids, and I was neither. I told him I wanted to be a psychiatrist, and asked if he had pamphlets I could look at or if he could explain to me how you got into college.

"College isn't for you," he said.

I never went near his office again. I started talking to Mr. Kelly, the high school guidance counselor, between classes sometimes. Mr. Kelly was very nice and non-threatening. I never told him about wanting to go to college. I already knew I was too poor and too stupid. But I did talk to him about missing my old friends and my old school and about wanting to graduate early. He said that school didn't allow students to graduate after the junior year. He said I could graduate halfway through my senior year, though. He checked my credits, and I had enough to do that if I took and passed Government during the first semester of my senior year. He promised to schedule me for the class.

Finally, there was light at the end of my tunnel!

Mr. Kelly wanted me to go to nursing school. He kept saying he could see me as a nurse. Later, he said he had applied for me to go and had an apartment set up for me. There would be money left over for my living expenses. He said I could even get help in buying a car. I thought this was not possible and I didn't believe him. We don't live in that kind of a world. I also didn't see how he could do this for me without my parents' permission. He said it was based on income, and I was on ADC (Aid to Dependent Children).

One day, I had it with the girls at school calling me a slut. I went and got my books out of my locker, took them to Mr. Kelly's office, slammed them down on his desk, and yelled, "I quit!"

He got up, walked over and turned off his office light, and then pulled down the "Out of Office" shade on his door window. He said, "I know it's hard to change schools and make new friends. Just sit here and relax. Take as much time as you need." He gently closed the door and went to lunch.

I sat there and cried for myself for the first time. I was so moved by his act of kindness. Harsh words had wounded me throughout my life, but the smallest amount of kind words or gestures seemed to heal me. It was like I lived in a world of darkness, but tiny bits of light popped into view now and then.

There had been the Sunday School teacher who told the kids to leave me be because I was full of the Spirit. There had also been a man digging a ditch outside our church in Beverly. A friend and I had started talking to him. As he continued digging, he answered all my intrusive questions. I tried to shock him, but he stayed calm and polite. Then he asked me one question. He said, "I bet you're smart in school, aren't you?"

I laughed and said, "No, I'm stupid."

"That isn't possible," he said. "You are very smart." When you are so mean to someone, and they respond with such warm kindness and respect, it can move you from where you are in life to where they are. You feel the energy in you change. They pass something onto you through the air. You feel it come in.

There had also been a preacher who visited the Open Door detention center. I liked to try to embarrass him with questions about sex and going to hell. He would blush and answer the best he could. His energy was so sweet and kind, I felt it.

I thought of every positive adult I'd met. Those small acts of kindness were few and far between, yet they filled every crack in my broken heart with a few kind words. It's like someone pouring water on a useless dried up plant, and it springs back in to life. I was overcome with appreciation. These were all my role models. I found my will once again with memories of every kindness I was ever shown. As I watched these scenes in my mind, it was like looking through a kaleidoscope. I could see my life unfolding and turning into something new. A healing was taking place inside of me. It was like a warm hug—it was insight and hope.

Molly began to stay with us off and on so she could visit her daughter. She needed her visits to be supervised. But Mom soon kicked Molly out and stuck her in an apartment by herself. Soon we got the call. She needed to be hospitalized again, but she refused to get into the squad. Mom drove me there to handle it. I walked up and told Molly to come on, I would ride with her, and she got in. I told Mom to pick me up at the mental hospital in Athens.

I got Molly settled in. Mom never came. Every time I called her, she said, "Okay," and hung up on me

"It isn't two for one sale day at the nut house!" I said. She couldn't just leave me there!

Eventually, Jack showed up with his wife Sis to take me home. There were a lot of detours because of a flood. It took forever to get home, and I fell asleep in the backseat of Jack's car.

The next thing I knew, the car was sinking in deep water. I thought we'd wrecked and landed in the river. Jack and Sis sat on the hood of the car. I was furious they hadn't even bothered to wake me. Water flowing into the backseat woke me. I thought, *I bet he remembered to get his cassette tapes off the floor, but not his little sister who was sleeping in his backseat.*

I was treated not just less than human, not just hated, but with complete disregard. A man on a tractor came to get them and take them to his farmhouse. They didn't even mention me. I think Jack would've been perfectly satisfied to leave me there and let me drown. But I caught the man's attention and got a ride back too. They pulled Jack's car out, let us and the car dry out, and we were finally able to get home.

I asked Sis why they didn't wake me up. She said when she gave up trying to get her door open, and was sacred because she couldn't get out, I reached up from behind her and opened the door. She said she couldn't figure out how I did that. She had tried and tried and it wouldn't open. I told her I hadn't, I was asleep. She assured me I had.

I shut down for a while. I stopped talking. I was on strike. Weeks went by and nobody noticed, no one at school or at home. I was mute. I saw it wasn't getting me noticed. I didn't know how to ask for help.

Then mom put a newspaper clipping on the hall wall that I couldn't miss as I walked out of the bathroom. It went on about how terrible kids are today, how they disrespect their parents, and won't even talk to them. I wrote a note on the clipping that maybe if parents would treat their kids better, they would talk to them.

The Will of a Wildflower

Mom wanted me as someone to talk to when Don wasn't home, but as soon as he was back, she was trying to get him mad at me and playing the victim again.

CHAPTER 8

MY HILL

We moved to Seedsville, Ohio, in the country outside of Peyton Plains. Every morning when I got on the bus, little kids flocked around me. I loved these little kids. They made me feel special like I was Snow White and they were my little dwarfs. They would fight over who got to sit next to me and talk to me. I couldn't understand why other high school kids just ignored them.

One day after I was seated on the bus, the kids were pushing each other. I told the kids they would have to take turns sitting by me. I realized the bus wasn't moving yet, so I looked up to see what was wrong. The bus driver was watching me. What had I done wrong now?

"What is it?" I asked.

She smiled. "You're going to make a wonderful mother someday."

There it was again—one of those blessings that just fell from the sky and pushed me forward. A nice gentle shower of love. I was learning to like myself again.

Yet there was one big girl on the bus who sat behind me every single day, and all she did was lean on the back of my seat and put me down. She was a few years younger than me, yet I was clueless about how to deal with her. She reminded me of Jack. You are this, you are that, nonstop.

She was very heavy but had long straight brown hair parted in the middle like me. I assumed she was jealous because I was so skinny, so I ignored it and tried to ignore her. One day I got on the bus with my hair still wet, and you would have thought I'd committed a mortal sin. She never let me hear the end of it. She looked for the smallest things to pick on me for and make a big deal about.

On the last day of school of my junior year, I broke up with a guy I'd been dating for a while. Before we moved again, I went to a party on the river with him. There was a big bonfire and I got drunk. I tried to go swimming. He said I was trying to kill myself. I don't know—maybe I was. I could hardly remember what happened. He said I kept trying to drown myself and jump in the bonfire.

I woke up in my bed the next morning covered in mud, with leaves and sticks matted in my hair. I couldn't remember coming home, or him dropping me off. Later in school, I asked him what happened. He replied, "You don't want to know."

He told me a few things and slowly some bits came back to me. Apparently, I informed him that I didn't love him and I was not marrying him. I told him I would always love Mike and I wanted ten kids someday.

He kept confronting me about what I'd said.

I couldn't lie—it was all true. I just needed someone—him—to get me out of the house for a while.

It didn't go well. Now I would be stuck home all summer with nowhere to go.

So now, this big girl on the bus who's been saying crap about me in the seat behind me all year, sat in front of me. She rubbed the break-up in my face. Because it was the last day of school, there were only a few high school kids on the bus and no little kids, so there were plenty of seats. I sat in the back alone—or at least tried to be alone.

As she started her usual list of insults, I glared at her. I didn't take my eyes off hers. I felt hell and fire boil up inside me. Rage spewed out of my eyes like a massive flow of evil energy. I had buried every insult that had ever been said to me. Now it all came out and directed itself at her through my eyes. Her mouth dropped. Her eyes went from proud to puzzled. She leaned back, and fear took over her face.

I didn't move or say a word. I just let all the anger that should've surfaced a long time ago flow out to her through my eyes to hers. It was telepathic hate, channeled like a sun ray. I didn't move or blink.

She backed up and moved to the next seat forward, then the next, not taking her eyes off me. I kept my focus on her. She started to open her mouth to speak, but she couldn't. She was finally speechless! She went to where other kids were towards the front of the bus. She started to whisper to them something about me, but she stopped herself because I was still staring. She tried to tell them to look back at me, but they ignored her. It was just between us. At last she kept her face turned around where it belonged! It felt like a scene out of the movie *Carrie*.

Early that summer before my senior year, Mom, Don and Kyle left and didn't come back for a long time. They took all the food from the fridge and from the cabinets. All they left behind was one bottle of beer sitting in the center of the top shelf. I would open the fridge door and study what the meaning could be behind that. It had to have been left there for a reason. The only explanation I could find was they hoped I drank it so they could finally prove to the probation officer that I broke a rule.

During that time, I had made a friend while walking in the woods one day. Her sister was in my class, and she was a year behind me. One day she came to my house. She walked in and we chatted awhile. She walked from the living room to the kitchen, and I followed her.

"What do you have to eat?" she asked.

"Nothing."

"Oh, you have to have something." She opened the fridge before I could stop her. I was terrified.

She saw all we had was one beer. She immediately went to the cabinets and opened them all—not one single item. I was discovered. I feared she would tell everyone at school and I'd be made fun of. She grabbed our phone off the wall and called her mom and told, even as I begged her not to.

She hung up and said I was going to have dinner with her family. She wouldn't accept *no* for an answer at all.

I went to her house, and her mom had a wonderful meal set on the table for us. I said, "Really, I'm not hungry."

"Eat," she said.

I enjoyed the spaghetti, the salad and rolls. It was the best meal I'd ever tasted. Halfway into the meal, her sister stood behind me. "What's *she* doing here?" she asked. "Why is *she* eating our food? Why doesn't she eat at her own house?"

I refused to eat another bite.

My friend said I was to spend the night there. I agreed, but said I was going home in the morning. I did, too. I was so uncomfortable with her sister looking down on me. I would rather stay home and starve to death than be humiliated like that again.

Eventually, Mom, Don and Kyle came back home.

I spent the beginning of the summer angry, and then lonely. I was tired of being a victim, a fool and stupid. I took long walks in the woods. It was good to be in the country again. There were no insults or threats in the woods. Nature, silence and time were healing me.

There was a tall hill out in the middle of a field that had been completely cleared off. I sat at the top of the hill and could see for miles—over tree tops towards town that was miles away. Seeing from high up and being able to be alone made me feel at peace. With the anger released, I think I found my soul again and was made whole.

I still hadn't recalled drowning when I was little. Yet it must have touched a soft spot deep in my soul to see again from the tree tops. I felt free and calm, and gained insight. I remembered God, and how I used to pray. I found the child I used to be, and the mother in me, and I mothered the child in me. I understood that when I felt the most hate was when I was the farthest away from myself and from God. I had to find myself first, before I could find God.

I talked to God on that hill like I never had before. My thoughts were so clear and open and honest. I could hear myself think. There were no distractions. I found forgiveness and acceptance—and I found hope. I heard myself speak loudly and clearly inside. I began walking to the hill to pray every day. I would sit there for hours. I was the one who'd left God, but He was still there when I came back to Him. I felt His love, warm and strong. I trusted Him to protect me and guide me. I was not alone on that hill—far from it.

I picked wildflowers and enjoyed the warm wind on my skin and blowing through my hair. I was safe out there. It was how I had felt while floating in space, looking down at the earth, during the rape. All the ways in which God had ever healed me now joined forces. The planets were lining up and things were coming together as they were meant to all along. I felt like a song playing in tune with nature. I found harmony in my heart and soul.

I felt God telling me he loved me. I felt security and hope for my future. I received healing on that hill.

Even though it didn't belong to me, I referred to this special place as "my hill," because I had a relationship with it. Each time I went, I knew what to expect. Some people turned to drugs. I turned to the quiet, peaceful atmosphere in nature.

I gained insight there. It was time to get my shit together. After the fall semester of my senior year, I would be free. I had spent every day in survival mode, but now I needed to start thinking about the future. Like that Wildflower, I had made it, but now what?

I prayed to God for hours on that hill. I prayed to move above the anger and depression that had plagued me. I prayed for help and guidance for my future. All that I wished for was given.

I wasn't a good student, and I would have no family support after I turned eighteen. Don had always threatened to kick me out. And soon, I could leave. But where would I go? What would I do? I needed a plan. I had worked, so that was helpful. I could get a job. I needed a driver's license and a car. I needed to stop partying and acting stupid. I needed to stop going out with anyone who asked me. I needed to respect myself even when no one else did. I needed to choose a man wisely, because I didn't want the father of my children to be anything like my father or stepfather. Choosing the father of your children is the biggest decision a woman makes. It impacts everything.

I wondered how different our lives would've been if Mom wouldn't have married Dad.

I needed to get over Mike before I could get on with my life. Mike. That was Step One. I went home and simply asked Mom if I could call Mike. She said I could. I called him and he answered the phone. We chatted a while, and he asked me out. I asked Mom, and she said I could. I couldn't get over how easy that was. Why hadn't I thought of this before? Sixteen months of insanity over this guy resolved in one call.

Mike and I went out and had a long talk. He couldn't believe I went out with Bug—he hated that guy. They were worst enemies and were always getting into fights at the vocational school. He couldn't believe I gave the engagement ring and necklace Mike had given me to Bug to give back to Mike. He asked if I had any idea how much that hurt him, to have that guy give that to him? I told him Bug said Mike wanted him to get it from me to give it back to Mike.

He said, "No way! I hated that guy!" He said Bug rubbed it in his face that I'd slept with him. How could I do that?

I didn't have words. I still couldn't allow myself to think about that night. I took the blame and felt ashamed. His color was not a factor to me, but I knew it was to everyone else. I couldn't even tell Mike what happened that night. It was still easier to let people think what they wanted and let their own prejudice be their punishment. I felt responsible for letting it happen because I didn't fight.

I knew now why Linda was so concerned about my bruises and wanted her cousin to take me to my dad's. It wasn't to help me or out of concern for me. It was out of Bug's hate for Mike. This was a conversation I didn't want to have. It was too ugly and painful. It was also beyond my vocabulary and comprehension.

One thing I was not going to do was let it make me prejudiced. My family was white, and they had hurt me more than anyone. I also wasn't going to tell anyone it was rape. That's what all white girls say after they have sex with a black man. I wanted people to stew on their own prejudice. They were the ones who made a big deal out of it. If he were white, nobody would've cared. It was easier to just be the dirty whore in the story.

I had a secret—I had many secrets—I never told. That was my life. Learn to take the hits and keep going. Nobody tells you why or says "sorry."

I told the brief version to the cops and case workers, and Bug was charged. I didn't know what more people wanted from me. I couldn't change it. It was this big black cloud over my head that gave people the right to hate me and abuse me.

No one asked me if I were okay. It happened to me—I did not do it. Still, I had no way to comprehend anything. Mike now judged me like my family had. I was past all that.

I wouldn't have been so afraid of what my family would think if he'd been white. My family wouldn't have been so eager to kill me when they found me the next day. My dad, Sam and Molly wouldn't have judged me so harshly when they came to visit me at the detention center. But because he was black, that's all they focused on. Not why I ran away or how I was feeling. His color gave everyone reason to hate me. They were stupid.

Even Mike couldn't get past it. He didn't mention Bug's skin color, but I knew it had something to do with him being so upset with me. Mike had gotten a girl pregnant, and her mom was trying to take him for everything he had. He worked hard and had done well for himself. He had a new Trans Am, a boat, and a new truck.

But all I heard was that he wanted nothing to do with his own child. I had wanted to have his babies, but someone else had. That's what hurt me, but I kept my hurt inside. I never asked the "How could you do this to me" questions like he had. The color and per-sonality of my rapist and his child stood between us now. We went out a few times, and things just weren't the same. We had both changed. Yet, I couldn't stop seeing him, after missing him for so long. I couldn't tell if I was afraid to love Mike again, or if I was falling out of love with him. But something was gone.

Before I introduced my friend Sis to Jack, Jack had gotten a girl named Carol pregnant from a one-night stand. She and the baby frequently spent the weekends with us. Even though Jack had married Sis, Carol was determined to get Jack to marry her. I asked Carol if she wanted to double date with Mike and me. Tonya had joined the Army and gotten married. Tonya's ex-boyfriend Mark, Mike's friend, was available.

I thought I was a good matchmaker. Things usually worked out with people I felt would hit it off. But I was just looking for dates for Carol to get her mind off Jack.

Mike, Mark, Carol, and I went to the river across from the pond where I had drowned when I was five, and went swimming. We were drinking and having fun. I was shocked that Carol was having sex with Mark because they'd just met.

Mike and I started arguing. I now saw we would never be able to get back what we once had. That made me sad. I kept trying to swim far out, and Mike kept stopping me. I got out and snuck over and climbed a tall tree and went far out on a limb that reached over the river. Mike stood at the ground yelling, "Get down right now!" He sounded mean.

A weird feeling came over me. Being over the water looking down from this height seemed familiar. I thought about death, but in a familiar, comforting way I didn't understand. Then I remembered all the healing I'd been doing, and the hope I had for the future. I was over Mike. He needed to get on with his life, and I needed to get on with mine. We would never get married. I fell out of love with him in that moment. I was finally free. Life now looked like a wide-open road with millions of possibilities.

We got in Mike's beautiful white T- Top Trans Am and he was furious. I was fine now, but he wasn't. He was yelling at me because I wanted to kill myself. He started going as fast as that car would take us, which was very fast. I watched the speed climb to over 100 mph.

He yelled, "You want to die, do you? Here you go!"

I told him to stop it.

"What's the matter? I thought you wanted to die!"

Well, not now, I thought. That was a few minutes ago. I was

fine now. I felt guilty for scaring Mike. If we wrecked, it would be my fault. I needed to stop acting stupid. I had more growing up to do—if I didn't die first.

We made it home safe and I never saw Mike again. While discussing his paternity suit against him, Mike mentioned we could run away to Canada together, and I had made the mistake of telling Carol. She told Mom. Mom and Don called Mike's parents, screaming and threatening kidnapping charges against Mike. As predicted, I was told I was never to see Mike again. Don was never going to allow me to be happy with Mike. I was only allowed to date guys I didn't like and go places if I wasn't excited about going.

I had learned how to live with a stark-raging-mad alcoholic. Never let them see you happy. Keep your head down and your excitement to yourself. They hate to see you happy. It is their mission in life to destroy you. If you're happy, hide it until you're out of the house, or they'll prevent you from leaving. Also, drunks forget when they ground you. Never assume you are grounded when they say you are. Make plans anyway, and wait to see if they remember.

I refused to live like that any longer. Those were Don's issues now, not mine. I was taking control of my life. I was over Mike now, and I was ready to move on.

Now Step Two. Get a driver's license. Suddenly Sam showed up out of the blue to teach me to drive. We no more got to town, and he put his filthy hand on my right upper thigh. I was wearing short blue jean shorts. I told him either remove that hand or I was driving his car straight into that utility pole. He laughed. I swerved. He removed his hand and said I was just crazy enough to do it. I said, "That's right!"

Sam said he had sex with all of Jack's old girlfriends to see who they liked better. He said they all liked him better. He wanted to know where Jack's fiancée Sis lived. I refused to tell him. She was my friend, and she wasn't like that. He insisted, so I drove him to her parents' trailer to make my point. She turned him down. He asked where Carol lived. I told him. He later told me he went to her house, took her out and had sex with her.

Don was always putting me down and comparing me to my friends, asking why couldn't I be more like them. He bragged how they were so much better than me. I never told him any different. I think he had crushes on all my friends. It was even worse with Carol because she was at our house almost every weekend. I had to hear how great Carol was and what a piece of shit I was non-stop. Finally, I got a gut full one day and said she had a baby and wasn't even married. Jack was a one-night stand. Then I informed them she'd had sex with Sam.

I think I may have done that for revenge, for her telling on me and Mike talking about going to Canada.

Carol had already admitted to me that she'd gone out with Sam and they'd had sex. She had begged me to not tell. She wanted my parents to like her so Jack would leave Sis for her. Everyone—but Carol—knew that wasn't going to happen.

Later, I visited Sam's wife. She started asking me questions about Carol. Then she asked me if what she'd heard was true. I told the truth again. It was funny how all the lies about me flourished, but the truth about them was to remain hidden at all costs.

I went back home and Sam came to our house. He said his wife was taking the kids and leaving him, and it was all my fault. He said he would get even with me if it was the last thing he ever did. He was so mad—and nobody else was home—I feared he would break my neck if I said a word.

He went on about how he was the only one who ever tried to teach me to drive. He brought up how he and his wife took me in once. Even though it was just over a year earlier, I could barely remember that. I had forgotten about it. All I remembered was fighting to get him off me while I screamed for his wife to come help me. She never came, and he finally got off me. He lied and told his friends that he'd had sex with me as I walked into his house that night. A neighbor of his told me that Sam had raped all the girls who lived on his hill so I had run away, yet it was like it had been erased from my memory.

I froze as Sam stood in our kitchen screaming at me. I didn't say a word. Luckily, he finally stormed out.

I had my driver's license now. The local nursing home agreed I could start work in January, as soon as my required classes were completed for graduation. I was over Mike now, and I could see I was getting out of this mad house soon. I still had to walk softly—anything could happen.

I asked Carol if she wanted to walk into town with me. There was a guy named Todd who'd wanted to go out with me ever since I'd moved to town. I had a strange feeling it was time now to go out with him. I just knew if I walked to town, he would be there. I don't know how I knew this.

Carol went with me. When we arrived in town, Todd was at the Dairy Queen with his friend Chuck. I felt Destiny was calling my name. I felt it to my core. I felt the right time was upon me. I knew this was a major event in my life. I knew this was the beginning of my life.

I asked Todd for the time. He replied, "Half past a monkey's ass and a quarter 'til his balls." He wasn't the Prince Charming I'd hoped for.

I told Carol to keep walking.

"Isn't that the guy you were looking for?" she asked.

I told her I was playing hard to get. Carol didn't understand that strategy. I told her to just wait, he would come after me.

Soon Todd and Chuck pulled up in Chuck's jeep and asked if we wanted to go mud running. I said I didn't know. Todd said, "Well, either you do, or you don't!"

Todd had asked me out several times before, and I always turned him down. The last time, he peeled out in his car, kicking up gravel. When I first moved to Peyton Plains, he asked me to go for a ride in his car, we smoked a joint and talked. He was getting ready to leave town for work in Chicago then. Earlier, when I was dating someone else, we stopped at Todd's trailer once and smoked a joint with him. I had sat close to him and we shared a bag of Doritos. I felt like I could spend the rest of my life sitting on the couch beside Todd that night. Now I felt the same way again.

I agreed to go. Carol and I climbed in the back of Chuck's Jeep.

The guys said they were taking us mud running at Boston Hollow. They described it to us all the way there. We didn't know what mud- running was, and had never heard of Boston Hollow. We were about to be introduced to the backwoods form of entertainment—tearing up vehicles and trespassing.

As the Jeep fell in deep ruts, Carol and I were bounced off the seat, up in the air. The top of my head was getting sore from hitting the roll bar, but I had never had so much fun in all my life. We couldn't stop laughing.

Todd and I spent every weekend together after that. During our first kiss, I saw fireworks exploding in the sky, just like *The Love Boat* closing scene when the couple finally kisses.

We both liked to smoke pot and listen to music. Some of Todd's brothers always had pot, and he liked to visit his family and friends. I was shy and a loner, so this was hard for me, but I tried to fit in.

In January, I started my new job as a nurse's aide. I was told if any of my patients died, I would have to give them a bath before the funeral home arrived to pick them up. When a patient died, I did as I was told. While bathing the man, I watched his spirit move out of his left side. Suddenly, there was a moth there that I hadn't noticed before. The moth went straight to his closed bedroom door. Without questioning it, I hurried and opened the door for him. He wanted out of there as fast as he could. He had waited so long. The moth went straight down the hall quickly towards the exit sign. I ran, yelling, "Stella! Mr. Smith wants out!" I opened the exit and set him free.

Stella said she would finish his bath.

I saved all my checks. I didn't buy anything. I knew Don would kick me out soon. Mom was mad that I wouldn't stay in school until June so she could continue getting welfare checks and child support.

Dad used to always yell at me at the table to eat. Molly would get so nervous from his yelling that she'd vomit. Now Don yelled at both of us so much that Molly was vomiting at the table again. I went to my room when it was time to eat.

Now that I was dating Todd, I think Don was afraid to hit me.

Todd was bigger and stronger than Don, but I think it was mostly because Todd's family were friends with Don's boss. I think Don was afraid I was telling on him to Todd. Don always tried to keep up public appearances.

My grandma thought Don was nice. Mom would send me to her house for days to "straighten me up." I would listen to lectures on how terribly I treated my mother and how terrible I was. I never defended myself. I wasn't told what I was supposedly doing that was so wrong. She just complained about "How you treat your mother." My mother played the victim, acting like she needed rescued from my horrible behavior. She found some satisfaction in this attention.

Tonya came home from the Army with her husband Bob and met Todd. She said, "Peg, you can fall in love with a rich one just as easily as you can with a poor one." She said when Bob's father died, Bob came into a lot of money. Bob was from Pennsylvania, like Don. Todd came from a poor Catholic family with twelve kids. Most of them were grown with their own families and lived in the area. Todd was between jobs and had to take me out in his Dad's old station wagon. I couldn't have been any happier.

My mom and Tonya would go on about how good- looking Todd was. My mom said she didn't blame me if I had sex with him. Then she made fun of my small breasts and told sex jokes about Todd and me.

Don accused me of having men upstairs in my room prostituting myself out, and accused Mom of having an affair with Todd. The day I turned eighteen, I made a solid promise to myself and God. I would never forget these childhood years. I would never say, "Oh, it wasn't so bad," or "I deserved what I got." Then I saw photos of kids' faces roll across my line of vision. I didn't know these kids, but I felt in my soul they were all still suffering like I had.

I promised God deep in my heart, that someday, somehow, I would do something to help abused kids. I was like a soldier who'd made it out of a prison camp while so many others were still incarcerated. I knew I couldn't just be free now and only think of myself. I had a responsibility. I must make people understand what I knew. I vowed to never forget.

Mom was stealing money out of my purse, even though she knew every day I spent there was another opportunity for Don to finally kill me. I needed my money to get me out of there. I needed to save for a cheap, dependable car and deposit and rent money. I didn't buy anything other than gas to get to work and back. I was using her car to get to work, so I didn't say anything about what she took. I just hid my purse.

I promised myself, ready or not, the first time Don told me to get out after I turned eighteen, I was going.

One day, Mom acted super nice towards me and asked if I wanted to ride to town with her. I said sure, and hopped in the car. We got as far as the elementary school when she said she needed five dollars for gas. I told her I didn't bring my purse. I hadn't planned on buying anything.

She started yelling at me. She was telling Don on me, and I'd better be afraid. She did a doughnut right in front of the school.

I told her if she would've asked me for money, I would've given it to her. If she needed money, just tell me. But she wouldn't calm down.

She drove extremely fast back to our house, swerving all over the road and yelling she was going to call Don, and I'd better be worried this time.

"Stop it, Mom. Kyle is in the car!"

We got back to the house and I ran to my room and packed a laundry basket full of my best stuff. I left the rest for her to sell at a consignment shop. I waited. This was it, either way.

Don came home mad. "Pack your stuff and get out!" he yelled like he had a hundred times before.

Only now I could do so without being sent to jail for it.

CHAPTER 9

HOMELESS

I called a friend to come pick me up. When I saw her headlights pull in, I went downstairs. I felt like a prisoner finally being set free—except I feared the guards would kill me just before I left as one last cruel joke.

As I reached the bottom of the stairs and entered the living room, Mom and Don stood quietly watching me, not saying a word. I walked to the front door. It couldn't be this easy.

Kyle looked up at me with his big brown eyes and said, "Take me with you."

I felt the glare of the guards upon me. I put down my basket. I hugged Kyle and said, "Kyle, I can't." I quickly grabbed my basket, opened the door, and didn't look back. I walked out into the night, off the front porch, and through the grass.

I held my breath until I got into my friend's car. As she pulled out, I took one last look at the house. I told my childhood goodbye.

Kyle's face was pressed against the window, as if he wanted to go right through it.

That was the price of my freedom. I recalled how much I had missed Tonya, when she left home. I prayed to God to please keep Kyle safe—let them be happy now that I was gone.

This was another step in the right direction—moving out— behind me. I was ready for the next step—a car. I bought a car from Todd's aunt for three hundred dollars. It was big, but dependable. The backseat made a nice bed, because the car was now my home.

I was very happy being a homeless person. I finally had my independence. Sometimes I spent the night with Todd, who lived in his brother Kent's trailer on their parents' property. Todd's parents came to the trailer one day and told me to get in the car, they were taking me to town. They took me to a doctor. The doctor handed me birth control pills. Nothing was said. I started taking them, and I got very moody.

One night, I told Todd there was something I had to tell him. He replied that he already knew—Kyle belonged to me and Don, not my mother. I couldn't believe he said that or thought that. He said everyone knew.

"Then everyone is nuts! Don and I can't even stand to be in the same room with each other, let alone would I allow him to touch me!" I'd been crying myself to sleep because I missed Kyle and worried about him because he was my little brother. If he were my son I never would've left him there with them.

"That wasn't what I had to tell you," I said after setting him straight. "I have something to tell you that might make you want to break up with me, so I'd rather you do it now instead of later." I took a deep breath. "I had 'sex' with a black guy once. That seems to matter to people, so if you want to break up, let me know now."

He said he didn't care if it only happened once. I knew Todd had other sexual partners, so what would it matter? Still, I knew this black issue was huge with people, for some reason. I also knew a past is different for girls. If I would fall in love with a black man, I'd be fine marrying him. There was nothing wrong with interracial relationships. But it made some people hate.

I was going to see Todd one day, and his friend Chuck stopped me in the driveway. He asked me why I was still with Todd. He said Todd didn't love me.

"He tells me he does, and we talk about getting married," I said.

"That's not what Todd tells everyone else."

One night, Todd had asked me to have sex with Chuck and I refused, so I wondered about Chuck's motives. It was clear he was trying to break us up. I walked in Kent's trailer and confronted Todd. I demanded to know if he loved me or not.

Todd laughed and wouldn't answer.

I told him what Chuck had just told me in his front yard.

Todd didn't deny it.

I grabbed the birth control pills that his parents put me on, showed them to him, and threw them in the trash right in front of him. I got my things and threw them in my car.

Looking back, the fact that Todd asked me to have sex with someone else was reason enough to know Todd didn't love me or respect me. I had pushed that out of my mind like I had everything else. I was too in love with Todd to let him go—until now. I think the pills made me aggressive—all we did was argue after I was on them.

I walked up to Todd's parents' house to get my car keys from his little sister Ryan. I had been teaching her to drive. I asked her where her mom was, and she said taking a nap in her room. I walked into her room and told her I'd just broken up with Todd because he didn't love me. I just wanted to say "goodbye" and "thank you" for everything. She and her husband "Pappy" had been very kind to me and welcomed me into their family.

Todd's mom cried. Tears ran down her cheeks—and they were for me. She leaned up slightly and opened her arms big for me to enter them. It felt like an angel had just opened her wings. I rushed to her arms and landed on my knees by her bed. It felt like I had waited my whole life for a warm embrace like this. For the first time in my life, I felt compassion for me. I would be okay. The slightest amount of kindness healed me, but this was love. I gained strength.

So, that meant I had to go on to the next step—get my own place. I'd heard that my Mom and Don moved back to Marietta, so I went to our old landlord and asked if I could rent the house. He agreed, and I paid the rent. He was very nice. I was afraid he wouldn't rent to me because I was so young. Moving in was easy, because I didn't have anything. Before my bedroom was upstairs, but now I used Mom and Don's old bedroom. I closed off the rooms I didn't need, to save on utilities. I was already used to keeping it mowed and clean.

Mom had left some furniture and a white antique cook stove

behind. I always loved that stove. The landlord said I could have it.

All I had to do was buy a few groceries each week. I gained ten pounds and grew an inch after I moved out of Mom's. By the time I graduated, I weighed ninety pounds and was 5'6".

Todd and I got back together. Sometimes he stayed with me at my house, and sometimes I stayed with him at Kent's trailer.

I took off work to go to my prom. I bought a silky white dress with a gathered bust. I was tanned and feeling special to have already started working and renting my own house before I'd even graduated. Our prom was on a boat. We went to the wrong boat dock and missed the boat. We rushed to the other boat dock, but they said they had just taken the last group over. I was so disappointed.

Todd took me out to dinner to try to cheer me up, but it didn't help much. I finally had the perfect date, perfect dress and perfect life, and I wanted to feel proud.

I soon had another opportunity to wear that dress though. It was white, so it worked well under my gown for graduation. As I stood in line with my classmates waiting for the ceremony to start, several of the girls asked me in front of everyone, "Are you living with Todd? I hope you're on the pill!"

They harassed me the entire time we waited to go in to be seated. I couldn't believe that my accomplishments and my nice appearance was crushed by the whore label again.

Even after we were seated, the rumors and insults continued. A photographer snapping pictures heard it all. I just needed to get this over with so I could get on with my life. School had been just one more thing I'd had to endure. People couldn't let me hold my head up high for one lousy minute. Everyone was so jealous, hateful and mean.

The previous fall, when they'd found out I was dating Todd, they would gather at the parking lot to say "hi" to him when he picked me up. They all flirted and wanted him to dump me for them, so I tried considering the source. After all the time's I'd been called a whore at home and in school and was looked down on, and after everything I had gone through to graduate, I wanted to have this moment to feel proud. But nobody would let me. I even passed up going to Canada with Mike because I wanted to graduate. Several times guys offered to let me run away with them to escape my home life. I always refused, saying, "No. I want to graduate." I tried to think encouraging thoughts to block the pain the girls caused. I refused to let them see they were breaking me.

I'd been through worse, and this was almost over. I could handle it a little while longer. I would never have to see these girls again. I had a job, I had a house, I had Todd, and I would be okay.

They finally called my name to walk up the aisle and receive my diploma. I proudly walked to get my prize for being a good girl. It was my moment. I held my head high. Then all of a sudden, from the top of the bleachers, in a voice so loud that it took over the entire auditorium, someone yelled, "Dog! Dog! You are a dog! Bark! Woof!"

I recognized the voice. It was Jack's. He was in the bleachers.

The room fell silent. I felt the gasps and shock of the crowd in the stands. Or maybe I hoped it, so I could keep my head high and focus on shaking the principal's hand as I walked across the stage.

I had won. I had escaped. Barking, insults, abuse, it all stopped right here, right now. I had stepped out of my past and into my future.

After graduation, the photographer said we couldn't go yet, we had to get a class picture. I felt like I had just been through hell and was about to escape, but wait, a group photo before you go! I tried to hide behind everyone as the "popular" girls rushed to be front and center. Finally, everyone was seated where they wanted to sit for the photo. Everyone got quiet to listen for the photographer to tell us to say "cheese." He stared at us. He stopped and looked at all of us like he wanted to discuss something. I was afraid the girls were going to get a lecture about how they had treated me. No one had stood up for me before, and I didn't need them to start now. That would just embarrass me more. I just wanted to get out that door. I prayed that wasn't going to happen.

He looked around at all of us. "YOU, up here!" He pointed to me. "Up front!" I knew by his demeanor that he'd heard the bullying and he'd had a gut full, too. Luckily, he didn't say anything. I still couldn't smile for the picture. I just couldn't wait to leave, walk out that door, and get on with my new life. I didn't have one smile left in me.

Mom and Don sat with Jack in the bleachers. They were watching me. As soon as the picture was taken, I hurried out the door, rushed to my car and drove away with Todd.

A month after graduation, I took my first at-home pregnancy test. I was living with Todd at Kent's trailer full time now. We were planning on getting married and buying Todd's brother Daniel's trailer. Renting was just throwing money away. Daniel's trailer was on a half-acre that joined with Todd's parents' property. We were both working and saving money to fix it up.

Todd and Kent left that morning for work together, knowing Todd would hear the results of the pregnancy test when they returned home.

I took the test, and it was positive. Overwhelming joy filled me. I ran to Todd's mom's house up the road to tell her. Todd's little sister Ryan was there too. They both laughed, hugged me and said, "Congratulations!" I was so happy I could barely contain it. When Todd and Kent walked in the door after work that night, they both looked at me for the answer. I smiled and said, "Yes!" Kent burst out laughing. He bent over and laughed so hard he couldn't stop. He reminded me of a child seeing their sibling get in trouble.

Todd's face went white. He kept looking at me like I was going to tell him I was kidding. He finally smiled and took a deep breath, like he'd just realized we had a lot of work ahead of us, and he was ready to accept it. He smiled big and started laughing. He was as happy about the baby as I was.

Some of Todd's older brothers' wives and one of his sisters did not want me in the family. They said I was a "nigger lover" and that I'd "had sex with gangs of niggers," and I wasn't good enough for Todd. They tried fixing him up with a cheerleader and started rumors that I planned the pregnancy to trap him. They said I wanted Todd for his money.

We both made three dollars an hour. Todd didn't even have a

job or a car when we met. He couldn't afford to take me on dates. I was always happy to just be with him. Todd and I both made the mistake of ignoring the rumors instead of stopping them. They had "meetings" at Todd's parents' to discuss what to do about me. His parents liked me, and some of the kids did too. It was just a hand-full of women who, I found out later, had cheated on their husbands. I was no match for their evil ways. Todd kept telling me to turn the other cheek. But doing nothing helped them get by with everything.

The ringleader was Todd's sister-in-law Janet. Todd said she'd had a crush on him and it was starting to go somewhere until we started dating. She told me she was from Kentucky, and "In Kentucky, if you're friends with niggers, you're to be treated like a nigger. You are a nigger."

One day I was at the laundromat. I was taking laundry out of the washers and putting them into the dryers when a woman walked up to me. "Are you Peggy"

I said yes, and she said, "Well, I'm Janet's mother, and I like Todd, but I sure as hell don't like you! By the time I get done with you, no doctor in this state will swear you were ever pregnant!" She turned around and walked out.

I didn't know if she had men out there with ball bats or what she'd gone after. I wasn't about to stick around and find out.

I grabbed my wet clothes out of the dryers and tossed them into my baskets, and ran out the door as fast as I could with them. My legs were shaking so badly I could hardly drive. I drove down Todd's road toward the trailer, and saw his sister Connie walking to work. I stopped, and she asked what was wrong. I told her, and she replied, "Well, your baby is a bastard."

I drove on home and ran into the trailer crying. Todd and Kent were working on the underpinning and saw me. I didn't like to look weak in front of anyone. I never confided in anyone, and now, when I'd told my problems to Connie, it hadn't gone well. I wouldn't be able to handle it if Todd or Kent reacted the same way.

Kent told Todd something was wrong with me. They both asked what was going on, but I refused to talk. I withdrew inside my shell.

I didn't have words. I ran into the trailer and went to bed, sobbing. Todd came in and asked me what was wrong. I finally told him. He went to his parents' house to use their phone. When he came back, he said Janet and his brother Donald admitted her Mom did say that. He said they wanted us to go to their house to "talk." I said, "They want to kill my baby! I'm not going anywhere near them!"

I wanted to move into our own trailer so bad, but Todd kept making excuses. He didn't want to marry me, so I left. He came and found me. He said he wanted the baby to have his last name. I said if I wasn't good enough to have his name, neither was my baby, so he reluctantly agreed to marry me.

His brother Daniel had said we could go ahead and move into his trailer—just get our loan and pay him later. I couldn't bring a baby to Kent's trailer. We were already in a child's-size trailer bedroom. There was only room for a single bed, and I wasn't putting my baby in a dresser drawer, which was all I had for a baby bed. My belly was growing, and the single bed was too small for us. I was working night shift at the nursing home lifting heavy patients, and during the day I moved our stuff and push-mowed the half-acre lot. And Kent's lot. I started bleeding.

I called my doctor, and he said I had to quit working and keep my feet up until the bleeding stopped, or I would lose the baby. I was three months. Todd came home after work and said, "I looked at rings today." He wanted to go to the mall and let me pick out my engagement ring. I had been waiting for this moment since we'd met a year before—a proposal. But we couldn't go. I was on bed rest.

I told him what the doctor had said, and Todd agreed we weren't going until the bleeding stopped. We were both very worried.

After a few days, the bleeding stopped and I went back to work to see if I could get light duty. My favorite patient, a jolly old man who loved visiting other patients and telling stories, was now bedridden. I was heartbroken. He became depressed when his children didn't show up for a visit. He was willing himself to die. I would sit by his bed and beg him to not do this. He would just shake his head. I watched him will himself to die. After he died, his children came and were upset. I didn't go near them—I was too angry.

A woman was brought in one night by her children. She had lived on her farm her whole life and was still active and healthy. She had just turned a hundred, so her kids told her it was time to go to a nursing home. She willed herself to die in only a few days.

I told my employer that my doctor said I couldn't lift patients, but they didn't make any accommodation for me, so I quit my job. I wasn't taking any chances.

One night I had a dream the baby was a boy. He had three eyes, one in the middle of his forehead. I didn't care—he was my baby, and I loved him no matter what. I told everyone from then on that I carried a boy, and his name was Cameron. I also planned to breast feed. Nobody understood that—formula was the new thing.

Todd and I talked to our priest about getting married, and the fact that I was pregnant. He said that proved "the willingness was there." He said a marriage wasn't a marriage if the willingness to have children wasn't there.

Kent's girlfriend Lucy came to Kent's trailer to tell me that Todd had told lies about her. She was my friend, but suddenly she wanted Todd and me to break up. Todd's friend Chuck got involved and convinced me that Lucy was lying.

Todd told me that Donald and his wife Janet had been going to his parents' house to have "meetings" with people to try to figure out how to stop the wedding. They said they weren't going to Todd's wedding because they weren't "going to watch Todd make a mistake." They said I had come from a bad home.

I didn't see where they were so perfect, but they must have thought so.

I think they just saw someone weak to pick on. We'd had chickens when we were little, and the chicks picked on the weakling. Todd and I were getting married no matter who liked it. I knew I was stronger than they gave me credit for.

The day of our wedding, Todd and I were busy cleaning the church, decorating it, picking up our cake, and doing all those last-minute details. Our wedding started at 4 p.m. At four, we were just getting in the shower, still hoping "to get to the church on time." We were laughing and telling each other to "Move, get out of my way!" As we ran out to get in the car, Lucy held out her arms and told us to stop, we were not getting married. I told her to move out of our way and go get her bridesmaid's dress on. She kept saying "No!"

We jumped in the car, and she threw herself on the hood. I got out, yanked her ass off, and said, "Get your dress on and get to the church!"

After I got to the church and got my wedding gown on—another hand me down from Tonya—and Todd's mom's wedding veil, I ran out to the kitchen of the parish where all the women were. They checked to make sure I had on "something old, something new, something borrowed, and something blue."

"Oh, wait, I haven't even looked in the mirror yet!" I ran back in the bathroom. The only mirror was above the sink, and it was so old and faded I could barely see. I wanted to see myself on my wedding day. I smiled big into the mirror. My face was fat! In a panic, I ran back out to the kitchen and asked the women, "What is wrong with my face?"

Someone said, "It's the mask of pregnancy."

"On my wedding day?"

The kitchen filled with laughter. I was four months pregnant, so I guess I had it coming.

I asked my grandpa to give me away, because my dad said he had to work. I could tell Grandpa was proud to have the honor. He wore a suit, walked tall, and held his head high. I will never forget his smile as he raised his arm for mine, then walked me down the aisle to give me away. It is my fondest memory of Grandpa.

I didn't invite Don, Sam or Jack. I told my mom that Don was not welcome. Todd had Tonya's husband Bob and one of Todd's brothers as best men. I had Lucy, Kent's finance, and Todd's youngest sister Ryan as bridesmaids.

I knew Todd was marrying me because he had to, but the truth was I had to marry him too. I had no family support to raise a baby on my own. I feared if I asked welfare for help, they would put me in a home for unwed mothers and take the baby away from me when it was born.

None the less, this was my dream wedding and the man I wanted to marry. I felt like a princess and Todd was my prince. My fairy tale had come true, and this was my happy beginning. I thought about all the frogs I'd had to kiss to get here. This was the happiest moment of my life. I loved Todd one hundred percent and was one hundred percent committed to this marriage and our child for eternity. I couldn't have been any happier. Todd seemed happy too.

However, my story doesn't end with "We lived happily ever after."

PART TWO

CHAPTER 10

STARTING A FAMILY

On our wedding day, Todd's family filled up one side of the church. My side only had five people—my grandparents, my mom, Tonya, and Tonya's husband Bob. After the wedding, we had cake and a small reception at the church. Everyone seemed happy and celebrated with us. Todd's parents promised they would take care of the reception at their house after the wedding. Then they informed me they didn't want my family coming to their house. I had to say goodbye to my family at the church. My grandma was disappointed they weren't allowed to come. I explained to her that it wasn't me, but what Todd's parents told me. She seemed hurt by this, and I was too.

When we arrived at Todd's parents, we were expecting a big party like they'd had for Todd's brother Eugene and his wife Norma a few months prior. This family was known for their big parties. Pappy and his brothers, and Todd and his brothers, liked to drink. Todd's mom was the best cook in town. Some of them liked to smoke pot. They had many friends, and everyone in town knew where the party was—it was somewhere on Pappy's farm. They had big parties every holiday on the calendar. Yet, hardly anyone was there for our reception. In fact, there was no reception.

We were both disappointed when we walked in and noticed nothing was prepared. Todd's family just stood there glaring at me. At Todd's brother Eugene and Norma's wedding reception, everyone paid to dance with the bride, and people were happy. I went home and changed out of my wedding gown and came back in my jeans. Todd's Uncle Frank looked at me and yelled, "I'd like to fuck that ass!" in front of everyone. The room went deathly silent, as did my heart. I told Todd I was ready to leave.

We went to a hotel room for the night. When we came home the next day, Kent's trailer was a mess. Lucy had burnt fried potatoes and got them all over the stove and counter, and left the mess for me to clean up. People had been in and out partying—hunks of mud was smeared all over the floors. Welcome back to reality. I asked Todd if we could start planning to move out. We bought sky blue carpet for our trailer, which spiced it up a lot. We also bought a wood burner to help with heating costs.

After Tonya and Bob bought a new trailer, she gave us all the furniture that came with it, including the curtains. She said she didn't need it, and it was about the same price furnished as it was unfurnished. I wallpapered the dining room. The wallpaper was white with big blue flowers and long green stems. Even though our trailer was old, it now looked pretty—inside.

I begged Todd to let me bring the white antique cook stove that Mom had left at the rented house, but Todd wouldn't let me get it because it was electric. The trailer had copper colored appliances, and I didn't like them. But our little home was like Heaven to me. I felt like I was living a fairytale.

Todd worked and I was a house wife and soon to be mother. Tonya was AWOL from the Army. She said if she had a baby they would excuse her, but she kept having miscarriages. She dyed her hair red and used a different name so they wouldn't find her. At least, that's what she said—you could never believe anything Tonya said. My mom always said, "Tonya started lying when she learned to talk."

When Bob got drunk, he sometimes talked about how he hated God because of their miscarriages. Sometimes at the parties at Todd's parents' farm, Bob would brag about killing "niggers" while he was visiting his mother's home in Pittsburgh. Bob said they all wore long black coats and big top hats, and went out and killed them.

I rarely talked to Bob. I wanted to report him, but everyone said he was just drunk and didn't know what he was saying. They said the facts he gave were not possible. Still, I didn't understand why he thought talking like that sounded cool. They liked you if you were a big mouth drunk.

My brother Sam would try to come to our trailer to visit. He always wanted to talk to Todd outside alone, even though I told Todd I didn't want Sam at my home, and he was to never come back. Todd would get mad at me and say, "I like Sam." It hurt me that Todd wasn't protective of me. It was the same thing when my stepsister Barb tried to come and bring her husband Jerry. I told Barb that she could come, but Jerry wasn't welcome. Todd was mad about that too. Everyone liked coming to our place because there were always a lot of people partying at the farm on weekends.

Todd didn't care how I felt. I worried about Sam's threat—that he would get back at me if it was the last thing he did, for breaking up his marriage. I was afraid he was trying to break up mine. Also, there was no way I was going to be friends with Jerry after he and his brother Joel tried to rape me when I was fifteen.

Todd's brother Donald and his wife Janet were still talking bad about me to everyone, hoping to break us up. They lived just outside of town. I had to see them at Todd's parents' house. Janet danced around in skimpy clothes, constantly drawing attention to herself. I tried to hide from anyone seeing me—the last thing I wanted was that kind of attention. The women would sit together and talk about me. They had to create something to make me look bad.

Kent and Lucy soon married too, so that made three young couples living in trailers near Todd's parents' house. Lucy would come visit me while our husbands were at work. She was a good listener and someone I could talk to about my past. I didn't entirely trust Lucy, though, since she tried to stop our wedding. Sometimes I wondered if she only pretended to be my friend so she could tell Janet everything I said. She insisted that I promise to take her with me when I went to the hospital to have my baby. I never understood why—Kent never let her go anywhere. She had to wash his clothes in the bathtub for a long time. One day he got her a brand- new washer and dryer set. It was a big deal. Everyone stopped in to see it because everyone bought things used.

Tonya was finally the sister I always wanted her to be. She and Bob visited us all the time. They now lived in their brand-new trailer in a trailer court about 45 minutes away. They purchased brand new vehicles too, because of Bob's inheritance. Tonya seemed very happy with her life, and I was very happy with mine. Tonya would stare out my living room window at Todd as he chopped wood, and then tell me how lucky I was. She made comments about his muscles, but it didn't bother me.

Jack came to visit once when Todd was at work. I let him come in and sit down, hoping the Marines had changed him. As soon as he was seated on my couch, he said, "You know, nobody would have married you if they hadn't got you pregnant." He started calling me a dog. I told him to get out of my home and never come back.

Tonya insisted on taking me to my doctor appointments. I appreciated her doing that and tried to give her gas money. She would never take it. She always bragged about how well off they were.

When I first started going to the doctor for my pregnancy, the doctor told me I should get an abortion. He said I was too young and not married, and I didn't have any support from my family. I refused to listen, and told him to never talk about that again.

I wondered where he got his information about my family. I never talked to anyone there about them. I loved my baby and would never have an abortion in a million years. I had never once considered it, and I never would. This baby and I were going to be just fine. My life began the moment I learned I was pregnant.

I noticed Tonya was very friendly with the nurses. I wondered if she was talking about me to them while I was in with the doctor. She seemed way too friendly with them, like she was having my baby. I assumed she was just excited for me, yet she had never been so good to me before. Why now? She seemed like she had changed. I had everything I always wanted—love.

I would go for walks and rub my belly, talking to Baby Cameron, telling him how much I loved him. I promised him so much love and to protect him my whole life. Maybe we would always be poor, but I promised to take care of him, and that everything was going to be wonderful. From the moment that home pregnancy test showed two lines, I was in love with my baby. That loved filled my heart completely.

My mother came to visit me once, when we still lived in Kent's trailer. Somehow, she had found out I was pregnant. I think she saw my baby as another welfare check, since mine ran out. She said she came to take me home. I refused. She yelled, "What will the neighbors think?"

I said, "What do you think they thought when you kicked me out, and I was living in my car?" I told her I could've been living in a ditch for all she cared. I told her to leave and never come back. After that, other than our wedding, I hadn't seen her very much.

So, I finally went to visit her one day, hoping things would be different between us. She instantly became hysterical and started yelling at me, saying it wasn't right that I made Tonya take me to my doctor appointments and never paid her anything for gas. She said Tonya was complaining to everyone about it. Then she said that Tonya was telling everyone that I was giving my baby to Tonya when he was born. She wouldn't give me a chance to speak. I left immediately.

Todd took me to Tonya's trailer so I could confront her.

She just smiled. "What's wrong, Peg? You don't like it when people talk about you?"

"We never, not once, said anything about giving you our baby."

She just smiled, enjoying the sight of seeing me crying and heartbroken.

When I got back in the car, Todd looked at me. "Why is Tonya laughing, and you are crying?" He had always wondered why I couldn't get along with my family. I think he was starting to see why. They had all re-entered my life just to cause problems for me. They couldn't stand it that I escaped their abuse and was happy. They thought I was too stupid to find out they were scheming against me. They didn't long for love and security like I did—they wanted revenge.

Later, Dad came to our door. He said Tonya sent him to pick

up everything she had given me. He walked in and took my dining room set, my living room set, and even a sewing machine she'd given me. I was more upset about that than anything, because Tonya didn't sew.

I pulled the curtains off the living room windows and gave them to Dad. "Here, she gave these to me too."

"She didn't say anything about those," he said.

I told him I wanted nothing more to do with Tonya or her things.

"I don't have anything in it," he said coldly. "I'm just doing what she told me to do."

This was the only time my dad had come to see me since I was a kid, but it was only to take stuff from me. I said, "You shouldn't have got yourself in the middle of it."

Who knows what Tonya had him believing about me and my baby? The sky was the limit to the lies she could come up with. I never even addressed it with him. He always believed Tonya and sided with her, and that would never change. I wasn't about to waste any breath on him. Neither one of them were worth it. I had my own family now.

I went to the doctor on my due date, and he said it would be another two weeks yet. Todd's brother Eugene and his wife Norma came to visit that evening. I felt like I was in labor, but I was afraid to tell Todd. I was scared—it was too real.

Norma talked to me and calmed my fears. She asked if she could go with us to the hospital. I knew Lucy wanted to go, but I didn't feel safe with her. Norma had just had their first child when I learned I was pregnant with Cameron. We had visited Norma in the hospital, and she kept laughing, saying, "Oh, you just wait!"

I agreed she could come.

I knew this would make Lucy angry, but I couldn't help it. I didn't feel safe with her, especially after what Tonya had just pulled.

My mom lived by the hospital. I called her from Todd's parents' house.

Don answered the phone.

"I'm in labor," I said softly and started to quietly cry.

"You want your mother?" he said kindly.

"Yes."

Mom came and sat in the hospital waiting room and was friendly. When we got to the hospital the nurses told me to keep walking. I got diarrhea, and Norma kept taking me to the bathroom.

"Nobody told me about this!" I said.

Norma laughed and kept making jokes the whole time. She kept Todd and I both relaxed.

They sent me to a room with Todd to finish dilating. A nurse came in to shave me. She cut me several times. Finally, I complained about it to Todd.

Todd asked her if she could take it easy. The nurse told my doctor she cut off a pimple.

The doctor came in wearing a black tuxedo and a white shirt with a white bow tie. He'd just left a party to come deliver my baby. He said he didn't see any pimple or anything on me earlier that day, or during any exam prior, but he had to take the nurse's word for it. I would have to have a C-section in case it was herpes. He said if he didn't, the baby could be born blind or even die—as could I.

Norma went home with news to report to Todd's family.

Deep down, I felt the doctor just wanted a quick birth so he could get back to his party. Yet, this was too serious for me to make that call.

My mom sarcastically told me Todd was "crying like a baby" and that he went to the bathroom to be alone. Todd and I were terrified and stunned.

I woke up after surgery and was told everything went fine and "It's a boy!" They held my screaming baby up in the nursery so I could see him as they wheeled me on a bed down a hall. I was so dehydrated that my lips and voice cracked when I boasted, "I told you it was a boy!"

My mom and Todd laughed. I couldn't imagine that anyone could ever be this happy or love a baby this much.

A few days later, we were in Todd's car bringing our baby boy home. I felt complete bliss and pride. I had done his nursery all in yellow and a little blue. It was bright and cheerful. It was the only room that had nice furniture now, but it was the only room that mattered.

Todd's parents gave us an old orange tweed loveseat and an old rusty metal table and chairs from their basement until we could afford to get something else. I was the happiest new mother that ever lived.

At least I had a rocking chair. I rocked my baby while I nursed him by the living room window and sang gospel hymns to him all day long.

Nine months later—a month after I had stopped nursing, we were hoping to get pregnant again. I fixed Todd's breakfast and packed his lunch for work while he was in the bathroom throwing up. He yelled out to me, "Woman, are you pregnant?" He felt like he had morning sickness.

He meant it as a joke, but I looked on the calendar on the wall, and yes, I was a week late.

I went to a new doctor. I felt the C-section had been unnecessary, and I resented the push to get an abortion when I was pregnant for Cameron. The new doctor told me I had to get my tubes tied after this pregnancy. He said once you have one C-section, they all had to be C-sections. He said my scar could rupture, and if I had more than two, they would have to have a helicopter on the roof waiting to transport me in case my scar ruptured. I was devastated. I went home and told Todd. He said I would get my tubes tied, and that was it. He refused to discuss it further. He didn't want any more kids, and didn't care that I did.

I got a second opinion from my old doctor. He told me none of that was true. He would let me have natural childbirth. I didn't know what to do or which doctor to trust. I told Todd to get fixed if he didn't want any more, because I wanted more kids.

"Nobody is touching me down there," he said.

I was depressed during the entire pregnancy. I loved my baby, but I didn't want this to be my last. I feared Todd would divorce me if I didn't get my tubes tied during my next C-section.

Meanwhile, Norma wouldn't allow me to use her bathroom when I visited her. She said she didn't want herpes. Todd's entire family talked about it. Now they had proof that I was a dirty whore. The story grew to I had "screwed gangs of niggers and a whole football team."

A third doctor informed me that I'd never had herpes to begin with, and my doctor could have done a simple test to find out and avoided the C-sections all together.

I wasn't about to tell his family the truth. I hoped it would keep the men from making passes at me. Maybe someone who wanted to rape me wouldn't because they thought they might catch something. I would use their prejudice to my advantage. They believed what they wanted. They didn't care about the truth as long as the story got them what they wanted—and they wanted Todd to leave me, and they wanted me to look bad.

But I knew the truth, and that was all that mattered.

When I was admitted for my scheduled C-section to have our second child, the nurse questioned why I was having a tubal ligation when I was only twenty years old. I told her I was afraid if I didn't do it, my husband would divorce me and take our babies from me. I didn't have any way to raise them on my own. I didn't have any family support and everyone would be on Todd's side.

She said she wouldn't do it if it were her. With a heavy heart, I signed the papers to have my tubes tied to avoid losing my sons. I felt I had to choose between them and having more kids later. I could never replace my sons, nor would I. Not for all the children in the world.

Now I know I should've torn up the papers. I should've been willing to fight for my rights as a mother, but I didn't have that confidence at that age. I should have had faith that nobody would ever take my sons from me.

I blamed myself for everything, and got used to nobody caring what I wanted. After I signed those papers, I was heartbroken. I knew if I didn't get the surgery and I ended up pregnant, Todd would be furious and divorce me. Catholics didn't believe in birth control, yet Todd insisted on this. I had thought if I married a Catholic, that meant I would have a lot of children. My dream of a large family was crushed.

I had my baby. Another beautiful baby boy. We named him Cole. It was bittersweet for me. I had a beautiful baby in my arms, but he would be my last. Cameron was mad at me because I was away for a few days, but he immediately adored his little brother.

A week after my C-section, a friend of mine named Ann came to visit. She told me Janet wanted to talk to me. Ann had told Janet what I'd said about Janet's mom threatening to kill Cameron when I was pregnant for him.

They all knew it was true. Janet's mom had admitted it to Todd a long time ago. "If her mom doesn't like people talking about her, she shouldn't go around threatening to beat up pregnant women and saying she wants to kill their baby," I insisted.

Ann said Janet was at Lucy's waiting for me. I agreed to go talk to her.

I took my babies to Todd's parents' house to watch while I talked to Janet. I told them I was tired of her pushing me around, and I wasn't putting up with it anymore. They warned me to not go down there. I said, "No, I'm sick of it."

Todd's little sister Ryan, who is a year younger than me, and Ann walked down the road to Lucy's trailer with me.

Todd always told me to not say anything back to anyone. "Turn the other cheek," he'd say. "They're just jealous." But Todd was at work and not there to stop me. This woman was bent on breaking up our marriage. I just got fixed to save my marriage, and I wanted her to see I wasn't afraid of her anymore. I had to start standing up for myself sometime.

Janet always bragged how she beat girls up in school. I was the type if I saw a fight at school, I'd tell them it wasn't cool and I wasn't going to watch. I'd just walk away, hoping others would follow me. People hurt others just for the attention, and the fighting would stop if people would stop watching it. It never worked. People always stayed to watch. I had never been in a girl fight in my life, and I wasn't going to start today. I knew it was possible that was all Janet wanted. Yet, I also knew I that was over eighteen now, so no one was allowed to hit me. I would make that clear if it came down to it.

They may hate me, but nobody would threaten my kids any

more. We walked down and saw Donald, Janet, their five-year-old daughter Faith, Lucy, and Norma, strut out of Norma's trailer in single file. Norma carried a plate with a sandwich and chips, and a glass of pop. She seated herself on the trailer steps laughing as she wiggled her large butt to get seated. She looked like she was about to enjoy a live show.

"This is going to be good!" Norma laughed with excitement.

I now feared that Janet was not wanting to talk at all. It looked like she'd sent Ann to get me just to fight. I wanted to turn around, but I was already there and wanted to speak my mind. I was tired of living in fear. For once, I wanted to stand up for me and my family.

Janet and Donald walked in front of Lucy's trailer. Faith sat down on a railroad tie that lined Lucy's yard from the gravel road to watch. Lucy stood back in front of her trailer to keep a safe distance. She'd known all along what was about to happen. I see now this was planned. My hunch about her was right all along—she never was my friend. She was just a spy.

I walked up to Janet. "So, you wanted to talk to me?"

She eyed me up and down as though sizing me up. "I heard you've been running your mouth about my mom, and I want you to shut up about it."

I shrugged. "You know it's true. Your mom never should have said that to me if she didn't want it repeated."

"You aren't going to the family reunion."

"I'll go wherever I want and you're not stopping me. You don't own that property—Uncle Frank does."

"Donald has been telling me stuff you said."

"Like what?"

Janet turned to Donald. "What did you tell me she was saying?" she said in her southern hick drawl.

Donald didn't say a word. He just stared in my eyes, as always.

I laughed. "You brought me here for this? I'm not wasting my time talking to you about something when you don't even know what you're talking about." I turned and walked away, feeling I'd won the argument.

Ann and Ryan turned around and walked away with me. We

held our heads high.

I strode past the bystanders and headed back to Todd's parents' house. Ann and Ryan caught up with me.

"Get back here!" Janet yelled. She had followed me and now stood with her fists up.

I turned around and laughed. "I am not going to fight you." Ann, Ryan and I again turned back around and continued walking. I took a step.

Janet ran up behind me, grabbed my long braid, yanked me backwards, and spun me around. I ran back towards Lucy's trailer trying to escape, but she wasn't letting go.

All I could think about was my new C-section incision rupturing. She pushed my back, and I fell to the ground face down. Janet jumped down on my back and started swinging her fists into the back of my head. I couldn't move. She growled like a dog and bit my right cheek. She wouldn't stop hitting my head, the blows were quick and steady.

I'd been beat a lot in my life. I tried to use my old technique to block out the pain, but it didn't work at all. When Don and Jack hit me in the head, I always passed out on the first blow. I never felt a thing. I was fully awake for this, and fully humiliated. I saw my little niece Faith sitting on the railroad tie right beside this attack. I recalled how horrible I felt when I was ten and saw my mother beating up Don's wife.

But Faith didn't move away—she just sat there watching. Finally, Lucy ran over, sat down and covered Faith's eyes with her hand. I was grateful for that.

Feet surrounded me, but they weren't there to help me. They were there to get a better look. I was afraid Janet was going to beat me to death. As she continued jumping on my back with her butt, I feared my C-section would open and I would bleed to death. The constant sharp blows to my head concerned me too. Then my body went limp. I was no longer pushing my body up to try to get her off.

Finally, Ryan jumped in and pulled Janet off me. "My God!" she screamed. "You're going to kill her!"

Janet was now off me, but I couldn't move. I just lay there

wondering if I were paralyzed. I thought someone would have to call an emergency squad for me. I wondered how I'd care for my kids if I were in a wheelchair.

"No, let them fight it out." Donald went behind Ryan and held her back, so Janet jumped back onto my lifeless body and beat my head some more.

I lay there thinking, Let them fight what out? I didn't even touch her. I told her I wasn't going to fight her. What was Donald getting out of this? I'd never done anything to him or anyone else. Why did me getting pregnant by Todd make everyone so mad?

Janet saying, "I am from Kentucky, and in Kentucky if you like niggers, you are to be treated like a nigger," played in my mind.

Was this all because I was a "nigger lover" or just plain jealousy? Or both?

After I'd had Cameron, Donald came to our trailer one day while Todd was at work. He asked me to smoke pot with him. I told him no, I was nursing. Todd and I had quit smoking for good as soon as we got pregnant for Cameron. "We are parents now," I'd said. He flirted with me as I made Todd's supper. I couldn't wait for Todd to get home. Now, as I laid motionless on the ground, I thought about how crazy Donald was. He switched from flirting to enjoying this girl fight. Was he getting off on this?

I didn't let any of Todd's brothers in our home after Donald made me uncomfortable that day. If Todd wasn't home, I kept my door locked. I'd ask through the solid metal door who was there. If it were a man, I told them Todd wasn't home. When Todd's brothers got drinking, sometimes one of them would make a pass. I always avoided it, and told Todd. He would say, "They're just drunk."

Maybe Todd wanted his brothers to flirt, hoping I'd cheat on him. Then he'd have an excuse to divorce me.

I lay there trying to make sense of Donald and Janet's anger. What was the cause of this rage? What had I done to deserve this?

Janet either finally got tired, or bored or thought I was dead, but she finally got off my back.

I didn't know if I could move or not. No one said a word or offered a hand. I got up. I had to get out of there quickly.

Janet stood beside Lucy, Norma and Donald, watching me.

I walked over to Janet and got close to her face. I wanted to show I still had my pride.

She smirked, looking pleased over the damage she had done to my face. And that was the answer to all my questions—that was the real issue all along. She was jealous of my pretty young face and long healthy hair. She was happy she'd butchered me.

They all looked satisfied. I was ugly now. They were finally prettier than me.

I then saw an image of Jesus on the cross. I wondered if this was what Jesus saw before his death—the heartlessness and cruelty of humanity.

I looked straight into Janet's overly suntanned smirking face. With a stone face and a calm voice I stated "That proves to me what kind of woman you are. I will see your ass in court." I refused to be humiliated. I had done nothing wrong. I couldn't even get angry.

I walked back to Todd's parents' house. Ryan and Ann followed close beside me, trying to tell me about my injuries. I told them I didn't care about that right now. I was walking tall.

They were very concerned, and I didn't want that. I always handled my pain alone. I was strong enough to take it. As we walked into Todd's parents' kitchen, Todd's dad screamed, "Oh, dear God!"

Cameron was eighteen months old. He smiled and ran to greet his mommy, when all a sudden he stopped dead in his tracks. He stood in one spot, shaking all over, bawling his eyes out. He trembled with his fingers stretched out in shock.

"Ryan, get him!" I yelled.

Ryan ran and scooped up her baby nephew and ran to her bedroom to calm him. I should have listened to them about how bad I looked. I needed to rethink my theory on self-preservation using denial. What worked when I was a kid was no longer appropriate now that I was a mother.

I asked Todd's mom if I could use her phone to call the sheriff. She nodded. I called and said I wanted to report an assault. They told me to come in and file a complaint. Ann and Ryan drove me to the Sheriff's Office.

By the time, they got me there, I had double vison so bad I could hardly see straight. I kept thinking there were two of everything. They helped me walk up the hill to the sheriff's department. Once we got there, I insisted on walking in without help. I put on my stone face. I still had my pride.

When I walked in, the deputies were relaxed with their feet up, chatting. As soon as they saw me, they jumped up, grabbed their gear, and demanded, "Who in the hell was he? We will arrest his ass right now! We'll teach him a lesson about beating on a woman."

"It wasn't a he," I said. "It was a she."

"There's no way a woman could do that much damage," one deputy said.

"She must've been one big woman," said another.

"About my size," I calmly said.

"No way! She must've worn brass knuckles."

I told them I had no idea. There were large lumps all over my face and head. My face was bloody and black and blue. The bite mark looked terrible. They took pictures.

They took our statements, and asked Ryan and Ann if they agreed to be witnesses. They agreed, and were interviewed. They both told them I never touched her, that I had refused to fight her, and was walking away when she jumped me from behind.

They sent me to the hospital, and the doctor documented my injuries and diagnosed me with a concussion. On our way home, I kept telling them to watch out, a car was headed towards us. I kept seeing four head lights instead of two. They had to keep re-assuring me nobody was in our lane. I kept wanting them to swerve to miss the oncoming car that was passing when there was none. If I would've driven myself that night, I'm positive I would've wrecked.

I picked up my babies from their grandparents' house and went home.

Todd came home and glared at me. "I already heard about it and don't know who to believe." He wouldn't let me tell my side. He said Eugene and Kent told their wives they should stay out of it, so they weren't going to testify for anyone. He said they had arrested Janet, and her mom was bailing her out.

Todd didn't care that I was badly beaten or that Janet didn't have one scratch on her. He was mad at me for going down there. I put our sleeping babies to bed, then went to the bathroom and shut the door. I looked in the mirror, and for the first time since it happened, I was mad. I couldn't get mad before. I just tried to understand. I just thought how stupid it all was. What was wrong with me, that I would just lie there and let someone beat on me like that? Had I thought I had to lie there and take it, like when Don beat me? Why didn't I even try to fight back? Once again, I blamed myself for what others did to me.

Now I was humiliated. Now I was furious, but it was too late to do anything about it. Just like all the other times I had been abused, everyone got by with doing whatever they wanted to me, and nobody ever cared about me. It was always my fault. I was always less than human. I never mattered. I never had family to back me up. I always fought my battles alone.

As I stared in the mirror and hated myself, like everyone else did, I loosened my long braid and started combing my hair. As I combed my hair, some fell out. I tossed the loose strands into the toilet, as I relived the night in my mind. After I had all the tangles out from her yanking it, I turned to flush the toilet. I was shocked to see that I'd lost so much hair. It was heaping over the toilet like bread rising-up from a bowl. NOW I wanted to kill her! But now it was too late for that. Where was that spirit when I needed it? I had never felt so much anger. I didn't know what to do with it all. I had been on numb mode for so long, I couldn't handle emotions. I always kept them suppressed. She had stolen my pride, the one thing that kept me together.

I wanted to show them they couldn't push me around, but instead they learned they could do whatever they wanted to me.

The weeks to come were spent waiting on a hearing. I met with the prosecutor, who asked if I was sure I wanted to do this. "These matters are often best handled within the family," he said. But he "would pursue it if I wanted" him to.

I explained that I'd waited years to have the right to not be beat. Now that I was over 18, no one was going to hit me. I needed to feel safe. Janet needed to learn this was not high school—this is real life. She couldn't just go around beating on people whenever she felt like it.

The prosecutor reluctantly agreed to file my case, although he didn't want to.

Todd's sister Connie moved her trailer near ours. It had been behind the store where she worked. She said she moved it by us because she "wanted to keep a closer eye on things"—meaning me. She wanted to spy on me, hoping for the slightest thing to go wrong so they could get Todd to divorce me. She thought she would see men coming and going from my trailer while Todd was at work. Her boyfriend's father was Don's boss. I can only imagine the kind of lies Don told them about me.

When Connie called my unborn son a bastard that day, I never forgot it. I never liked her after that. When I had Cole, she came in my trailer and screamed that she was sick of everyone having boys; she wished someone would have a girl for once.

"I'm not fat," Connie would say. "It's just that everyone else is too damn skinny!" One sister-in-law would measure me and put me on the scales to see what I weighed. Skinny was now in. My years of starvation from neglect was now envied by my sisters-in-law's. I ate whatever I wanted, and it made them mad.

At Warren Elementary, I was often made fun of for being "too skinny." My classmates would yell in disgust, "Your arms are only that big around!" as they used their fingers to illustrate my stick arms. Now I was bullied because my skinny body was envied by grown women.

Before we were married, Todd made me promise I'd never gain weight. He said he saw good-looking women get fat after they were married, and he wouldn't put up with it. I was sure I'd never have to worry about my weight.

Connie had a five-year-old son "out of wedlock," and nobody called her a whore or her son a bastard, or spied on her. She lived with a man, and her son practically lived with her parents. I was a lot younger than she, but I was raising my sons without help. She had married a man once that was already married, but he wasn't the father of her child. I never judged her.

She came to my home and put me down for pressing charges against Janet. "That isn't how we treat family!" she said.

"No," I replied, "you just beat the shit out of them and they are supposed to forget about it!"

Connie went on about how her Dad had beaten their mom all the time when they were growing up, and nobody pressed charges. Todd and his siblings told me their dad beat a baby out of their mom, and the baby came home from the hospital in a shoe box. She is buried in the cemetery at the old church. Her name was Loretta; she'd be my age if she were alive. Connie told stories about her mom abusing her, making her change diapers, and rubbing a dirty one in her face once. She never got along with her mother, but was close with her Dad.

Todd's dad asked me several times to drop the charges, and I refused every time. He said it was causing a lot of trouble in the family. I said she shouldn't have done it, then. They didn't want to "air dirty laundry "in public. They never missed church on Sunday or a religious holiday—and neither had Todd nor I since we'd started dating. I tried to be the perfect wife and mother. I did everything by the book, and nobody was going to beat on me anymore. I was putting my foot down.

Finally, we had the hearing. The prosecutor said he wanted to give us all time alone "to try to work it out because family matters don't belong in a courtroom." Todd's oldest brother's wife was ready to lie under oath and say she was there and I started it. They lived thirty minutes away, and she was nowhere near there that day. Her husband and her were fighting about this and about ready to divorce because he told her to stay out of it.

There were also two mean-looking ladies there whom I'd never seen before in my life. They were ready to lie under oath and say the same thing—that they were there, and I'd started it.

I knew they were just trying to intimidate me, but it would never fly. I had sworn statements from Ann and Ryan, who took me to the sheriff's office that night. I also had medical records of my injuries.

I kept remembering what Todd's dad had said. If Janet were found guilty, she'd serve six months and not be home to be with her kids during Christmas. So, I said I'd drop the charges if she promised me this would never happen again. I needed to feel safe. I told her I didn't want to see her go to jail for six months.

"I am not going to jail!" Janet screamed. "You're the one going to jail!" She bragged about her witnesses.

"You mean all those people who weren't even there?" I asked. "Fine. We will go to trial then."

The attorneys came in and continued the hearing. I knew right then this family was protected by the county.

Meanwhile, at home, Todd said it was my fault he couldn't see his brother Donald now. He asked if I was happy that he wasn't getting invited to any of the parties on the farm. We'd sit on our porch swing on weekend nights and listen to them partying.

Todd was left out, but we were starting to bond more by just having each other. He was siding with me now, even though it was hard for him to do.

I wanted our own family time, and to start our own family traditions at holidays.

A common saying about Todd's family was, "If you go up against one, you go up against them all." I always fought my battles alone. They would never know what inner strength was. They always had someone fighting their battles for them.

CHAPTER 11

THE BULLSHIT

Todd's parents said they sided with me. Their own kids were mad at them, even though they still wanted me to drop the charges. One day Todd's dad asked me to drop them for his wife. He said the kids were making her so nervous he feared she would end up back in the mental hospital. Todd's mom had a chemical imbalance like Molly, only she wasn't mentally delayed like Molly. She often told me her husband didn't allow her to go anywhere and told me he beat her often.

One day she took me by the arm. We walked off their farm, up the road, and through town. She said she'd never been allowed to do that before. It was an important moment for her—her dignity was restored. I didn't know if she was off her medication or if she really had been that controlled by her husband. She held her head high and kept ahold of my arm.

I loved both of his parents. I knew Todd's dad, "Pappy," was far from perfect, but he was like a dad to me, and his mom was like a mom. My love for them was unconditional, as my love for Todd was. I told Pappy I would drop the charges for his wife's sake, even though I didn't want to. He said he knew the kids would all say it was because I knew it was my fault, but he said he and "Mommy" knew better. He always referred to his wife as "Mommy."

I dropped the charges out of love for them.

I knew they used my love to save their family name, but I would do anything for them. I also wanted to take the strain off my marriage that this was causing. The court hearings kept getting postponed, which was dragging it all out. I could tell the county didn't want to do anything. Todd's dad was a township trustee, an elected position, and they were protecting his reputation as well. This could cost his dad votes, and he could lose his job.

Soon there was another party at his parents' house. The women stayed upstairs this time, and the men stayed downstairs. Finally, it was late and I needed to get the boys home and in bed. I walked down to the basement. It was quiet, so I walked softly and listened to the conversation. It sounded like they were having a meeting. Todd, his dad, his uncles, and his brothers were all telling Todd he had to divorce me and take the kids from me.

I couldn't hear Todd talking, so I peeked around the corner to look at his response to all this. Todd stood there with his hands on his hips listening carefully to their advice. When he saw me, he jumped and smiled at me because he was caught. He pretended to be innocent and asked if I was ready to go home.

I looked around at their faces. They knew I'd heard them. Todd went with me, we got our boys and headed home.

As Todd drove, I thought, This is what a nervous breakdown feels like. There it was. I always worried that someday it would happen. This was the day. I had handled everything life could possibly throw at me, but I could not have my babies taken from me. I'd tried to block out everything going on around me my whole life in order to protect myself. But here it was. I could not protect myself now. I had blocked out the fact that Todd didn't love me since the day I'd fallen in love with him.

Reality overwhelmed me.

Now, just like Dad standing up in court and admitting he didn't want me, I had to face the fact that my husband didn't want me either. I withdrew deep inside for protection from the outside world.

On the outside, I was calm and silent. Inside, I was fading quickly. It felt like a silent murder—there were no screams or blood, but my soul had been killed.

Todd kept looking at me, knowing I was reacting to what I'd just witnessed.

Todd carried the boys in and laid them in bed.

I felt like a mindless shell, as I walked to the living room and looked at the wall above my rocking chair. I raised my arms and carefully took down the framed 8 x 10 picture of our boys sitting together. I went to the bathroom and shut the door.

I sat down and held the picture close to my chest. I rocked back and forth without saying a word. I was holding on to the only thing I had left of my family with all my might. They had won. They were taking Todd and my kids from me.

Tears fell like a downpour of rain, yet I remained emotionless.

Todd kept asking if I were okay, but I couldn't respond. I had slipped far away. I kept rocking back and forth in silence, looking straight ahead. I was afraid I'd be locked away in a mental hospital and do this for the rest of my life, just rocking and clutching the photo. I wanted nothing to do with reality. I was leaving, sinking somewhere deep inside. It was a slow fall into dark nothingness. It was intentional, not out of my control, I was willing it to happen.

Todd peeked in and saw me. "Please don't do this."

I realized he was pacing the hallway and didn't know what to do. Every time he opened the door, I saw him, but he felt distant. I moved further inside myself, where I could disappear forever. Life without my boys was a life I refused to live.

Then I realized he was seeing his mom in me right now. Compassion for him drew me out of the void. The next time he looked in on me, I softly cried, "I don't want to lose my family." I was then able to take a deep breath in, as if I had been drowning under water and came up for air.

"You're not," he said softly. "I'm not listening to them. A divorce is what they want—it's not what I want." He helped me stand up, and together we put the picture back on the wall. It signified our commitment to our family. I then glanced at a plaque also on the wall, a picture of Jesus on the cross. At the bottom, it read, "Father, forgive them, for they know not what they do." That plaque became my spiritual guide whenever I felt I couldn't take his family anymore.

When I was pregnant for Cole, Mom came to our trailer one day and said Don had been arrested. She said after I left home,

Don started abusing her instead. She'd been having nervous break-downs because of his abuse. He treated her like he used to treat me, accusing her of things she didn't do, like sleeping with other men. She'd been seeing doctors and was on a lot of nerve medication to deal with Don.

She had put us kids through his abuse and never felt sorry for us, yet now she wanted my sympathy. I never got medication or therapy.

I held my tongue and listened. I cherished the differences between me and her. I couldn't be cruel.

She said the other night Don came home and said he was getting a gun. He made her and Kyle get into his car. He told her he was taking them out to kill them. He would kill Kyle first and make her watch, then he would kill her, then himself.

On the way, she talked him into stopping at the truck stop at the bottom of the hill by the hospital. If he was going to die, he might as well have his two favorite things in the world first—coffee and a cigarette. After he was done with his coffee and he went to pay for it, she got the attention of two men sitting at the counter. She mouthed the words, "He is going to kill us."

The two men told Don there was a problem, and he needed to go have a seat over there until the police came to sort it out.

"Peg, he terrorized you kids all those years, but he didn't stand up to those guys." He was a "big pussy" because he just sat there and waited like they said.

He was forced to get counseling.

"Will you leave him now?"

"No," she said. He had just found out he had a bad heart and was on a waiting list for surgery. At first, he was fine with it, until he saw how long the list was. He would die before he had the surgery, and he knew it.

I told her I was worried about her and Kyle, because Don had nothing to lose now.

She said she wasn't leaving because she wouldn't get any money when he died if she did. She wanted his retirement and social security.

I was worried about Kyle being left in that situation, yet I knew there was nothing I could do.

Later, she called me and said Don wanted to come visit me. I told her they could come for dinner. I made a big meal, mostly from our garden, homemade spaghetti sauce and a big salad. Todd's aunt had given us some nice ripe spaghetti squash. I cooked that and baked homemade bread.

As soon as Mom and Don came in, Mom yelled, "Don can't eat any of that!" She said it would cause him to have a heart attack.

I apologized and offered to make something else.

Don smiled and said it was fine, he was eating every bit of it. Don was from Pennsylvania and always boasted about how the vegetables grew bigger there than anywhere else.

I was proud to show off my gardening and cooking skills, and my happy home. I always canned and kept a clean home and kept our yard mowed and trimmed. I was proud of who I was and glad Don could finally see it.

As they were walking to their car to leave, Don kept coming over and standing closer to me as he talked to Todd. I kept moving back away from him a few steps. Mom whispered that she thought Don was trying to apologize and he wanted a hug to know I forgave him. He'd been making his rounds to see everyone, and this would likely be the last time I saw him.

I told her I couldn't. The dinner was all I could do.

My family didn't hug. What was she thinking, asking that from me? I had never received a hug the whole time I was growing up from anyone. All Don ever did was hate me, beat on me, and want to kill me. He had just tried to kill my baby brother and my mother. He was lucky that I forgave him enough to invite him to dinner. But I kept my mouth shut.

A few days later, Todd's mom knocked on our door early in the morning. "Peg's mom called. Her stepdad died last night."

I covered my face and ran to my room. Todd thought I was upset, but I just didn't want them to see me happy—they would think I was terrible. Don would never threaten to kill anyone in my family again. I was glad he was dead—I only wished it had happened years before.

At the funeral, the line of people pushed me up to the casket. I didn't want to go. I glanced at the casket and imagined Don would sit up, grab me, and drag me down to hell with him. I was hurrying towards the exit when a woman stopped me. She held out a business card for me.

"I was Don's counselor," she said. "He told me everything he did to you, and he wanted you to know how sorry he was. Here is my card. Come talk to me if you ever need to."

I looked at her, took the card from her fingers, and dropped it in the trash can as I walked out the door. I could never forgive Don. His death was the only thing that prevented him from wanting to see someone else die. I lived in fear of dying by his hands for years.

That night, I was sound asleep when I suddenly sat up. Don stood at the foot of my bed. I'm not sure if I saw him, but I am sure I felt him and knew exactly where he was standing. I felt he wanted me to forgive him just so he didn't have to go to hell.

"Too bad," I said. "You should have thought about that before you did all those things to me. I didn't want to see your face when you were alive, and I sure as hell don't want to see it now that you're dead!" I lay back down and fell back asleep.

Ann told me one day that Janet was in her Bowling League and was pregnant by another man. Janet didn't want Donald to know she was pregnant. She was divorcing him, telling him it was temporary, that she just wanted to be on her own. She had never had a job or been on her own before. So, Donald was giving her the new doublewide and the property, since they'd just bought it from Uncle Frank.

Todd had been saying for a long time that Donald complained Janet "wouldn't give him any."

I told Todd what I'd heard, and he told me not to say anything. "She's the whore now, and I have to keep my mouth shut? Nobody ever made her keep quiet when she spread those lies about me, and now I can't tell the truth about her?"

I was beginning to lose trust in Todd, and wondered if things were really over between him and Janet. This was his brother who was being fooled and the home place at stake. Why would he take up for her?

I went to visit Todd's parents one morning, and Donald was sitting at their kitchen table. He was in the middle of explaining to his parents why he and Janet were getting divorced. It was the same excuses Ann had told me—Janet had never been on her own before and just wanted to try it.

Todd's parents said that was a poor excuse to get divorced, but pretty much were keeping their opinions to themselves like they usually did. They made themselves busy in the kitchen to avoid the conversation.

I sat down at the table and listened to Donald as he spoke. He looked at me when he talked because I was the only one listening. He explained how he was giving Janet the house, the land, the kids, and they would get back together later. "She just needs to be on her own for a while." He reminded me that I was on my own before Todd and I got married, and Janet never had that.

When he stopped talking, I calmly said, "That is not what I heard."

Donald was still looking at me. I told him what I'd heard and who told me. I informed him the father was some guy who worked on gas wells.

Donald looked square at me for a minute. I thought maybe he would fly into me—I had no idea how he would react. There was a long pause.

He then sat back and said, "That explains a lot of things." I could see him processing what I'd just said. He said he was going home and kicking Janet out, and she wasn't getting anything. "And I can't wait to see the look on her face when I tell her who told me," he said and then left.

Todd told me later that was exactly what Donald did, too. I would have loved to have been there to enjoy the look on her face like she enjoyed the look on my face after she beat me up. My hair grew back and my bruises healed, but she would live with this forever.

She moved in with her lover, and it wasn't long before they broke up. Her mom had moved to Florida, so she took her kids and moved there. I never saw her again. Donald rarely saw his kids. I felt satisfied that the truth finally won over lies.

My mother would visit us and make inappropriate sexual comments about Todd. She was lusting after my husband. Sometimes she made sexual advances to him right in front of me.

Todd and I would just laugh it off and shake our heads. My siblings all had children and were divorced. I kept in contact with Mom, Tonya and Molly sometimes, but mostly I stayed home. Tonya had two sons now, each a little younger than my two boys. We never talked about the past in my family—or in Todd's—but nobody was very close. I continued to bury everything that happened in order to get along.

Molly had to be hospitalized again and asked Todd and me to take custody of her son who'd just turned two, Ty, so we now had three boys. Mom asked me to take in her third husband's three grandsons, so we had six boys in our trailer one summer. Mom and her husband wanted me to adopt the three boys, but I knew Ryan and her husband wanted a baby. I felt selfish having six when she had none. I asked the mother if Ryan could adopt the youngest one. The mother agreed, and said she would contact the child's father to sign the adoption papers.

Mom and her husband got mad when they found out Ryan had the baby. They demanded I go get him, but I couldn't do that to Ryan. I told them if they took that baby from Ryan, to take the other two from me too. Mom and her husband went ahead and got the baby and brought him to me. Ryan was devastated. I told them to take them all back with them.

They took them home, and they were neglected by their mother and put through the system. All I had was one small bedroom for six boys. We couldn't have adopted them anyway.

Ryan rarely spoke to me again—she told everyone I wanted the baby.

Ryan told me that the sisters-in-law would start lies about each other, and when they were caught, they'd blame it on me. I caught them doing this once when they were all saying Todd's sister Sarah was having an affair. I stood up to everyone and said that Sarah was not like that. Yet when I told Sarah what they were saying, they convinced her I was the one saying it. Sarah rarely spoke to me again either. Todd knew the truth, he was a witness, but refused to stand up for me.

Ryan and Sarah had been the only ones I trusted of Todd's siblings. Todd's brother Randy got divorced and moved in with his parents. He went on for hours about his marital problems. Everyone danced with each other at the parties, and while dancing with Randy one night, he suddenly told me he loved me. I told Todd to tell him to stay away. Randy kept coming over when Todd wasn't home, so I stopped answering the door again. I took pride in being a faithful wife. I had never looked at another man since I'd met Todd. I was never the least bit interested in anyone else.

Todd's brother Rodney got divorced and then engaged to an old high school bully of mine, Sue. They put their doublewide down the hill from our trailer. One morning, on his way to work, Rodney stopped at my trailer to tell me he wanted to marry me. I told him to leave.

After that, I had to start watching out for his hands, like I once had to with my own brother. One Christmas Eve before Janet was caught cheating, Donald came and was drinking with his brothers, and then we all walked down to their sister Connie's trailer. In front of everyone, Donald said to me, "I would leave my wife right now, if you just said the word!"

I yelled, "What in the hell is wrong with him?"

Nobody said one word. It seemed I was always under a microscope, but everybody else could say anything, and it was never to be discussed. Todd would ignore all my concerns about his brothers and would never intervene. I still felt at times that Todd was having them do these things, hoping I would go along with it. I still wondered if Todd wanted to justify leaving me to his parents and his church.

One night we went to a party at Chuck's girlfriend's house. Todd yelled at me all the way home, saying that he wanted out of the marriage. He wanted me and the boys to get out. I think he was envious of Chuck's freedom.

I was afraid of Todd, so I locked the front door after I got the boys inside. I put them to bed and went to bed. I enjoyed my new power—until I heard the back- door open. I had forgotten to lock that door.

Todd just went to bed.

The next day, I took my boys and drove to the low-income apartments. Jack's ex -wife Sis lived there. I asked her how I could get an apartment there. I learned there was a long waiting list to get into low income apartments, so I went back home. I talked to Rodney and Sue next door. I didn't know what to do, or where to go. I was surprised to hear them say Todd had it made, and he didn't know it.

Todd's brother Rodney and his wife Sue said I was a good wife and mother, and they didn't know what was wrong with Todd. They couldn't understand why he was acting so crazy, and were concerned about Todd's mental health and excessive drinking. They said everyone bragged on what a clean home I kept, and called me "Miss Susie Homemaker." Husbands complained to their wives, asking them why they weren't more like me.

Apparently, public opinion had changed. Todd was now not good enough for me, instead of the other way around.

CHAPTER 12

THE MIRACLES

Todd's Catholic religion taught me rehearsed prayers and going to a priest for confession instead of calling out directly to God in my time of need. When Cameron was a baby, I started having dreams there was a fire in the hallway of our trailer. I was walking through fire and I couldn't get Cameron out.

I told Sarah about it, and her husband Shawn overheard me. He told Todd to go with him to check out the trailer to make sure everything was all right. When they returned, they looked at me very seriously. Shawn said the heat tape on the water lines had a short and was causing a fire. The wood under my washer, which was in the bathroom between from the bedrooms, was black from the fires. He said my washer had a leak, which was keeping the charred wood wet. Shawn said eventually it would have caught fire, right where I dreamed, in the hallway. Todd and Shawn fixed the short and the leak, and repaired the wood.

One night, Chuck told me Todd was outside trying to set the trailer on fire. He said Todd would carry fire from the burning barrel to the trailer, and Chuck had to keep putting it out.

I developed irritable bowel syndrome and vasovagal. It got so bad that I was throwing up and passing out two-to-three times a week. I got down to ninety pounds.

One morning Todd told me to lift my nightgown. He took my picture because he thought my skinny legs were sexy. I couldn't understand why he thought me wasting away from sickness was sexy.

I was a slow learner, but I was starting to catch on.

I finally learned if I cooled down with a floor fan and a cold cloth, the nausea would pass. I still couldn't eat if I was upset about anything. I had to wait until I calmed down first, or I'd get sick. I had been diagnosed with a "nervous stomach" when I was little. Apparently, I was nervous now and didn't know it because I had shut down. Now that stress was making me sick, I was forced to pay attention to it.

I told Todd I couldn't handle living in that Peyton Place any longer. Even though some of his brothers' trouble-making wives were gone because of divorces, I still needed to get out of there. We needed to move.

We could afford to buy a house. We now had free gas because a gas well was put a certain distance from our trailer. This would increase the value of our property, plus we had sold our old trailer and bought a newer one from his brother. We had built a big living room on the back, a back deck, and a front porch. We would get enough out of it for a nice down payment on something somewhere else.

Todd's dad had never agreed to sell off any of his property before, but he offered to sell us thirty acres so we wouldn't move away from them. He said we would have to sign something saying it would stay in the family if Todd and I split up. I told him no. He was deeply hurt. He asked if I knew how many times his kids asked him to sell a piece to them, and he always refused. I didn't trust him, and I needed out of there.

Donald was mad because his Dad wouldn't sell to him. He said his parents gave him away when he was a kid. He was raised by an aunt and uncle two hours away because his parents had too many kids. He was upset because he believed his parents loved me more than him.

I explained to Pappy that I had to get out of there, his kids were driving me crazy with the constant drama. Plus, I could hear him and "Mommy" fighting from our place. I asked him if he had any idea how bad it upset me to know he was hitting her. She was too old to be beat on. I saw the bruises on her, and it needed to stop.

He had recently knocked her down the front steps. Her entire arm was covered in bruises. I would see him passed out at the kitchen table, sleeping on his beer can. When he woke up, he finished the can off. It was disgusting.

He looked at me like nobody had ever put him in his place before. Soon afterwards, Pappy confronted me. Donald told him I was telling people that he killed Loretta when Mommy was pregnant for her. I told him that was what his kids had told me, so talk to them. Pappy said Donald said that I regretted naming Cole after him.

I agreed. If I would've known he would get drunk and brag that Cole was his namesake, no, I wouldn't have named Cole after him. I told him it wasn't right to not care how his other grandchildren felt and he should see their faces when he spoiled Cole and ignored the other grandkids. I also got upset when he wanted to hold Cole when he was too drunk to even stand—and then refuse to hand him back to me.

I always told Pappy the truth about how I felt. If he picked on someone when he was drunk, I let him know he was being an ass.

Nobody else stood up to him, but I was picked on my whole life, so I couldn't stand by and see it happen to someone else. Pappy and his brothers had farms and were the elders, and everyone bowed down to them. I wasn't afraid to speak up anymore. At parties now, I played with all the little kids and ignored the adults. I was bored with drunken conversations and the same songs being sung by a bunch of drunks. I no longer tried to fit in. I wanted out.

We bought 20 acres in another county. We planned to start building a basement in the spring. I went to the doctor one day to get some moles removed from my neck and chest. The doctor looked at my file and asked why I'd had my tubes tied so young. He asked if I knew that could be reversed now—a doctor in town just started doing it. I could have fallen off his table! I begged Todd to let me do it. He refused. I saw the doctor any way. He said I was a good candidate and our insurance would cover it. I begged Todd for months before he finally said yes because I would "never shut up about it".

The doctor said every woman has a five percent chance of an ectopic pregnancy, but a reversal would increase that risk to ten percent. He told me to think about that, and discuss it with my husband because I had other kids at home who could be left without a mother if I had a ectopic pregnancy. I was scared, but I had the surgery.

We had put our trailer and half an acre lot up for sale and were surprised that it appraised for $23,500. We had only paid $2,300 for it originally. Todd's sister Connie kept running her mouth, saying that "Some people think they have more than they do!" She said we would never get that amount. I couldn't wait until we could move. She walked in and snapped at me anytime she felt like it.

Todd was making more money at work now, and seemed happier. We had saved and stayed on a tight budget. One month after the surgery, my period was late. I went to my doctor to see if I could be pregnant already. They did a blood test and an ultrasound, and said they would call me. They called and said yes, I was pregnant—pregnant for twins.

I walked out my front door to go tell my sister-in-law Sue who lived down the hill. She was in her yard, so I yelled, "I'm pregnant with twins!" I fell to my knees in my front yard, crying tears of joy and disbelief.

On Easter Sunday 1986, life had never been better. We were standing on the spot where we planned to build a new home with our own hands. The three boys were running and playing nearby. It was a beautiful spring day—and the happiest moment in my life.

Todd and I stood on our hill, and he explained to me how the house would sit even with the road as you saw it coming around the bend. He explained what a transit level is, and how things needed to sit eye level. He told me to draw the house plans, and he would build it however I wanted. I'd taken a course in designing a floor plan in high school, so I was excited to pretend to be an architect. I was so excited and couldn't wait to start.

I stood there on that hill for a moment wondering how I got there from where I'd been so long ago. I once had no love. Now I had my own family, whom I loved with everything I had. I had once been homeless. Now we were building a new home. I had once been sterile. Now I was pregnant with twins. I once sat on a hill praying, not knowing where my future would lead. Now here I stood just seven years later on my very own hill. I was consumed by bliss.

Cameron screamed, "Mom! Cole!"

We knew something terrible had happened to Cole. Todd took off running in the direction of Cameron's scream. I stood there, frozen in time. I couldn't move. I refused to go see my baby Cole dead.

I began to pray on top of that hill. I couldn't move. I needed to be there with Cole right then, not in the time it took to run to him. I immediately put my faith in God to save Cole. He had to. I feared I wouldn't get there in time if I ran.

My legs couldn't move. One second I was in complete bliss, and the very next I was in complete terror.

I prayed so fast and hard, it felt like I melted into the prayer. Then I was in the air, hovering over the field towards the creek. I was in two places at once. On the hill, and above the field in the air. Somehow, I could almost see, or know, what was going on with Cole. Or I just felt I knew. I gained insight. I could tell he'd fallen in the creek. He thought it was deeper than it really was, so he was trying to swim instead of just walk out of there. The creek had always been ankle deep, but we'd had a lot of rain lately. Still, it wasn't so deep that he couldn't just walk out of there, if he would just calm down.

In my prayer, I said calmly, "Cole, calm down. It isn't that deep. Put your feet down and walk out of there." I started to relax and trust that God was working with me. I needed to be sure. I felt I needed to offer a sacrifice.

I told God if he needed to take a child from me that day, to take my twins. I hadn't seen them yet. I loved Cole so much and I wanted my twins so badly and loved them already too. Yet I could not live one day without seeing Cole's face again. I wouldn't be any use to anyone, not even myself if I lost Cole.

"God doesn't give us more than we can handle," I told God.

And I couldn't handle losing Cole. It was not possible. I thought of his sweet face, those big blue eyes and chubby little cheeks. Cole had thick, dark brown hair. He looked so much like a My Buddy doll, that I got him one. He cuddled it and his My Little Pony so tight before bed in his fuzzy blue pajamas. I treasured every inch of him, showing him to God. He had a sweet, overly-sensitive personality. Cole was one of those babies who never gave you one ounce of trouble. He was born naturally pure and good and beautiful. We couldn't lose him—the world needed more boys like Cole. He would be a wonderful husband and father someday.

I continued praying. I now stood in the back field. I had slowly walked there while praying in a trance. I still feared my son was dead. I couldn't bring myself to go to the creek and see him for myself. I couldn't. I wouldn't. I watched as Todd jumped through weeds to find the boys.

Just as Todd was about to jump down to the creek, I saw Cole's head come up from the creek bank. He didn't even glance at his dad, who was standing right by him. He walked past him and headed straight to me, like he was in a trance. He never took his eyes off me. I feared I was seeing his ghost. It was too good to be true.

Cole came up to me and stopped. He looked up at me. "Mom, was you worried about me?"

I fell to my knees and cried and hugged my baby tight. "My God, Cole, you are my baby!"

I thanked God with all my heart that Cole was okay. I knew what I had just offered God in return, but I never told anyone.

Sometime after Cole's near drowning, I started having pain. I called my OB/GYN several times that week. He kept assuring me everything was fine, saying, "The ultrasound showed both babies are in the uterus, so don't worry. It's not a tubal pregnancy."

I had to stop what I was doing and lie on the couch because it was so painful. By the end of the week, I could no longer walk, the pain was so bad, and then I started bleeding. I passed something, and I wasn't sure what it was.

I told Todd to take the kids to his mom's, then come back and get me. I needed him to drive me to the hospital. I had heard once that if you miscarry at home, you should take the fetus with you. Maybe they could tell what caused the baby's death and prevent it next time.

I carried what I had passed in a baggy and held it in my lap during the hour drive to the hospital.

My pain got worse as we got closer to the hospital. I looked down at the baggy of bright red blood and tissue, and cried out, "I never thought this is how I would hold my babies!" A deep sorrowful cry slipped out of my lungs.

Todd didn't say a word. Just before we crossed the bridge into town, my pain suddenly faded. It faded in a strange way, a way that made me feel I was fading along with it. Wherever the pain was going, that's where I was going. I didn't want to admit it to Todd, but I thought I was about to die. In fact, I knew I was. I told myself to hold on until we got to the hospital.

When Todd pulled into the emergency parking lot, I told him to drive up to the entrance doors. I didn't want him to leave me alone while he got a wheelchair, so he helped me walk in. I told the triage nurse that my symptoms were no longer pain. Now I was about to throw up, or I was about to pass out. I wasn't sure which one would happen first. I told her I feared I had a tubal pregnancy.

A nurse had Todd stay and fill out forms while she took me back to a room. She put me in a wheelchair and handed me a blue bowl in case I got sick. As she started down the long hallway, I wanted to reach for the blue bowl that sat in my lap. I thought I was about to throw up. But I couldn't move my hands off the wheelchair armrests, or even my fingers to reach for the bowl. My hands remained still. I had lost the ability to tell my body what to do.

My head dropped to my chest. I hoped I could aim my vomit so I wouldn't get it all over me. As my head dropped more, I realized I wasn't going to throw up after all. I was passing out—right then.

Suddenly, I am in a dim, narrow tunnel and I am flying fast, straight up, like I was shot like a rocket. In an instant, I am far out into space. It is a bumpy ride, like a roller coaster. There's vibration and a knocking noise as the strong wind crashes into the sides of the tunnel. I am in a force of speed. The wind speed forces me up, making a loud "swooshing" noise like a rocket does when it's launched.

I have just died.

I am dead.

The words *I am* seemed to consume my thoughts.

I am headed to Heaven, but I don't want to go. I am too far out in space to turn around and find my way back to my boys. I can't plot an escape, and I never will be able to return. My boys are all I can think about. I am being taken far away from them—way, way out into space. Forever. I have lost it all.

Then the loud bumpy, swift ride ends. I am at my destination, floating, still and quiet, in a bright white light. I still feel like me, but as I look all around me, I can't see me. I hover inside the light. I can see through myself. Up, down, and in between is all white light. I wondered if this is all there is to Heaven

There is no sound nor movement. I didn't think I would be all alone when I died and went to Heaven someday. Will I be all alone forever? Have I done something wrong that would keep me like this for eternity?

The only thing I care about is my three boys. I don't care about anything or anyone else, not even my life, except I need my life to take care of my boys.

I wish I wasn't alone. Then suddenly I realize I'm not. There is a panel of people up ahead, slightly to my right. I can see an outline of them, like a shadow. I look at them and feel them looking at me, even though I only see an outline. I squint as I scan the outline, trying to focus better. One sits up front and center, and I know that must be God.

Now I have someone to blame. I scream at Him because I need to be back there for my sons. I am rude and disrespectful, basically saying, "Hell, no! I won't go!"

I sense I am at an entrance, and if I stay, we'll move farther into Heaven. God shows me a vision of what he wants me to understand. I see a child in a store demanding something while his parents calmly tell him "no." The child kicks and screams and throws a fit, acting like a spoiled brat, not respecting his parents' authority.

They know what is best for him, and the answer is simply "no." The parents patiently give the child time to accept it. They are not stressed by his behavior—they just observe it.

Then I understand. I am the brat in this scenario. The answer to what I want is no, and they are patiently giving me time to accept it.

My temper tantrum will not get me where I want to be. I have to change to be heard. God is the boss here, not me.

I humble myself before God and beg Him to allow me to return to my sons. I blurt out my reasons, which come out as one long scream like projectile vomiting.

I tell him of every abuse I endured in my childhood, and how I grew up unloved, and how I need to keep anything like that from happening to my sons. I can't bear for even one bad thing to happen to them. I was an overly-protective mother. I rarely let anyone else watch my sons. I had to keep them safe. They have a mother who loves them, that shouldn't be taken away from them. Some kids don't have that, but my kids do. A mother's love is priceless. I don't trust anyone else to take care of them.

All that comes out in one long scream, like vomit. It disappears into the white space.

God and I communicate through our thoughts. I feel like I am still using words, but when He talks, I hear a male voice inside me, not outside of me.

I humble myself before God again, telling Him I know He is Omniscient. I know He can see into the future. If He will look and see that if my boys will be better off without me, then I will stay. If they will be better off with me, then I beg to return so I can raise them. I know God would do what is best for the children. He loves children. I trust Him completely.

I am shown a vision of the future, how life would be for my boys if I died. It was like a scene out of The Christmas Carol. Jesus and I hover over our trailer. It's dark outside and the boys' bedroom light is on. We see in like there's no roof over their room. They're in their bedroom, standing in front of the bunk bed.

We drop nearer to get a closer look. They are crying and wishing Mom hadn't died. In this future scene, their Dad has a girlfriend, but she doesn't love them the way I did. They miss me terribly. Cole starts crying so hard that he becomes angry. He doesn't care that I am dead, he just wants me back—right now!

I feel Cole's intense pain and start bawling. I know now this is not God's fault—it's all my fault. I got my tubes tied. I had them reversed. I caused the ectopic pregnancy that caused my twins to die. I caused my death. I caused all of this, not God. I did this to my boys, and to all of us. I withdraw.

I weep uncontrollably with my arms wrapped around my head. I notice I am lying down beside Jesus's feet, surrounded by the bright white light again. I am back in Heaven. I am filled with gut-wrenching anguish and despair, bawling from guilt, shame, remorse and heartache. Then I slightly lift my head trying to look up at Jesus, who I feel is now seated beside God. I cry out, "Who else will teach them about You?"

CHAPTER 13

AFTER EFFECTS

Suddenly, I was back. Briefly for a moment, I was in the florescent light on the ceiling of the Emergency Department hallway. Then I entered my body. My hearing came back first. The nurse was talking to another woman. I didn't know when that woman joined us, because I wasn't there. Then I felt my hands on the wheelchair armrests. Next, I felt a wave of warmth run down the inside my body. I waited to feel my feet—they were last. Once I felt them on the foot pedals, I knew I was fully back.

My first thoughts: What the hell was that?! I was just in Heaven. Now I am back. How did that happen? I couldn't comprehend it. Then I felt annoyed that no one even knew I'd died. That nurse was too busy socializing to know her patient just died! Then I thought, I can't think about any of that now. I had to focus on how I was going to stay alive for my boys. God let me come back, but what if I didn't have much time to save my life? I had to make my doctor see I was in trouble here. He had blown me off all week. What if he didn't believe me and I died again, this time for good?

My pain had stopped, as had the bleeding, nausea, and feeling I was going to faint. Physically, I felt fine now, but because of what I'd just experienced, I knew I wasn't fine at all. I was going to die without medical intervention. I hoped my doctor would see what was wrong when he examined me. I couldn't tell him what had just happened—he would think I was crazy and not take me seriously. I didn't want to be sent to the mental ward because something was very wrong with my physical health that needed immediate attention.

I knew in my heart there was no hope for my twins. There was nothing I could do for them. I had to save my life so I could stay and raise my three sons.

Ty's permanent custody hearing was next week. His life depended on me to be here. I couldn't let Molly down, either. If I died, Todd wouldn't adopt Ty, and he would eventually be sent back to his alcoholic father.

The nurse took me to a room at the end of the hall and told me to get on a bed that was jacked up high. There was a big lamp over the bed. Todd came back and kept asking for more warm blankets for me. I was so cold my teeth rattled, like my body temperature was now low. My knees knocked together, and I shook so hard I thought I'd shake right off the table. Todd had to hold me down.

My doctor was on call. He came in and prepped me for a D & C, thinking I must have miscarried. I cried as I prepared to have my babies yanked out of me. I felt this would be the moment of their death. After examining me, he sat me up, looked at me, puzzled, and said my uterus was intact. I was still pregnant. He said the pregnancy was fine. He asked me why I kept insisting I was having a tubal pregnancy. He said I'd told the nurse that when I came in, and he'd already told me it wasn't tubal. The ultrasound he did before in his office showed both babies were in the uterus.

He looked at Todd, as if he were trying to figure out if I were crazy or not.

Todd chuckled and shrugged his shoulders. "I don't know."

The doctor said the blood that I passed was just tissue. I was fine and the babies were fine. But since I lived an hour away, I could spend the night there if it would make me feel better, even though there was nothing wrong.

I knew I had just died, so something had to be wrong. I said I would stay.

Todd and the doctor went home. I was put in a private room. I lay in bed, afraid to fall asleep, fearing I would never wake up again. I was afraid I'd return to Heaven, knowing I'd been given a second chance to raise my boys, and I'd blown it. I didn't know if I could make it until morning. Whatever caused my death was not fixed. I thought it was a tubal/ectopic pregnancy, but the doctor said that was not possible. I could only pray that I would live through the night, and that my doctor wouldn't send me home in the morning. If he did, I would quickly die. I knew this with certainty.

I prayed that my doctor would keep me long enough for another ultrasound and find out what was wrong, before it was too late. I knew I would never hold my twins in my arms like I'd hoped, but saving my life was all I could focus on right now.

Eventually, I fell asleep, then woke right back up because of pain in my right hip area. I felt sick, so I sat up and reached for the blue bowl. Then I woke up, covered in vomit. Nothing went in the bowl because I was passed out when I vomited. This happened several times during the night. The large nurse got upset with me and told me to use my bowl. She was tired of coming in my room to clean me and my bed.

I told her there was something wrong, and asked her to call my doctor. She snapped at me, saying, "He is home in bed, and I am not going to call and wake him up!" She demanded that I just use my bowl.

I was sad. No one ever took me seriously. People always assumed I was dumb and my opinions were discounted.

The next morning, an orderly came to take me to Ultrasound in a wheelchair. I warned him I would pass out if I sat up in the chair. He said he didn't have an order to take me down in my bed, so I had to get in the wheelchair. He said he'd get a sheet for my lap and be right back. I did as I was told. I sat in that wheelchair, knowing what would happen next—I would pass out.

The next thing I know, I was lying back in my bed and several nurses were gathered around, looking down at me. They looked worried and were trying to wake me up. One waved smelling salts under my nose. They said the orderly had returned with a sheet and found me with my head on the floor. I was mooning him, and it scared him to death.

140

They now were sending me to ultrasound in my bed, because for some reason I passed out every time I sat up. I was frustrated that it took so long for people to get it, yet I was glad now they finally did.

As the orderly pushed me and my bed into the elevator, Tonya was there. She said she wished she could trade places with me.

"No, you don't. I'm dead."

She giggled and said she wanted to see the ultrasound of the twins.

"They're dead," I said.

Again, she ignored me and continued smiling and rambling.

This world is dumb. It wasn't just me after all—the whole world is dumb, I concluded.

When the ultrasound began, I turned my head away from the screen, toward Tonya.

"Oh, look, Peg! I see them! I see the twins!"

I refused to look. I knew they were dead.

Tonya coaxed me, and the ultrasound tech wasn't saying there was a problem, so maybe—could I have been wrong? Was everyone else right? Were the babies really fine after all?

I would have loved to enjoy this moment with Tonya and look forward to my babies being born in seven months. Could I be crazy? How I wished that were true. If the trip to Heaven last night was just my imagination, then my babies were okay. I knew what I saw, felt, and heard, but if I were crazy, that would explain everything. Crazy would be great right now, instead of me and the twins dying. As much as I always worried I'd end up mentally ill like Molly, I now wished I were, if that meant my twins were okay. I felt a flicker of hope and excitement. As the picture of bringing my twins home returned, I turned to look at the ultrasound. Just as I did, the tech grabbed the screen and turned it towards her so I couldn't see it. I looked at her face. It went white, and she looked scared to death.

She jumped out of her chair so fast, it fell backwards—and she didn't care. She ran to the emergency phone on the basement post. She paged my doctor, yelling "STAT!" Then she ran out of the room.

Well, I'm a goner.

I hadn't been wrong, crazy, or misled by my visit to Heaven. It was true—I had died last night. I somehow stayed alive all night, by the Grace of God, and finally they saw what I knew all along—something was very wrong. My twins would have to be removed. I only hoped they would hurry now before it is too late for me to survive.

My doctor quickly came in the room and did the ultrasound himself. He looked at me. "Peggy, it's the worst thing imaginable. Internal bleeding is filling your entire abdominal cavity. You have blood clear up to your chest."

He said because I was an organ donor, I had to go back to my room to sign papers to donate my organs. He would scrub up and see me in surgery.

I was put in a room by myself to sign each organ away. I asked if they had a form that said "Take it all!" But, no, I had to sign to release each organ individually. I was afraid I wouldn't get to surgery in time. I feared too much time had passed, and it would be too late now. I imagined all the people who would benefit from my healthy twenty-five-year-old body.

I was angry. I wanted to spend my last few moments alive being mad, not giving my body away. My death was now about me, not my boys. I felt very selfish. I was too young to die. I was pretty, too, damn it! I shouldn't die!

I was taken to the operating room. My doctor looked down at me and apologized. A tiny tear filled one eye and I watched it roll down his cheek.

I turned my head away from him. I hoped he never forgot me and how I died because he refused to listen to me. At this moment, I believed it was all his fault. I was back to anger and blaming, being self-centered and selfish and bitter, believing I would never wake up from surgery. I thought about calls being made to people who would be excited to get my organs. I thought about my eyes and parts being cut from my pretty young body, and I was pissed off about it.

When I awoke, I was in my room. My anger was replaced with relief for me and grief for my babies.

My doctor came in, held my hand, and apologized again.

Quiet tears of acceptance and forgiveness fell down my cheeks.

He said he knew how much we wanted those babies. His compassion comforted me. He said one baby was in the uterus and the other was stuck in my right tube. He said it had almost made it in. I gained a visual picture of this and thought about how they must have suffered. I mourned the loss, and knew I had caused it.

He said I was famous at the hospital—it was the biggest tubal pregnancy the hospital had ever seen. The babies were growing and thriving, and it was otherwise a healthy pregnancy. Doctors would be poking their heads in to look at me. I was the talk of the hospital.

I was a little irritated that he thought being famous at the hospital for a day or two because my babies died would compensate me.

My doctor said that I'd taught him a lesson—to listen to his patients over his machines. He said I kept telling him something was wrong, but the ultrasound showed both babies were in the uterus. I hoped my babies hadn't lived and died in vain. Maybe this would save the lives of other babies. I asked how big they were, then I asked to see them.

His face dropped. He said they were put in the incinerator with other body tissue and parts.

I imagined they were thrown down a laundry shoot and landed in a heap of disgusting biohazard waste like they were nothing important.

They were my children. Tears rolled down my cheeks again. My doctor looked like he didn't know what to say.

Todd came in, smiling. He said my dad was outside my door, and he had told Todd not to come in because I was in there with another man—a tall, blond man.

My doctor and I laughed as I wiped my tears away.

Todd said he informed my dad the man was my doctor. We all got a chuckle out of that.

Later, after Todd left, my dad came in my room. He was rambling on, saying Molly didn't need custody of Ty, and he would go to court for me against her. I told him court wasn't against Molly—she asked us to take Ty. Court was so Molly's ex-husband couldn't take him. Molly knew she couldn't take care of Ty, but she had to try.

We didn't even have a lawyer. Molly's lawyer was asking for custody for Molly, but if the court found she couldn't raise him, then she asked that we get permanent custody. She gave us temporary custody when he was two, two years earlier.

But I didn't want to talk about any of that right now. I was grieving. Two of my children had just died. I felt a wave of grief returning.

I looked over at my dad. "Do you love me, Dad?"

He immediately started bashing my mother, blaming her for everything that went wrong in their marriage and in our lives.

I quietly turned my back away from him and blocked him out, hoping he would go away. He finally did.

It was now time to mourn my babies. The due date was all I could think about. I couldn't let go of the dream that I would bring them home. I could see it so clearly, one in each arm as I smiled down at them, yet I knew it would never be. I felt so alone. I didn't have anyone to comfort me.

Tonya said that during my surgery, Mom was mad, saying my funeral arrangements would be left up to her because Todd would be too upset to do it. The whole family had been called and told to come in right away because I wasn't going to make it.

Sam came in my room. He said when he got the call, he left work and came straight there, but Todd left work and went home and took a shower first.

Just like when I was in the Open-Door Detention Center, I felt everyone made everything about themselves and their anger, and didn't care how I felt.

I spent a week alone in the hospital and was given a lot of blood. I did a lot of crying. I fell into a depression that I couldn't escape.

I went home and drew house plans all day at the kitchen table. I told the boys to stay in the living room and play with their toys and watch TV. It allowed me to disappear for a while. I cooked and cleaned and did everything I had to. I closed myself off from everyone. I had three beautiful boys. I should be happy. But I wanted my twins too.

I felt selfish for grieving when I had so much to be thankful for, yet I had an empty womb.

One week after I lost the twins, just after I got out of the hospital, I was on the witness stand all day fighting for Ty in case Molly couldn't have him.

Molly's ex-husband's attorney ended an argument with, "You just got out of the hospital, didn't you?"

I answered, "Yes," firmly, with a raised eyebrow that said *You better not say I wanted Ty just because I can't have kids.*

He backed off, so I didn't have to say the words. I was glad. I was exhausted by the end of the day.

Mom and Tonya sat with me. At times, I would sit behind Molly and her lawyer and give them more fuel against Molly's ex. Mom testified. She lied and denied things she'd told me had happened between Molly and her ex. Mom stated she'd done a lot of "soul searching" and determined Molly should get custody, not me.

When Mom was done tearing down what Molly and I had been working for, she came back and sat next to me again. I put my arm around Mom and comforted her.

Tonya sat smiling, just watching it all unfold.

The judge looked at me, confused. I think she wondered why I would comfort someone who'd just stabbed me in the back, and why was I helping Molly and her lawyer. I think she saw I was the mother in my family. I was the youngest, but I was the protector, and the only voice of reason in the case.

Todd and I were given permanent custody, and the parents were given liberal visitation rights. A few years later, Molly and her ex asked us to adopt Ty. They knew it was best for him, and we were happy to do that.

When Molly was pregnant for Ty, Mom insisted that Molly get an abortion. She said Molly couldn't raise her first child, so there was no way she could raise this baby either. She said due to Molly's mental illness medications, the baby "wouldn't be right."

I reassured Molly all through the pregnancy that she didn't have to listen to Mom. If she couldn't raise him, Todd and I would. Every time I visited Molly, she would tell me Mom was still after her to get an abortion. I would explain to her again that she didn't have to. It was Molly's decision, not Mom's, and Molly always said she didn't want an abortion.

Molly wanted a happy life like everyone else. She wanted a marriage and children, but her illness took everything from her. I wasn't about to harm her in any way, and I despised anyone who did. Yet, we had to ensure Ty's safety, and Molly was all for that. Despite her illness, she knew what was best for her son, and was willing to sacrifice herself for him. She also loved me, and knew I would take good care of him. It was the best thing that came out of our family.

One month after I lost the twins, I was pregnant again. I couldn't handle it. How can you be happy about having one baby when you just lost two? I knew nature wouldn't allow me to keep it. I was going to die this time. I had blocked the Heaven experience completely out of my mind because it was too frightening. I was so torn. I wanted to live and raise my boys. I wanted my twins. I wanted this baby. I wanted more babies in the future, yet getting pregnant now meant dying. I knew now how fast death happens, and how real it is.

I couldn't get attached to this baby. I was too afraid I'd lose it too. My heart and mind were in a constant battle, and I felt like I was going in circles, not able to find a resolution. I was withdrawing from my beautiful little boys and couldn't help it. I thought I would die anyway and not get to raise them.

I had no one to talk to, and, as usual, no one cared. I felt like a selfish loser. I felt guilty for being the healthy sister and getting Molly's child. I had three, and she didn't have any with her. I should be happy, but I wasn't. The last time I was happy, Cole almost drowned, the twins died, and I died. I was lost.

One day I couldn't deal with it all anymore, so I ran outside. I grabbed a garden hoe and started chopping down all my flowers that were growing tall and beautiful in front of my trailer. An elderly lady next door had given me flower bulbs the fall before, and they had done very well. I had no idea why I wanted to kill those flowers. I was angry they lived and my twins didn't . . . and I knew this baby wouldn't either. The flowers were growing and thriving with ease, like they were showing off how easy fertility is.

What should come naturally, I had destroyed in myself. I hated myself for having my tubes tied and causing this. I directed my rage for myself to those flowers.

When I was seven weeks pregnant, I was very worried. I'd lost the twins at eight weeks. I worried that I would die in my sleep. Without pain to warn me, my tube would just rupture, and I would bleed to death.

We went to a family reunion for Todd's mom's side of the family. As everyone lined up to get a plate, I heard a child crying. I asked people in line if they heard it too. Everyone said no, and was just focused on the food. I followed the sound of the crying and ended up in a field. I looked all around me, but I couldn't see anything. I knew what I'd heard, but it had stopped now. I felt led, like there was something there. I sensed it in the air around me.

But why?

There was something there, but what?

I noticed some high grass. I walked over and looked past the grass, even though it didn't make any sense. Then I saw a tiny boy floating face down in a narrow ditch. His shoulders were jerking slightly. I reached down and pulled him up by the back of his shirt. He landed on his feet, and looked up at me like he'd seen a ghost. He was soaking wet and his eyes bulged out as he stared at me. Water flooded down his face.

He quickly ran off to his parents. I saw him at the entrance of our picnic shelter, pointing to me, and telling them what had happened. They looked confused as they looked towards me out in the field, standing alone.

When I pulled him up by his shirt, I felt myself miscarry. I went to the outhouse and confirmed it. I had Todd and the boys come sit with me under a tree to eat. I didn't want to be around people. This was hard enough to deal with on my own. Todd never wanted more kids.

When they were done eating, I told him I needed to go home. I had lost three babies in two months. I wasn't done mourning the twins yet, now this.

Since the tubal pregnancy, I had longed to hear the old church hymns I'd grown up with. Catholics don't usually go outside their religion to other churches, yet I begged Todd to take me to my grandma's church.

He finally agreed, but wasn't happy.

With an angry husband standing by my side and a lump in my throat, I sang the hymns, and my heart tenderly healed.

As we walked out of grandma's church, Todd warned me to never ask him to do that again.

Sarah's boys played at our place a lot. One night when she came to pick up her kids from our home, I asked if she'd heard we lost the twins.

"Yeah," she said. "I heard you were pregnant, but I didn't know if it was true or not."

It sounded like she thought I had lied about being pregnant. All she wanted to talk about was winning $50 on a lottery ticket. I had watched her kids all day, and she couldn't spare one minute to console me.

After I miscarried the second time, I knew better than to reach out to anyone. The people I thought were good Christians proved it was all about religion, and nothing to do with love or compassion.

We had to go to a party at Todd's parents' house. I was so sad, and still not one person could be the tiniest bit kinder to me. They ignored me and treated me like I wasn't worth speaking to at all. I had hoped we were past that. Apparently, we never would be. I would always be just a "worthless nigger-loving whore" in their eyes.

I went outside to be alone. I was tired of trying to make the world like me. I was tired of trying to get them to see me as human. I was tired of trying to turn people who hated me into my family. I couldn't even play with the kids.

I sat in the yard, in the wet grass, alone in the dark. It felt good to be away from all the people in that house. A group gathered on the front porch. They grew drunker and louder. I looked up at the night sky and blocked them all out. It felt good to release myself from trying to fit in. I knew now these people would never like me.

If they couldn't care about innocent little babies who were their own blood dying, there was no way they would ever care about me.

I realized the problem lay in them. For the first time in my life, I just let it all go. I got so lost in the beauty of the night sky and the twinkling white stars that I felt I was inside the sky. I just glided up there for a little while, feeling the warm summer breeze on my skin as I floated weightless among the stars. I was consumed by bliss in space, safe away from this earth.

I slipped away, far away. I completely let go. Then I watched the entire incident of me drowning when I was five—from start to finish. I was fully there and not here, and it was all okay. It played like a movie screen inside my eyes. When it was over, I sat up from the wet grass. Did I drown when I was little? I had no memory of drowning at all until this moment, but now it was as fresh as if it had just happened. I had been transported back in time. It was such a smooth transition, going there and coming back. There was no denying it. This was such a personal and private moment. This was not for anyone but me.

I decided to go see my family in Marietta the next day to find out. I'd never had a memory just come out of nowhere like that before. It was so vivid and clear. It had me captivated from start to finish.

I visited Mom, Tonya, and Jack each alone, one at a time at their homes. Yes, I had drowned when I was five in that pond just as I remembered it. I only wanted the facts. One, did it happen? And two, how did they find me?

None of them recalled how they found me. Jack said all he knew was that he got in a lot of trouble that day because of me. He added that he was always getting into trouble because of me.

Tonya remembered when I drowned too. I think they had forgotten all about it until I brought it up. It had never been discussed before. If I hadn't recalled it, I doubt anyone would've ever told me.

Years later, Mom said she'd thought more about the day I drowned. She thought that after she noticed I wasn't there, she made Jack find me, since he was the last to see me. She thought he felt around until he found me down under the water, and then pulled me out. Mom said she thought she had lost another kid that day, and knew my dad's family would blame her for that too, like they had when Junior died. I think she kept my drowning a secret from my dad all those years so he wouldn't blame her for it.

Back then, I didn't know there was such a thing as Near Death Experiences ("NDE") or NDE after-effects. All I knew was that weird things happened for a while after I lost the twins.

One night, after I finished supper dishes, I stepped down to our new living room that we'd built on the back of our trailer. Todd and the three boys had fallen asleep, curled up beside each other on the floor in front of the TV. I sat down and gazed at them, appreciating them, thinking how cute they all were and how lucky I was. I realized I was back to my old self, feeling bliss again.

Suddenly I was gone. I was five. I was in my nightgown, standing in front of the bathroom door at night because I had to pee. I knocked on the door and now Dad was mad. He slammed the newspaper shut so loudly and angrily that I jumped.

I was gone. I was afraid. I couldn't see my living room, Todd, the boys or anything. I was in 1966! I jumped up and ran, trying to escape what was in my vision. I fought to come back to the present. I ran out the back door, into the night, and right into a friend of Todd's. He was standing on our back deck. He said he knocked on the front door but the TV was on. He thought we didn't hear him, so he came to the back door. I hadn't heard him knocking—I heard myself knocking on the bathroom door in 1966! I was now in two places at once, twenty years apart! I was struggling to come back!

I could see him and hear him, and I knew I was outside, but this vision was also still going on. The past was in my vision more than the present was. I was terrified of my dad being mad at me while I was in the kitchen needing to pee, and terrified I was losing my mind on the back deck at night outside of my home. I was in a time warp. I assumed I had gone crazy, and if I didn't pull out of it, I would be hospitalized.

I had never remembered this incident before, and didn't

understand why I was so afraid, or why it was so powerful, or why it took control of me like that.

Todd woke up and came to see what was going on. His friend told him there was something wrong with me, and that he needed to see if I was okay. Todd invited him in and they left me alone outside. Todd's friend was still concerned, but Todd couldn't care less.

I paced back and forth, forcing the present to come back to me. I forced myself to think of anything else, touch things outside, anything to stay in this time. Once I calmed myself, I went back inside and pushed it out of my mind.

I got excited about moving to our new house, so one day while Todd was at work, I moved us out of the trailer and into the basement. Todd came home from work and was befuddled. I told him we could get more done on the house if we lived there, then trying to find the time after work. Soon afterwards, someone bought our trailer and half-acre lot for what it was appraised for. It paid for our property and our basement.

Soon we finished the basement and built a concrete patio, retaining walls and a long deck.

One day I walked through the living room, headed to the kitchen to start supper. The boys were down for a nap, and I paused to watch Oprah for a minute. She was new then, and I wanted to see what she was talking about.

Oprah was interviewing a group of people who claimed they went to Heaven and came back. I immediately decided they were liars. I stood there arguing with the TV, saying nobody was that stupid, nobody was going to believe that. I felt so strongly that these people were just like Tonya, telling tall tales for attention and hoping to find a sucker dumb enough to believe them. I yelled at the TV, telling those people how stupid they were. I never scoffed at anyone so much in my life.

I stepped back away from the TV and took a step to leave when something they said felt so familiar. I paused in silence for a moment, sensing.

It all came back to me. It was real! It really did happen! I covered my eyes and my mouth with my hands and shook all over in disbelief. It was true! I couldn't deny it, but how could it be? I had to tell Todd, but I was afraid to tell anyone. But I had to!

I continued a dialogue with myself for a few minutes as I paced back and forth from the living room to the kitchen. It seemed like Oprah was even skeptical. I certainly understood that. How I just felt about those people was how people would feel about me. Their so-called experiences sounded ridiculous, but it happened to me.

I made dinner. When Todd came home and the dinner dishes were put away, I asked the boys to play quietly in their room for a while. I needed to talk to Dad. I sat down at the kitchen table and told Todd about dying and going to Heaven. As I told him, I started to shake all over. I felt like my soul was fighting my mind, like my soul had to break free of my mind to express itself. I felt freezing cold, just like I had when I woke up after I came back, when Todd had to keep getting me blankets in the exam room. Or, maybe I couldn't stop shaking from the shock of remembering. I wasn't sure.

I relived going through the tunnel and being in the light and wanting so badly to come back. I was so afraid of what I was saying. It sounded impossible and crazy, but it happened.

Todd looked at me, and when I finished, he said, "As crazy as it sounds, I know you wouldn't lie and make that up." He said he believed me because of how I looked when I told him.

Then he told me he had seen and heard an old man with a wooden leg walking in his parent's old house before it burnt down. He said nobody believed him, but he saw the man.

I felt better knowing something happened to him that he couldn't explain as well.

Later, I told Tonya and Chuck. They didn't say anything. They just looked away when I was done and changed the subject. I figured I'd better forget about it—I didn't want to be weird. It was lonely not to have anyone who could explain it to me, and to be the only one this had happened to. I was sure our library wouldn't have any books about it. Other than those weirdos on Oprah and me, no one else had ever experienced such a thing, as far as I knew.

Not long after that, we were driving through Gallia County. All a sudden, I told Todd to pull over. I didn't know who lived in that house, but I had to go there. I was led. I knocked on the door, and Sis, Jack's ex, answered. It was her sister's house. I didn't know that.

Sis was babysitting her nephew. I no more than walked into the living room when Sis's nephew came in from his bedroom. He was choking on Easter basket grass. I grabbed him, ran to the bathroom with him under my arm, and turned him upside down over the tub. I turned on the water, got my fingers wet, and stuck my fingers way down his throat. I kept pulling the plastic grass out until I couldn't feel any more.

He started kicking and wanted down, so I let go. He was fine.

I went back out and got in the car. I told Todd who it was and what happened. As we drove home, we would glance at each other in silence occasionally. The unspoken words between us were *What is happening to me?* First, I heard that little boy crying when nobody else did, and I saved him from drowning. Now I suddenly had to stop at a strange house, where my friend just happened to be babysitting, and as soon as I walked in, her nephew was choking, and I save his life too!

Sis had no idea what to do. She got out the phone book and was going to call her sister and say she couldn't handle him. She didn't know he was choking and wouldn't have known what to do if she had. (Sis has some learning disabilities.) She said I saved his life. To this day, she says he would've died if I hadn't been there.

One day, while Todd and I lay out in the sun on our deck, I heard a soft scuffing noise. I told Todd, but he said he didn't hear anything.

"I'm going to check it out," I said.

Todd went with me. We didn't see anything, but we kept walking anyway. I told him I saw a shadow at the top of the hill, across the road. Maybe it was dirt, but maybe someone went off the road. We walked on up the road. A car was parked on the right side, but there was no noise at all. As we grew closer, we realized the car was actually off the road because it had hit a tree head-on.

We looked in the car. Two men sat in the front with their heads leaning on the dash. We thought they were dead. We spoke to them and their eyes turned to look at us, but otherwise, they didn't move at all.

Todd looked over the cliff, and two men had been ejected from the backseat. They were way down below in the creek. Todd told me to go call for help and bring boards for their necks. I ran back home and called for help. I told them to send a life flight. We tried to keep the men calm until help arrived. We were told later that we had saved their lives. The two men in the car kept dying in transport, and would have been paralyzed if we hadn't supported their necks.

Years later, I felt led again. I sensed there was something wrong in the backyard. I walked back to the dog kennel and found a dog that didn't belong to us. The kids had found it and chained it up because it would dig under the fence. The chain was wrapped several times around its neck, and it was dying. I unwrapped it, but it died before I could get it all untangled.

My mom was there and told me to leave it alone, it was dead. I kept nudging it and talking to it. I threw water on it, and it came back to life. Then it staggered off.

Mom looked at me in amazement. "You brought that dog back from the dead."

CHAPTER 14

BACK TO WORK

One day I looked in the classifieds and saw a job opening: child assault prevention workshop leader. I interviewed for it and got the job. I was to teach in three counties about child assault prevention. I had always been so shy and couldn't express myself before. Now I couldn't believe I was standing in front of strangers giving speeches and demonstrations. It wasn't long before they made me head workshop leader. The position only lasted that school year, as the grant expired.

The following fall, Ty started school, so I got a job at a doll factory. I quit when school was out. The next fall, I worked at a formal clothing store doing alterations.

One day, the older lady I worked with suddenly stopped her sewing machine, turned around, and said, "Why don't you get out of here? You are young enough. Go to college. Don't waste your life here." Then she turned right back around and continued sewing.

I stopped sewing, sat back in my chair, and thought about what she'd said and how she'd said it. I was wanting to quit my job because school was about to be out for the summer and because they refused to give me the twenty-five-cent raise after six months as they had promised when I was hired.

I couldn't afford daycare, so I never worked in the summer. Todd said I couldn't quit. He said, "If you start something, you have to stick with it." When I wanted to start working, he told me *no*. First, I wasn't allowed to work, then I wasn't allowed to quit. We had just gotten a loan and built the shell of our house. We could afford for me to quit. I wanted another summer home with my boys.

Even though I was twenty-eight, people often said I looked eighteen. Maybe the other college students wouldn't notice I was too old to go to college. My only knowledge about college was that it was for smart, rich kids. I had wanted to be a psychiatrist when I was in high school. I even started talking about it again after we first got Ty.

Mom heard me talking about it, so she brought me a letter from my old high school. She said it came in the mail after I graduated.

It said my test scores were so low that all I would be good at was crafts. She sat in my living room, putting me down, saying I was too dumb for college. She laughed at me for even thinking about it. She told me to go to beauty school so I could fix her hair. She rambled on, then she fluffed her short permed hair and told me how she wanted it fixed. I wondered what was wrong with her.

Ty had social delays from being raised by Molly and her husband for the first two years of his life. He also had seizures, which they failed to inform me of when we got him. I found out the hard way. He stopped breathing and turned black one day.

I got him to where he needed to be for his age pretty quickly. The seizures also stopped. His neurologist had written a letter for the permanent custody hearing praising me, saying even though Ty wasn't born mentally retarded, he had become so due to his environment before we got him. He added that Ty now was doing very well because he was with us and he was exceling in Head Start.

I wondered if I had been retarded due to my environment too. And maybe I wasn't retarded anymore either. I wondered if I would do better in school now that I wasn't at home.

I enjoyed taking those three boys that summer when Mom and her third husband asked me to. After they returned to their mother, children services in Marietta called me. They wanted me to keep the boys. They said the boys kept talking about me. I wanted to, but we lived in the basement and still didn't have room. We also were still having a hard time making ends meet sometimes.

Later, Mom asked me to take in my aunt's two unruly teenage granddaughters after my cousin died. She insisted I take in kids again, but I didn't mind. I was glad our family thought enough of me to ask. I'd heard when I was growing up that my dad had molested my cousin, the girl's mother. I felt this was a way to make up for that to her—since he was my dad, I felt I owed her. Plus, my cousin was so kind. I would want someone to take good care of my kids if I died. We had a small third bedroom. The girls could share a double bed. It wouldn't be for long, and I could use the friendship.

We made a game out of getting our chores done quickly so we had time to play games or do make-overs or just watch a movie and hang out. We called ourselves "The Time Sisters" because we kept track of the time it took to do a chore, and we were pretty fast. I kept them about six months, until they started acting wild.

One day while I was in the bathroom vomiting from the stress they caused me, they body-slammed Cameron on the basement floor, and then they stole my car. I called the police. They had driven to Peyton Plains to one of Todd's brother's houses. They called me and let me know they were there. The girls were sorry. The Juvenile Probation Officer went there and got them. He said he didn't want bad kids from Marietta in our county, and to never let them come back here.

When I had moved to Peyton Plains, I was harshly judged because I was from the "city." By then, I had lived there ten years and was still considered an outsider. The county revolved around who you were related to. Everyone knew everyone's business. If the girls stayed with us, they would now be labeled. Plus, my boys came first.

Outsiders were never trusted in this county. The long-timers seemed to live in a protective bubble, like this was the only place on earth. Everyone was told to not even shop outside the county. "Keep your money here," they said. Some had never stepped foot out of their hometown. Even though there weren't any jobs, they stayed right there. Nobody we met had ever been to college.

I knew of two cousin marriages just in Todd's family and among his friends. Some people talked so "hick," I would sit and laugh because the accent sounded so funny. Before I knew it, I was talking just like them. I came to believe it was the safest place to live, and that eventually I would fit in.

Children Services put the girls in the Open Door. We had an argument a few days before they ran off, because I'd overheard them talking to their friends on the phone at the Open Door. They thought it was funny how their friends were beating up kids at the Detention Center. I was upset they found it so funny, and they turned on me, so I grounded them from talking to those kids.

I got a call from Children's Services later that my nieces were begging to come back. The oldest one was sent to a home for unwed mothers, and the younger one was beating on the caseworker's desk demanding to come back to our house. I turned her down. I was told she'd had a growth spurt, and was even beating up the boys now.

Later, I remembered that I promised myself and God ten years ago that I would do something to help abused kids. I felt I was ready now. I wanted to work with troubled kids. We had built a story and a half onto our basement, so we had room now.

I finally felt confident in who I was and what I had to offer in life. Maybe I could use what happened to me growing up to help kids, because I knew what it was like. Most people don't have a clue.

I asked Todd if I could quit work when school was out, and start college in the fall. I was tired of making four dollars an hour. He said *no* and wouldn't discuss it further.

I was pulling weeds one day and got into poison ivy roots, and my hands became swollen with poison ivy. I couldn't even bend my fingers. I went ahead and quit my job, since I wouldn't be able to sew for weeks anyway. Todd was mad at me for it.

I decided on a college. It was an hour's drive away. I had been accepted to begin classes for my Associate's degree in Human & Correctional Services in the fall of 1989. A friend decided to go too. I was so nervous my first day that she had to drag me out of the car. I kept thinking about how bad my grades were in school. Who did I think I was, going to college? College was for smart people. I was so dumb! I was so shy, there was no way. I finally made a deal with myself—if I would study ten times harder than everyone else and get a C, I would be happy. I figured nobody there knew how dumb I was, so I'd fake it. If I failed, I wouldn't tell anyone my grades.

Starting college was the first time I ever went against Todd's wishes. I told him I would not leave for school until the kids were on the bus. I would be back before they got home. I would still have supper ready and on the table at four p.m. every night when he walked in the door after work, like I always had. Grants covered all my books and tuition. I would never eat at school. All I needed was gas money.

Todd was pissed off at me from then on. I kept my word, except I did eat lunch a few times.

At the end of the first quarter, I couldn't believe it. I'd made the Dean's List. I made it every quarter and even got a 4.0 once. I did have to study a lot harder. I had to be alone to study, and had to talk to myself aloud to hear myself think. My short-term memory was terrible, so I wrote everything down, and rewrote it later. I was fascinated with every class I took and liked all the instructors.

One day, Todd said, "I hope that school teaches you something. You sure as hell don't know anything now!"

That cut me like a knife, and I never forgot it. At least I was trying to get smarter.

One day I was reading the newspaper and noticed an ad for Therapeutic Foster Care. It was a new program they were just trying out to keep kids from going to mental hospitals and detention centers. I called them, and after our training, Todd and I became Therapeutic Foster Parents. Todd refused to do it at first, until he met the staff. We all got along very well. Todd was good looking and charming and everyone easily respected him. He always left the child care to me, which was fine. I was just glad he enjoyed going to the meetings and trainings.

By the second quarter, I was getting paid to do what I had been doing for free—taking in other people's kids. Our first foster child was the sweetest teenage boy. He stayed with us for a year and a half, until he turned 18. Then he moved in with his dad. About a year after he came, we got the sweetest wild-child teenage girl ever.

They both were so good, we had no issues at all. Our boys loved them too.

After I graduated with my two-year degree, I transferred to Ohio University as a junior, studying for a Bachelor degree in Criminal Justice. Todd was furious because grants no longer covered my books, so I got a part-time work-study job in the Social Work Department. I was the first person in my family to attend college.

Our house was now finished, so I was also the only person in my family to ever have a new home. My mom's parents and some of my aunts and uncles showed up on Christmas Day one year. They came to see our new home. They were very impressed. I was so honored to have them there, and so proud of the beautiful home we built ourselves.

My confidence was building, but I still carried a lot of heartache that I had no one to talk to about. I just kept very busy.

Todd's youngest brother Kent and his wife Lucy came to our house one night. Kent started putting me down, saying I would never get a job unless I took one from a man. This was 1992. He went on about how a company must hire a percentage of women and blacks now. He thought people who went to college were rich snobs. Kent couldn't get me mad enough, so he started putting Lucy down, saying she wasn't pretty and she knew it. I had stuck up for her in the past with Pappy. I wasn't about to again—Lucy needed to learn to stand up for herself like I had. She never stood up for me when Janet beat on me. Then Kent started saying "niggers" needed to go back to Africa.

They knew nobody was allowed to use the "N" word in my house. I told them to get out. Lucy stood up and started screaming in my face as I sat on my couch. She said nobody was right, not me nor Kent. I stood up and told her to leave right now, but she wouldn't. I pushed her out of my face. I said, "Now leave!" They finally left.

Todd didn't like the new me. I wasn't taking anything from him nor his family—nor my family—any longer. I had learned a lot in my psychology and drug and alcohol classes about the cycle of violence. I wasn't allowing any negatives into the life we'd made for our kids and foster kids.

Todd began to drink more. He had lost control of me. We had never fought much because I went along with whatever he wanted most of the time. Now his drinking was an issue, so I made him a deal—he could drink all he wanted, just not at the house. He was happy because he could stay as late as he wanted at the bars now.

Todd was no longer a laborer at work. He worked in the office, and it was going to his head.

Todd and his boss took secretaries to lunch and then to bars after work. He said, "Don't ask questions" when he came home in the middle of the night. This was how his dad treated his wife, and how some of his brothers treated their wives. He said they went along with it, and I should too. He didn't care what I thought. I wanted my life one way, and he wanted his another. We were going in separate directions now. We were no longer the kids we were when we got married.

I allowed myself to see what was going on all along. Todd had gotten sympathy from his family for doing the right thing by marrying me. He thought he was a saint. He constantly told people, "See what I have to put up with?" and he always told me, "You already got the best—you got me. What more do you want?" I came to see that Todd could only love himself. I wanted him to be free of me, but I was too in love with him to let him go. I came to realize I was in love with a person who didn't exist. He wasn't the person I pretended he was. It seemed selfish of me to make him stay married when he didn't want to be.

My brother Sam showed up at our house one day with his third wife. I ran him off too. For the first time, I confronted him about the attempted sexual abuse while I was growing up. I didn't care what Todd thought about it anymore—it was my house too. Sam said he was the only one who tried to help me, and I had run away from his house.

I said, "What choice did I have? Get raped by you, or let Don kill me?"

Funny, I don't remember staying with him very often—just here and there.

Jack came one day with his family and his immaturity. I didn't encourage them to come back either. My brothers never attempted to see me again, except when Sam introduced me to his fourth wife. They just came once, and I was civil.

In 1992, I quit college at the university to accept a position at Children Services as a Child Abuse Investigator for $6.68 an hour. The Therapeutic Agency we worked for begged me not to take that job. They said the county was corrupt, and I wouldn't want to work in it. They offered me $30,000 a year to stay home with one child who had extensive mental health issues. They were making a name for themselves with the good job we were doing for them. They said they could increase their program if I could successfully help this one severely mentally ill girl. I declined. I wanted to use my college education to investigate abuse.

I also didn't want to put my kids in danger by seeing a child so mentally ill every day. It wasn't easy growing up with Molly. Sometimes Molly would smile at me while holding a butcher knife, or come in my room at night naked, asking if I yelled for her. She had burnt down her apartment, tried jumping off a bridge, and tried stabbing Ty's father because she was upset after having a miscarriage. She never knew what she was doing. She turned from kitten to killer in an instant.

My first month at Children Services, I followed the other investigator to learn the job. We went to a home where I immediately became concerned about a newborn who was alone in a room, sitting in a carrier on the floor. He looked as if he'd been put there when his mom walked in the door, and then forgotten, like you would drop your purse or something. The other investigator didn't see a concern at all. He said to tell our supervisor if I was concerned.

I told our supervisor my concerns, and that at first glance, I thought the baby was dead. He was gray and lifeless, and he didn't grip my finger or notice me. I put my hand on his tiny heart to see if he were alive. She explained this to the Supportive Services Case Worker who was working with the family. That worker was so mad, she told everyone I just wanted her job. To prove her point, she refused to see the baby had an issue. Three days later, the baby was taken by squad to a hospital and was admitted in serious condition. He had failed to thrive.

The doctor refused to release the baby to the mother, and wanted that Supportive Service Worker off the case. The supervisor put the baby in foster care just to get the doctor off the worker's back. In thirty days, the baby was returned to the mother out of spite to me and the doctor. A few months later, as I was investigating another complaint at the home, the baby was having seizures and the mom needed a ride to the hospital. I rushed a few blocks back to the agency and told the supervisor. She said the worker had to take her, I couldn't. The worker screamed that she closed the case because the mother "completed parenting classes at the Health Department." She glared a hole through me. She was convinced I was trying to say she wasn't doing her job.

I told the supervisor I would take them then, since she didn't have an open services case. This was an emergency! The supervisor coldly told me *no*. I was shocked. Everyone acted like I was just trying to show that worker up. She could have her popularity contest—but this baby needed to go to the hospital right now.

"I'm calling the squad for her then," I said. "I promised her I would get her a ride immediately."

My supervisor walked into my office and put her finger on my phone, hanging it up as I was calling for help for this baby. "No, you're not."

Were they all insane? Why couldn't anyone care about this baby? Were they protecting this worker's pride? Just then, it was 4:30—quitting time. Lights went out at exactly quitting time every day. It was so dark you couldn't find your way out if you didn't hurry. I drove home crying, fearing I would be fired or arrested if I took this mom and baby to the hospital on my own time. This made no sense. Was I retarded? What was I not understanding? This moment will forever be in my list of biggest regrets.

I should have said to hell with them and driven back to the apartment and took them to the hospital, but self-preservation won, and I drove home instead. I told myself the mother would see I wasn't coming back, and she would find a ride. But I promised her, and the baby was having a seizure, and I was told to do nothing. I had no one to call to complain to. I was sick to my stomach all evening from stress and worry for the baby.

Three days later, again, my coworkers huddled in that worker's office, reading the newspaper. The baby had been air-lifted to Children's Hospital. He was now a vegetable because he didn't receive treatment in time.

This case became my fuel for every case after that. From then on, nobody stood in my way. I no longer asked permission—I just did my job—and, often, everyone else's. I began to believe this neglect was intentional because the baby's father was in jail for murdering someone. I wondered if this baby suffered as a payback for something. I couldn't tell anyone—there was no one to tell.

I told the prosecutor, and he said if the family sued it would be an easy million dollars, and our county couldn't afford a lawsuit like that. I thought at the very least he could ensure this never happened again. I was the only thing standing in the way of this county corruption, and I didn't plan to budge on my principles.

I was in the prosecutor's office a few times when someone would walk in and start right off saying who they needed them to go after or back off from. The Office was like a grocery store for favors. They just took note of what they wanted and agreed. I was shocked at how casual and open it was.

I worked there seven years. I investigated seventy-five percent of all the child abuse reports our county received during my first five years there. After that, I requested to be cut back to fifty percent, as I was getting burnt out. My supervisor told me she and her superiors said they had never seen anyone like me in all their years working for the county. I was very thorough with my cases. My files were thick, while the other investigators might have a couple of pages of notes. Everyone admired my guts and insight, but they wanted to control my case dispositions, and I wouldn't let them.

I wasn't trying to please them or show anyone up. I wasn't trying to be a hero. I felt worthless every day as I struggled to keep calm as I witnessed harm to children by their parents and by my coworkers. I was just doing my job. Every case was important, not just the "important people" in town.

Many professionals who reported abuse would only report to me. They didn't trust anyone else in the office. If coworkers wanted a case swept under the rug, they gave it to someone else. If I found out a child got hurt again because of this and I reported the worker to the director, everyone got mad at me for not being a team player. I didn't care about their team—I cared about these families. The team was hateful to me and to families. They made it clear they only cared about vacation, wage increases and retirement.

The supportive worker was threatened by me because I had a college education, while she was just a high school graduate. She often boasted that she got the job because she worked at a nursing home and took such good care of a commissioner's mother. She ran the office because our supervisor was always drunk. They allowed this situation to continue so they could do whatever they wanted on cases.

The supervisor missed so much work that workers had to go drag her out of bed and bring her to work to keep the director from getting mad at her. The supportive worker was also having an affair with someone who wanted the supervisor's position, and she feared I might get it instead. I assured her I was not interested in her job or the supervisor's job. I was doing exactly what I wanted, investigations. She told me some days she felt like bringing her cases over and throwing them on my desk, and yelling I could just go ahead and have her job. Nothing I said to her mattered. She had me all figured out in her mind, in a neat little package. Why confuse that with the truth?

Several alleged child victims reported a worker several times for allegedly having sex with the children's mother in exchange for not removing the children for neglect. Nothing was done. A new worker told me that he frequently had to sit outside in the car for an hour while that investigator went inside a client's home. I wondered why we were never allowed to remove that child from that alcoholic mother. I would hold back a large lump in my throat whenever I witnessed him yelling at young mothers and degrading them, like he was beating them into submission. They were always young, thin, and weak, and often chemically dependent.

It was seven years of pure torture, seeing kids abused by their parents and by the system. I always felt if only God would have made me smarter, I could solve this problem. I waited, and each day I only felt more lost. Being hated by my family and Todd's family was practice for being hated at work too. I felt God gave me a job that was too hard for me, and wondered why.

I took the side of a defendant once. This was never done. The prosecution and workers teamed up against people like it was a sport, not caring about the truth. I sided with the opposing team. It was a high-profile case—one that took up forty percent of my time for two years. Everyone who was anyone in the county was mad at me because of it. They wanted to believe the father was sexually abusing his children, when the real problem was his ex-wife wanted revenge. I knew it from the first time I met her. I always wondered why they cared so much about this case, when so many others were discounted, or even dropped. I was firmly told to "close" several horrible abuse cases without any explanation. Those were the most gut wrenching moments.

The director called me into his office one day and had me bring all the files on the high profile case, and bring my supervisor with me. He had me go through each one, explaining my conclusions. When I finished, he said the stepmom did it. Call and report her to that county's children services, and say she had done it.

I refused. There was not a shred of evidence to indicate that the stepmother had done anything. The director reminded me I could be fired for refusing a direct order. "Not when that order is illegal," I pointed out. He told me I was excused and told my supervisor to report it. She did.

The children happened to be American Indian, and they got in trouble for not following rules. My supervisor said she and the director had to sit in a "Pow Wow" all day with Indian Affairs. I found out there was a conflict of interest for the director to be involved in this case, and this false report was to influence a custody battle. I documented this information in the case file, but that's all I could do. There was no one to help workers concerned about injustice.

From day one, my supervisor was drunk every day and rarely looked at any of my cases. She even refused to send me to training when I was a new employee. I had to start signing myself up and just go. Yet, she was reviewing my case notes in this case. She told me the director said to tell me he didn't want to see his name in any children service's file—even if he were the reporter and instigating a case against someone for his own personal reasons. These children were being repeatedly interviewed and examined for sexual abuse that didn't exist.

I asked for the current date, and she told me. I asked for the current time, and she told me. Then I read her my latest entry, stating what she had just advised me.

I wasn't omitting pertinent evidence to a case for anyone. The safety of these kids came first, and I didn't care who liked it.

That case went all the way to the Supreme Court. I was the only one in the county who was right.

Long after the case was over, I went to training on the subject. The law professor went into length about this case and how interesting it was. I never mentioned I was the worker on it, even when he mentioned he would like to meet that worker. I didn't want to discuss the case. I was too afraid of what the director would do to me.

The director tried everything he could to get me to quit. One day, he set me up, hoping I would divulge personal information about a client over the phone to someone claiming to be from social security. It didn't work. He called and demanded to know why I hadn't provided the information. He slammed his phone down so hard that he broke it.

I knew he was coming after me. He barged in the office and demanded that I go in a closed office alone with him. I said, "Not until you calm down."

He kicked the door and forced me to go in. I knew he was coming, so I grabbed a sick leave form and quickly filled it out, and handed it to him. I told him I needed to leave right then. I didn't feel safe. He demanded answers, hoping he finally had me for refusing an order. I informed him everyone in the office heard him screaming at me over the phone—I had witnesses to this abuse.

He stared at me for a moment like he wanted to kill me. He signed the paper and threw it at me. I grabbed it, made a copy and ran out. I shook all the way as I started to drive home.

I called the prosecutor and reported this workplace violence, stressing I needed to feel safe in my own office. I wanted to file domestic violence against the director. I accepted violence by clients while working outside the office, but I needed one place where I felt safe to work.

He laughed and said to take tomorrow off. Give the director time to cool down. He explained the director acted like this at meetings in front of him too, and everyone knew how he was.

When I came back to work, my supervisor said the director wanted her to ask me if I was on my period. She said she was on vacation when he called her about this and forced her to get back to work to ask me that. She said he'd called her names and put her down. I told her we should not live in fear. I felt like I was back home taking the abuse so my mom didn't have to.

I told her I was filing a civil rights complaint on behalf of everyone there. The director called an agency meeting and gave us all nice raises. He was a hero now. Nobody was going to talk against him. When he screamed at me, everyone in my unit hid or ran. After I went home that day, everyone said they'd never seen him that angry before, and they had seen him get very angry. Everyone was afraid and talking. Now, after getting a raise, everyone went silent.

After the raises, they all got together and agreed to keep quiet and say they didn't see anything. This was told to me by the Child Support Supervisor, who then handed me a notarized statement for Ohio Civil Rights saying that. He also stated in the letter that a coworker asked him why he still talked to me. What could I do for the supervisor that the director couldn't—suck his dick? I mailed it to show retaliation. It was ignored.

One older lady who was about to retire told me that other ladies at the office appreciated what I was doing, and told me about sexual advances from the director in the past. She told me this by taking me in the bathroom, so I knew she was too afraid to tell anyone else. The Ohio Civil Rights Commission said my complaint was unfounded because I wasn't singled out—he treated everyone violently. I was fighting the whole state now.

For a few months, we had a new investigator. He came to me one day and said the director hired him to get rid of me. He said he was promised the supervisor position if he could. He was to watch me and report back to the director. He said his reports read that I have more fire in me than everyone else there put together. He then resigned. He was a retired Columbus police officer. He was disgusted with the corruption in our county.

The director was mad that I wouldn't do what he wanted on the high-profile case, and mad that I had filed a complaint against him. He ordered everyone not to speak to me. The secretary wouldn't even give me messages. I kept working. Eventually, the prosecutor's office backed the director. The director paid for the prosecutor's investigator out of foster care funds. They refused to allow children services to investigate sexual abuse cases, just to piss me off. I kept getting complaints from parents that nobody was investigating the reports, so finally I confronted my supervisor about it. Later, she said we could do all the interviews except the prosecutor's office would do the perp interviews. I kept track on a legal pad of the perps who were supposed to be interviewed by the prosecutor's office, but weren't. They didn't interview any of them. They wanted me to get mad enough to quit. I was onto them, and they knew it. Child abuse cases involving drugs were not being investigated. Certain government officials' names were coming up.

My legal pad had alleged perpetrator names on every line and half way down a second column. I kept showing it to the supervisor, telling her I assumed it was legal to have sex with kids in this county now. This was no longer just retaliation for me complaining to Civil Rights. It was about a young female getting too big for her britches in a male-dominated mafia. They were showing me they could do whatever they wanted, and getting me where it hurt me the most by hurting my clients.

When I started college, I was tested by the Myers-Briggs Personality Inventory test. I am an I.N.F.P. One percent of the population has a personality like mine, which is compared to Joan of Arc's personality in commitment to a cause. It also stated that I would become emotionally paralyzed if I didn't have harmony.

The director had a copy of my testing. I wondered if he was making sure I never had harmony and was intentionally blocking my cause, wanting to burn me at the stake.

Finally, I had no choice. I told the parents the truth. They reported the prosecutor's office to the attorney general.

The prosecutor called me into his office and yelled at me for it. I stood my ground. His assistant came in when he overheard the prosecutor yelling at me. He knew nothing about what was going on. I saw in his eyes that he was concerned that the prosecutor had interfered with our investigations, and didn't like how he was talking to me. He apologetically said, "Peggy, you're excused." I exited immediately.

One day the sheriff's department called me personally and told me to come remove two little boys because they were arresting the dad. I wondered why they didn't get the case assigned to an available worker as usual. I drove out in the woods to the address given. Several cops stood behind their cars like they were afraid they would get shot. When I got out of my car, they told me to go knock on the camper door and tell the father that I was taking his kids, then they would arrest him.

I said no, you arrest him first. I can't call the judge and get custody until they are dependent children, right now the kids are with their father. I didn't know this family and didn't know what was going on.

They said there was nobody to take the kids, and they had talked to the neighbors and they said they couldn't take them.

I refused to walk up there when they were hiding from him behind cars. It was a trap—they wanted me to get killed.

They finally arrested the man, and then said the neighbors

would take the boys. I wondered what kind of sick joke they were playing on me.

As I started to leave, a deputy came over to my car and said there was something he wanted to show me. He took me to the camper. It was empty except for a gun and ammo on the floor at each window.

The deputy said the father had told them if anybody tried to take his kids, he would shoot them. He looked me in the eye and said, "That's why we called you."

I drove back to the office. I was on my own. They were all in on this. I didn't have a state or anyone to report anything to, and they knew it. This incident was a way of bragging they could do anything, even kill me, and get by with it.

I began to think hard about if my problems with Todd's family and my problems at work could be interrelated. My supervisor told me about the attorneys and judges doing people favors. She said they had little black books of favors they hid whenever there was a drug bust or murder in town. She said she didn't stick her neck out because she had a son. I asked her if that was a threat regarding my sons. If she was threatening me, I wanted her to come out and say it, not imply a threat. She didn't say any more.

When I first started working there, I was on a case with the investigator for the prosecutor's office. He told me he used to work for the sheriff's office, and they tried forming a union because of the low pay. My director called him into his office and threw a folder down in front of him. It was an old child support case. He said it was a threat that if he didn't stop this union nonsense, he would be sued for back child support to someone he didn't know.

He refused to back down. He said then he got a call from his eighty-year-old mother to come right away. When he arrived, the police had her face down in the gravel and handcuffed behind her back. They had planted drugs in her home.

I didn't believe him. I thought he must be trying to scare me out of my job so I would quit. But he wasn't. He was warning me what I would be up against if I worked there.

One day my supervisor said the director wanted me to go watch a court case and come back and report to him what was going on. I sat in the courtroom all day listening to testimony. The sheriff at the time was being sued by an ex-son-in-law for a similar situation that the investigator told me about. Corruption seemed to be a standard practice here.

I talked to an attorney outside of the county about suing on behalf of my clients. I knew of several cases that could easily be won for clients, if they only had a voice. The attorney told me everyone knows how this county was, and he was not about to go there and tell them how to run their business.

At the civil rights mediation, the prosecutor represented the director. They offered me a job at another county children services and a "nice severance package." I told them my reputation meant more to me than that. I wasn't about to move my kids and leave the home we built, nor act like I was in the wrong by leaving. This was to make everyone there safe, not just me. Yet no one stood up for me.

I was told to not speak to the director. If I had an issue, I was to take it to the assistant director, who would turn on his tape recorder when I entered the room.

Right after this, the sheriff's office didn't page me through EMS as required after hours, but once again called me directly to go out on a case. This time I was home. I believed they didn't want it on the record that they asked me to come and get involved. If I were killed, I was just on my own time—the sheriff's department wouldn't be negligent. I went there as requested, and cop cars were lined up and down the road with flashing lights. A father had assaulted his son in the yard, and people driving by had seen it. I had placed the boy with his grandmother that day due to horrible bruises by his father. The father was mad about it. The father assaulted an officer and fled in the woods. Deputies ordered me to sit in the back of the cruiser with the child victim while they searched for the father. "We aren't ready for you yet," He said

A deputy then came and got me, and said they found the father, and he wanted to talk to me. I refused. He had just assaulted his son and an officer. I said I would talk to him once he was behind bars.

A deputy forced me to go. He forced me to walk over to the left side of the yard. It looked like every cop in the county was there. They all stood in a perfect circle watching. The deputy made me walk into the center, where this very large and very angry father stood. He said I was the reason for all the unruly kids in the county because I told them their parents couldn't hit them, so they got in trouble. He said all of this was my fault. I ran to my car and went home. I knew it was another set up.

I kept documenting and kept working; the kids needed me. I was unstoppable. One day I went to a home and a grandfather got my back up against the door so I couldn't get out. He picked up a hatchet off his dirt floor, got in my face, and said he should do it. I imagined the hatchet swinging down from the angle he had it raised above my head and landing inside my skull. I imagined he would bury me behind his house in his junk yard. I didn't dare blink—he had complete control over what happened next, not me.

My home and sons were only a few miles away, and here I was about to be murdered. He finally lowered the axe and I moved away from the door and walked to my car. He followed me and said, "Now go back and tell them I said to never come back here again."

My hands were shaking so badly I could hardly get my key in to unlock my car door. I cried and trembled on my way home. Once I got home, I called my supervisor and told her. She said to call the sheriff. I called the sheriff, and they coldly said to come in and make a complaint. I asked them to come to me. I was too shaken up to drive. They refused.

When Todd got home, I asked him to drive me. He didn't want to, so I called them back and said I would file the complaint in the morning. The man only got thirty days. He moved, and a worker from that county called me to tell me he came to her office with a knife threatening to kill her. She said her county wouldn't do anything either. She said he had bragged to her about what he had done to me. She said she wanted to know what my county had done. I was now paranoid. I wondered if the caller was really a coworker, just wanting to know how I felt about the county not giving a damn.

I had warned the staff in my unit about this man not long before this happened. He had threatened to kill staff at the high school and had threatened me before. They scoffed at me, saying he was harmless. They acted like I just wanted attention. I was taught in college to take all threats seriously. Now I had almost been killed, and everyone acted like I was being a baby or that it was my fault. The mental abuse was taking its toll. I felt like a rope was tightly squeezing my stomach all the time. I was resorting to the candy and pop machines for comfort.

The police called me one night and told me to remove a baby. I had helped the mentally ill mom before, so I didn't feel threatened. I told her it was just over night, and as soon as she left her abuser, she would get her baby back and I would help her get her own place tomorrow. She said okay and handed me the baby. As I started to walk down the hill with him, I overheard police officers inside her trailer talking to her about me. Suddenly, she jumped off the porch and landed on top of me. I was now on my back cradling her baby so he didn't get hit by her flying fists.

One officer walked over and just stood there. I yelled for him to get her off, she was hitting the baby. He calmly told her, "Leave her alone." He was just watching and wasn't going to help me, so I pulled my feet up as far as I could. I pushed her off me with my feet, then I ran down the steep hill. I drove myself and the screaming baby directly to the emergency room. We were treated for cuts and bruises caused by her attack on us both.

The prosecutor's office didn't want to file charges because they didn't believe a mother would hit her baby. They thought she just hit me. I said the officer just stood there and watched her. How else did the baby get cuts and bruises? They also said the mom was mentally ill. She didn't know what she was doing. They finally filed the complaint and charged her, but then dropped it without consulting me. The message was loud and clear: anyone who wanted to harm me was protected. I was a sitting duck.

That was when my PTSD and anxiety began. The cop standing there not helping me as I was on the ground being assaulted reminded me of Bear standing there while Jerry and Joel assaulted me in that field at Tonya's. The circle of cops reminded me of the circle of men in my bedroom when I was little. The director's rage reminded me of my stepdad, and my supervisor's codependency reminded me of my mom. My vindictive coworkers reminded me of my siblings and Todd's family. I felt safe nowhere. I was afraid to go to work. I now needed counseling. I needed time off to wrap my head around everything. I needed somewhere I could feel safe.

I tried to get workman's comp, but the director refused it. He blamed me for the hatchet attack and said I was there during "personal time for personal reasons." I had a complaint and it was during working hours! The director had me play act what exactly happened the next morning—over and over. He made me use a newspaper to illustrate the hatchet. By doing so, I couldn't forget the incident, which was my coping mechanism. Finally, I got so upset I threw the newspaper down and began shaking. The assistant director told him that was enough and let me go. My supervisor didn't do anything. All of these events were swirling around in my mind like a merry-go-round of memories. I wanted to jump off and couldn't.

Meanwhile, Todd was becoming more violent. He wanted a brand- new boat. He handed me papers to sign for it. I refused, telling him we couldn't afford it. He glared a hole through me. He said I was forcing him to make a decision he didn't want to make. In other words, he was threatening to divorce me if I didn't sign. I signed. I knew he wanted the boat to impress his secretaries. I knew this was part of his mid-life crisis. He was going to the tanning bed and doing his own laundry. He wanted his jeans pressed with a crease down the front. He had become exactly who he wanted to be. I was so sick of his line, "I just need space." That meant he wanted time away from me. The more time he had, the more he wanted. I had no choice but to set him free.

Todd got his freedom, and I received a peaceful home without him drinking in it. He was off having fun while I was home alone. The boys were running around with their friends or having them over. We had turned the basement living room into a game room for them. Their friends came and went from the basement glass door off my old kitchen. I usually didn't know who was in my house, but they were such well-behaved kids that I didn't worry. Yet, I had no one to hang out with anymore. My family was outgrowing their need for me. Loneliness became my only companion.

One morning, Todd said he was taking me and the boys out in his new boat to watch fireworks on the river that night. I was excited that he wanted to be with us. I had always wanted to see fireworks from a boat. He said he was going to the hardware store and would be right back. It was five minutes away, and across the street from the local bar. When late afternoon came and he still wasn't back, I knew where he was and what he was doing. He would come home drunk and there would be a fight. He knew I wouldn't allow the kids in a vehicle or boat with him if he had been drinking. The only thing I asked for, insisted on, would be up for debate.

Todd came home drunk. "I know how you feel about me drinking around the kids," he said, "so I will honor our agreement. I won't make you guys go. I'll just go to Donald's and see who wants to go. Maybe people from work will want to go."

"Wow, I appreciate that." I said. "I'll take the boys to dinner and a movie, and then school clothes shopping."

He agreed and left. I felt satisfied that maybe our marriage would work after all. It wasn't perfect, but it was manageable.

After he left, I realized I'd been made a fool. He had gotten drunk on purpose so he wouldn't have to take us. He'd stiffed his family for the secretaries again. I was helping to pay for that boat, but I couldn't even get to see fireworks in it.

But I was happy to have a fun evening with our boys—he could have his drunk sex party on the boat. He had what he wanted, and I had what I wanted.

The boys and I got ready to go to town and were about to leave when Todd returned home.

He said nobody wanted to go with him, and, therefore, he wanted me and the boys to go.

"No, we are not," I said. He was drunk. "The boys and I have plans, and that's what we're doing."

He was a happy drunk before he left, but now he was a mean

drunk, like Stepdad Don drunk.

Todd said we were so going, and leaving as soon as he got out of the shower. As soon as he got in the shower, I rushed the boys out the door and into my minivan. As I was about to start backing out of the driveway, Todd ran outside on the porch in broad daylight *naked*! He said something told him I was leaving while he was in the shower. He ordered the boys to get back in the house—they were going on the boat with him.

"No, they are not!" I yelled "You are drunk. You're not taking them anywhere!" I told the boys to stay in the van.

They started crying. Fear of their dad—and not me—made Todd win. They got out of the van.

Since they were out, I got out. I told them to run down to the basement door. I didn't want them to have to go in the front door with their dad standing there naked on the front porch. I was appalled that Todd would do this to our children. This was the sort of thing I never wanted my kids to go through. This was not the sheltered happy life I promised I would give them.

I ran into the basement behind them to make sure they were okay.

I talked to them in their rooms and calmed them down, and said it was okay, I would take care of it. I apologized to them for them having been put in the middle of that.

I heard Todd coming down the stairs. I told the kids to stay put. I jumped up and ran towards him. I told him we agreed to never let the kids see us fight. I ran upstairs to take the argument there.

I ran past him, I told Todd, "We are not going." He yelled that we were. I said I was calling the sheriff, because he was *not* doing this to our kids. He ran after me.

I leaped into the kitchen, grabbed the phone off the wall, and started pushing the familiar number in the phone. I was humiliated to be the one who needed help instead of one of my clients. I realized in that moment how I had put myself above them, but now I was one of them. I was the one who needed help. Who would help me? The sheriff's department would get a good laugh out of this call.

I wasn't sure if I got all the numbers pushed to make the call. Todd was in the kitchen facing me as I held the phone in my hand. His eyes bulged with anger because I had just defied him.

Todd threw the table upside down. I recalled Lucy telling me Todd had gotten mad at her recently at Norma's trailer, and had done the same thing. I stood there in disbelief. This was a movie about domestic violence. This was not my life. Todd was so angry and frustrated at me that he was crying and moaning in rage at the same time.

My life with Todd flashed before my eyes. One night I asked him if he were going to kill me. He had paused and said, "You know, you hear about someone on a rooftop shooting people. Everyone says he was such a nice guy, they can't believe it. I think that's going to be me."

I also recalled Todd telling me once that he would never hit me, because one hit would kill me. I'd seen Todd get in a few bar fights. One hit knocked grown men out cold.

After Todd flipped the table, he came towards me and pinned me against the wall with his forearm. The anger and pain in his face showed me he was considering killing me in order to end his pain of being married to me. The moment of truth was upon us. A saying I had heard once came to mind: "The graveyard is full of women who believed their husbands wouldn't really kill them."

I thought about what I had told women in these situations— that the next time he might go too far, and it would be too late. This was my too late. This time I was going to die. I thought of all the times Todd had been angry. He'd never done anything like this before. I had stayed too long. He'd made it clear he wanted out all along. Why had I stayed? Why had I waited for him to love me? He didn't love me. He never had.

The poor guy wanted out so bad, why hadn't he divorced me? It is amazing how time slows down in these moments. Your soul can have so many clear thoughts when your life is threatened, but in real time it happens in an instant.

I looked in Todd's eyes as he pressed me tight against the wall, calling me a bitch and slobbering tears of anger and pain. My life was in his hands, not mine, just like it had been that day the man with the hatchet threatened me. It was his choice. I had no control over the situation.

"Hello? Hello?" a voice spoke from the phone in my hands.

Todd's eyes bulged and he stepped back. His perfect image was blown. The call had been made after all, and the sheriff's department heard it all.

"HELP! HELP!" I screamed into the phone from a distance.

Todd grabbed the phone out of my hand and hung it up.

I ran to the silverware drawer. I stood there with my fingers on it but not opening it. I had instinctively wanted to grab a knife to protect myself from Todd. A vision grabbed my attention. I was on trial, and each member of Todd's family testified against me, one by one. I was found guilty of murdering Todd.

My fingers let go, never opening the drawer.

He would have to kill me, if that was what he wanted. Todd said, "Get in the truck." He got the boys and we walked outside. Knowing he was drunk, he wasn't thinking clearly. I would use that to my advantage. He didn't want me to be mad at him and go to the police. I would use that to my advantage too. Like the man who had kidnapped and raped me when I was sixteen, Todd was happy he got his date—I just had to play along.

As we headed to the truck, I said, "Can I drive the boys in my van and follow you, because it will be crowded in the truck?"

"I don't care," Todd said.

I felt a moment of great relief and breathed in air. I was getting my boys and going to file charges on Todd.

Then as drunks do, Todd quickly changed his mind again. He said Cameron was riding with him, though. I was relieved to have Cole and Ty safe with me, but I couldn't leave Cameron behind. I would have to follow Todd and wait for an opportunity to get Cameron out too.

Todd said he was stopping at the store for drinks and ice. As I drove behind him, I plotted my next move, and prayed it would go well and not make things worse.

Todd pulled into the store parking lot, and he and Cameron went in.

I grabbed a pen and paper and wrote down Todd's boat trailer license number, and then wrote, "Please help! Send police to the Coolville Boat Ramp. We are forced against our will to go in a boat with a drunk." I jumped out of my van and handed it to the first person I saw.

The lady looked at it and smiled.

"This is not a joke," I said. "I'm serious. Please call the sheriff and tell him this. Tell him I was the one on the phone screaming for help a few minutes ago. My husband is drunk. I'm afraid my kids will drown in the boat."

She was still smiling.

I ran back to my van before Todd got back. Again, I felt like I was living a movie—this was not my life. How did I get myself into this situation? I knew it was from staying too long, waiting for him to change, loving without expecting anything in return as I had done my whole life.

We got to the boat ramp. I begged Todd to stop, let me take the boys and go. He refused. He unloaded the boat in the water. I was not leaving any one of them behind. I was not letting them go without me. Todd had never put the boat in the water at that place before. He wasn't an experienced boater. The boat was new to him. He was drunk and crazy and unpredictable. And it was so dark out. It was a long ride to the fireworks from there. My anxiety was saying something terrible could happen.

Todd kept saying it would be fine, get in.

I made sure everyone had on life jackets, and the boat started moving. I sat quietly in the back with the boys. Cole and Ty looked worried. Cameron was having fun and didn't seem to notice there was a problem. He was happy to be upfront with his dad doing something together at night.

Soon Todd started in on me. He demanded that I come sit with him upfront. I told him I was fine in the back. He started getting mad again. Cole whispered to me that he was afraid. I told Todd to stop, Cole was scared.

"Your mom is a bitch, boys!" Todd yelled. "She is ruining our fun. We were supposed to have a good time tonight and see fireworks!"

Then he turned around again and pointed at me. "You're not going to ruin this. Get up here and sit by me, *right now!*"

"You got your way," I said. "We're here. Can't you leave me alone?" It was pitch black out. I was so scared one of the boys would fall out of the boat and we wouldn't find them if Todd wrecked or took a wave too hard.

Todd suddenly whipped the boat around and headed back to the boat dock, yelling, "See what your mother did!"

It was my fault we couldn't go. But I was relieved when we got back and started to get out.

Then Todd changed his mind again, I was too get out, but the boys were going with him.

Terror filled my throat. Cole cried. He wanted to go with me. Cole and Ty climbed out and headed to my van. I stood there waiting on Cameron to come too.

Todd changed his mind again, and started loading the boat on the trailer. He and Cameron got in his truck and left.

I drove to the sheriff's office. As soon as I walked in, I told them I was the one screaming for help on the phone earlier. The deputy said he didn't know what I was talking about. I asked if someone called in with Todd's trailer number.

"Yes, you had your friend call."

He didn't believe I was in trouble. He assumed I was trying to lie about Todd, and had a friend helping me.

He refused to let me make a report. He said the child was with his father, and they can't go pick him up. He wasn't at the house anymore—wasn't that what I wanted?

"He could be there now," I said. "And, if not, he will be back."

"Well, when he comes back, call us then."

I insisted on filing a complaint. I told him to give me a witness statement form. As he handed it to me, he said I could fill it out, but he wasn't walking it down to the prosecutor's office.

I told him I would be there Monday to walk it down myself. I filled it out and left it on his desk.

I drove home, worried sick about Cameron. I was relieved to see lights on at my house. Cameron was safe and home, but Todd's truck sat in the driveway. I drove up the hill to a neighbor's house and asked to use their phone. They didn't know why, but let me use it. I called the deputy and told him Todd was home, so arrest him now.

They said I wasn't home, so I wasn't in danger. I had to be home and in danger.

I said I was earlier when I called you and was screaming for help. I have to go be in danger again and then call? What if he doesn't let me?

I gave up. I drove to a Motel and Cole, and Ty, and I spent the night. I knew better than go to my Mom's house because I had tried that once and she boasted about Todd all night. She didn't care if anyone wanted to kill me as usual, as long as she thought the guy was good looking!

The next morning, I went home and walked down in the basement. Todd was running the sweeper, something he had never done before. This was as much sucking up as he could do. I nicely asked if I could take Cameron with me, we were going to get school clothes. Todd pouted "Go ahead, nobody cares what I want anyway." Cameron got in the van and we went back to the Motel.

The next morning, was Monday. I went home and let the boys get ready for school and drove them to school. Todd never missed a day of work, I knew he would be gone. I went to work and called a lawyer in town about the domestic violence report and need for a restraining order, and wanting to file for divorce. He filed the paperwork with the Prosecutor's Office for me. Todd pled "No Contest."

The child support supervisor once told me I was hated by everyone because they were jealous. He said I was famous. He explained the lawyers and judges in town were all talking about me. The sheriff and the prosecutor would call on me to handle high profile cases. I just had a natural talent for investigating, interviewing and uncovering the truth. Yet now, I knew the sheriff deputies were jealous too. One told me one day that it wasn't fair that I had the title of investigator, and they didn't.

I should have left Todd sooner. About a year before this, Todd and I were coming home from a night out. Todd got mad at me and started hitting the steering wheel and dash, then he busted the driver's window out, as he was driving. I had my hand on the door latch, feeling I would be safer if I jumped out of a moving vehicle than alone with him. I made myself stay put. Once we got home, I ran to the basement and called a friend who was a police officer.

He told me to get the boys and get out of there right now. I was afraid to go upstairs. I was afraid Todd was loading his gun. He told me to do it now. I quickly woke up my boys and rushed them upstairs to go out the front door. We had to step over Todd's blood all over the entry. It looked like a crime scene. His hand was apparently badly cut. We got in my vehicle and drove away as pieces of glass blew back on us. I had the kids keep their faces covered and heads down.

Chuck was dating a friend of mine from college, so we went there. I told him we needed a place to stay for the night, and if Todd came, he better not let him in. If he did, I would have to call the police. Todd came and Chuck talked to him outside for a long time, then he left quietly.

My cases took priority over my own life. A young woman called me at work and reported she was worried her dad was doing to her little sisters what he had done to her. She had a baby by him as a result of his sexual abuse. I talked to his sister, and she said he had sexually abused her as a child too, and he'd had sex with little girls while in Vietnam. She said he went from church to church with a hard luck story so people would take them in. She said they were never Catholic until the local Catholic Church took them in.

I went to the school with a tape recorder. All three little girls, one at a time, told of sexual abuse by their father, believing it didn't happen to the youngest, but it had. The dad told them he would go to prison if they told, and they would never see them him again.

When I let them know that may happen in order to keep them safe, they each said that was okay. When I interviewed the parents, they admitted this was going on and were relieved it was over.

That night a Catholic nun called me at home and said I put words in these girls' mouths, and that no more Catholics had better go to prison. She spoke about a Catholic attorney in town who was recently convicted of child sexual abuse. She was rude and threatening. The next night after work, my supervisor, who rarely got involved in my cases, went to the prosecutor's office with me on this case. They called the nun, put her on speaker phone and discussed the case with her. As soon as we walked in, they offered us a beer, and my supervisor started sucking them down one after the other. I refused to drink on the job.

I couldn't understand why we needed this nun involved in the case. It was explained to me that an attorney was selling a house to the church. This case would cause him to lose the sale because this family lived in that house. The Church provided this family with a place to live.

I left confused. They told me to postpone the case until after the girls had their first communion and the house was sold. I refused, but they controlled when it went to trial, not me. The dad confessed and got a plea deal of counseling, without going to trail.

I was sick to my stomach, knowing these girls were not protected. Their mom now knew, their dad had confessed to authorities, yet he was still in the home. He could continue to assault them. I could only imagine how they must feel. They depended on me, they trusted me, and I had failed them.

Many cases were just as devastating. I would uncover abuse and torture to children to be told they couldn't afford to put kids in foster care or the family would simply request a different worker, one who the supervisor knew would look away. Some families were protected—this I knew for a fact. When a case came in, family relationships were discussed between my coworkers. I didn't play that game, and I was the black sheep because of it. Every day was pure torture for me. I was in a position to help kids, kids like I once was, but often "politics" stood in the way. If I removed the children, the supportive worker quickly put them back and told families I was crazy. If her friends removed children, she worked with the families. That is why I hung on to cases as long as I could. I did what

I could for them in the thirty days I had to do an investigation. I began using the option of fifteen-day extensions as well.

As I struggled to make sense of this, one day I feared I stumbled onto something unbelievable as a possible motive. I was on my way to the hospital to see a baby girl brought in for sexual abuse/molestation. I stopped at the sheriff's office and asked for a deputy to assist me. The Catholic deputy was there. He handed me a camera and said to take a picture and bring it back to him. I said she was touched, not penetrated, so there wouldn't be marks. I told him I didn't feel comfortable taking pictures. He insisted. I did, and I turned the camera back over to him, but I felt sick, like I had gotten porn for him. I wondered what he would do with it.

One day, the fraud worker asked me for my socks—someone was into smelling women's socks, and wanted to buy mine. I was starting to wonder if there were a child sex ring running in this county. I had assumed they just flat out didn't care, but I was starting to wonder if it were more sinister than that.

One day I was forced to hear workers laugh when a dad broke a girl's nose. They said she deserved it. My stomach tightened and I thought I would be sick.

I had to jump in front of a mother once so she couldn't throw her daughter off the courthouse balcony. The mother saw her child on the balcony with me, ran up the street, up the courthouse steps, and tried grabbing her, threatening to throw her off. I risked my life to save that girl by putting myself as the one who would get thrown off instead. The supportive worker and her lover/day care worker were in court recommending she be given back her kids, despite my daily protesting. The mom didn't even want the kids and said if she had to take them, she would beat them up.

When they came out of court, I told the day care worker and a deputy what the mother had just done. The deputy ignored me, and the day care worker replied, "She deserved it. She's a brat." They forced that child and her two siblings to get in the car and leave the state with that mother. The workers did not want to pay for three "brats" in foster care. Foster care money was sent to the prosecutor's office to pay for his investigator instead, so they didn't have to pay for him themselves. I was constantly told to not remove kids for long term care because there was no money for foster care.

The mother's boyfriend had sexually abused them, but the mother insisted her girls seduced her man. The supportive worker had refused to remove them, so I did. To spite me, she was putting them right back with the mom. She had just told the judge to send them back, and told the mother to dump them somewhere after she passed the state line. The other investigator soon got a call from another county, saying they picked the girls up along the highway and they had just left our custody. He told them to put them in jail, not foster homes, because they were delinquent brats. I sat at my desk, over hearing the conversation, and wanted to vomit.

Another foster child had this same supportive worker as a case worker. The worker sent the child to jail without an order twice. Once the judge took her in and let her live with his family. Then he ordered the worker to find her a home. She said that was how she came to live with me. I had no idea.

Later, a worker's child died. A coworker told me the worker's husband wrestled him the night before over an argument about a ball game, and it got out of hand. I didn't know if she was making conversation or a report. We were standing right beside the Intake Log. I feared this was a set up. Everyone in the county would be out to get me for making his death a report. I wondered if the worker was afraid to report it herself. Either way, I wanted no part of it. I feared for my life if I reported that. I told a coworker what was told to me and by whom, and said that she could handle it, because I wanted no part of it. I felt it was a lie and a trap to get more people hating me. This was a very serious situation. I knew the supervisor would go off on me if I filed out a report on this. She was constantly covering this worker's butt.

I never saw it on the Intake Log. I never heard discussion of it as anything other than a mystery as to how he actually died. The grieving worker left the unit because clients blamed her for her son's death.

Before the child died, her husband bragged to everyone in the office that they had gotten life insurance on his wife's children. Since no one, as far as I knew, had ever reported this for an investigation, I wondered what else I could do. If I reported that to the life insurance company or the coroner, it would be a huge mess. I was sure the reporter would recant—she was best friends to the workers—and I would be sued and charged. There was never "Internal Affairs" or anyone higher up the chain to get advisement from.

Too many times, I was made to feel like I was the problem. Life would go smoother for everyone if I didn't seek the truth. I was in a constant battle to survive the waves I made. I knew this was one wave I would be thrown out for. The entire community supported this family, and I didn't have the heart to cause them harm in this tragic time. I don't know which was greater—my compassion or my fear. Yet I would wake up feeling this dead child wanted justice. I wasn't brave enough to speak up. I let it be. There was no one I could trust to tell. I had reported the sheriff deputies to the FBI when they tried to kill me, but I was never questioned in person. I had hoped I could spill the beans about everything, and someone would listen.

Every time I told anyone any of my concerns they shrugged it off, and said it was the same way everywhere. When I would tell them I would change it, they would laugh at me and assure me it was not going to change. Everyone knew what I knew, but flat out did not care. I refused to accept this.

CHAPTER 15

DIVORCE

A few weeks after I filed domestic violence charges on Todd, he called me. He hadn't seen the boys at all. He said he refused to visit the boys unless I dropped the restraining order. I tried to explain to him that he could see the boys anytime he wanted, he just had to stay away from me. He still refused to see them until I dropped the restraining order. He was firm on this. I called the judge and told him exactly what Todd said, and explained I wanted my kids to have a dad because I knew what it was like to grow up without one. He urged me not to, but I dropped it anyway. I couldn't harm my boys in any way for any reason.

Our divorce was to be final right before Thanksgiving. He didn't have any trouble coming to a divorce agreement. We were fair with each other. Neither one of us were greedy people. The few months leading up to the divorce, I tried talking to Todd to see if this was what he really wanted. He'd just say he didn't care either way. I thought, on one hand, if he didn't care either way, then we shouldn't be married. On the other hand, I still loved him and hoped he would change, I had a marriage that I wanted and I cared about, so I was keeping it. I knew it may take years for him to change, but eventually he would. I dropped the divorce because I was hoping for a miracle—that Todd would someday discover he loved me after all.

I kept seeing a vison of me looking down at a dirt-covered grave. Our marriage was dead and buried, but I still stood there waiting for it to rise from the dead. I waited for a miracle. No miracle was coming, but I couldn't stop hoping, wishing and waiting. I needed to walk away, but I just stood there. I couldn't leave. Now I was free. Poor and alone, but free. I was glad I had gone to college and had a job—otherwise, I wouldn't have been able to make payments on the mortgage that came with getting the house.

Meanwhile, tensions grew at work. A mental health therapist called me and asked me to meet a client at the sheriff's office for a joint interview. A child had been raped at the county fair months earlier and was just now willing to report it. She had been in counseling. She said she didn't want to tell her story twice. The prosecutors were still refusing to do interviews, but I couldn't tell her that. I informed the sheriff's office I was coming for a joint interview, and, surprisingly, they agreed. I was proceeding with this case no matter who liked it or didn't like it. They would have to tell me to my face that they were not doing sex abuse cases anymore. I was done with this.

When I got there, my client wasn't there. I asked where she was, but they didn't want to answer me. I persisted. Then they said they didn't know. I persisted again. Then they said they sent them to the prosecutor's office. I went there and asked them where my client was, explaining the sheriff's office had sent me there. They called the sheriff's office to see what they were talking about, then they hung up and laughed. "They sure don't like you, and they didn't want you there, so they sent her home."

They went about their business, blowing me off. This was a Friday afternoon. I could imagine how horrible that girl felt, finally having the courage to tell, and being dismissed. I pictured her at home, thinking nobody cared, not even children services or the police—the way I had felt at her age when I was in the Open Door. All of my good intentions were worthless. Someone was always there to block me from helping on every case. I knew this was done to her because of me, because they didn't like me. Maybe if I'd quit, they would hire someone else, and children would get helped again. Then I recalled when I was first hired, they bashed the former worker, who had a Master's degree. I went to her home one day and asked to talk to her. She told me she had experienced everything I was going through. They had run her out because she was too smart. They wanted dumb people—or ones who would look the other way.

The following Monday morning, our office clerk left a vague message for me about a call concerning the worst sexual perp in the county. When I asked her for clarification, she said she didn't have to talk to me. She was busy gossiping with the former supportive worker, who no longer worked in our unit. I told her she didn't have to like me, but she needed to respect me enough to work with me. She looked me up and down like I were garbage and snapped, "You? Me, respect you?"

Even though she was over three hundred pounds, I had never looked down on her. The old, unhealed, deep-seated belief that the world saw me as less than human surfaced. It was the worst thing anyone could have said to me at that moment. It was the straw that broke this camel's back.

I went to the assistant director and told him what she had done and what happened on Friday at the sheriff's office and the prosecutor's office. He coldly told me to tell my supervisor and go through the chain of command. I went to my supervisor and told her, knowing she wouldn't do anything—she never did. She had come to work drunk every day since I'd been there. Several times I overheard the other investigator on the phone telling our supervisor's son to keep his mouth shut when he called to report his mother for neglect. They all covered for each other. Even when he overdosed on alcohol in rebellion against her drinking and having no one to help him escape it, everyone just stuck their heads further down in the sand.

I never needed a favor. I never needed my ass covered, nor did I cover for anyone. I was on my own.

After I told my supervisor my complaints, she admitted that she'd told the staff they didn't have to speak to me. I told her I quit. I went to my desk and packed my things. She stood in front of me and said, "I beg you to reconsider. Think of what you're giving up."

"Get out of my way," I said. I walked out the door and never looked back. She called me several times asking me to come back.

I asked her, "What part of *I quit* don't you understand?" Despite our differences, she considered me a friend. She knew I was good at what I did and she admired my spunk. I always believed that deep down she was rooting for me and hoping I'd eventually beat the system. She had told me once that she was just like me when she started, and that someday I would accept the way things were. I assured her I never would. I promised myself I would change things. I knew now they were right. I couldn't change anything. It was just the way it was everywhere. If you fought it, they would run you out. One way or another, they would win. There were too many of them working together to keep the good ol' boy system of favors and pay-offs running smoothly.

I had never stayed for retirement benefits and pay increases—that was never my mission. If my clients weren't being served because people didn't like me, then I had no choice but leave. They got me where it hurt—my clients.

Later, the janitor told me the director sent flowers to the clerk, congratulating her for getting rid of me. He promoted her to his personal secretary.

Before I quit, Todd's mom filed domestic violence charges on Todd's dad and filed for divorce. His sisters went to the prosecutor to get the charges dropped, saying she was just copying me. They said it had gone on for years and was nothing new. There wasn't a problem anywhere—the only problem was—me. I would have loved it if my mom would have had the guts to file domestic violence charges against Don when he was still alive. I was disgusted that this sweet lady's kids did this to her. What if she died from his abuse? What about Loretta? Their sister who died from his abuse? They marched at every abortion rally, but what about that baby? I threw in the towel. I was defeated. You can't fight crazy.

Todd bought a trailer and put it on his parents' farm. Sometimes he lived there and sometimes he lived at our house. He wouldn't sell the trailer and commit to the marriage again, but he frequently showed up for sex. Each time, I thought it meant he'd decided he loved me. I was slow to realize that it only meant that he could have his cake and eat it too.

Todd kept going back and forth, wanting the divorce, not wanting the divorce, depending on when he wanted sex. He had told me he wanted "space" for so long, I was tired of hearing it. He just needed to divorce me, but I couldn't do it.

While separated, I became pregnant. Todd was not happy at all. Seven years of trying since the miscarriage, and I got pregnant when our marriage was about over.

Todd came to pick me up to take me to a Valentine's party at the gun club. I told him he needed to take me to the hospital instead—it was another tubal pregnancy. The memory of the tubal pregnancy never left me, and the pain in my hip bone was all too familiar.

He acted mad that he'd have to miss the party.

My doctor said it was too early for the ultrasound to tell if it were tubal or not. He would have to take my word for it. He said if I were wrong, the surgery would kill the baby.

I wanted this baby. I had never stopped praying for a baby. I hated the thought of having surgery to kill it. But I knew it was tubal, and those kill both the mother and the child in the first trimester. My boys still needed me.

My doctor asked me if I wanted him to go ahead and take the tube out so I didn't have this problem again. Todd quickly answered for me, saying, "Yes," and my doctor agreed that was best, and wrote down Todd's answer.

I spoke up and informed them nobody was making that choice for me again. I told my doctor to save my tube if he could. I planned to see a fertility specialist to repair my tube when this was over. I add that Todd and I were getting divorced, so he didn't get to decide what to do with my tubes any more.

My doctor walked out. Todd sat by my bedside as I waited for surgery to remove our baby. He didn't say a word—he was angry. I lay there thinking, "The next time I'm on my death bed, I will have a husband who cares!" I was so hurt and angry about losing a fourth child, and its father sat there only thinking of his *space*, and how he would rather be at the gun club drinking and flirting with women in front of me.

In the few weeks this child was in my womb, it had made a

huge impact on my life. It gave me the determination to fight for the right to be loved. It helped me see Todd for what he really was, and not through rose-colored glasses. I fell out of love with Todd. I would always love him, but I was no longer *in love* with him. How could I be, when he didn't care about the death of any of our unborn children?

I knew then what I wanted. I wanted a divorce, and I wanted a man who wanted to have babies with me, a man who would love me and hold me when I was sad. That man was NOT Todd. I didn't know who he was yet, but this baby taught me a lot during its short time here. I was determined to make sure I never lost another baby in my tube again. After the surgery, my doctor told me the baby was in the tube and he removed it. He said I have even more scar tissue in that tube now due to this surgery.

I later had tests done to explore that tube further and was referred to a fertility specialist in Columbus. Todd drove me to Columbus and went to my appointment with me, even though we had no intention of having another baby together. The doctor did more tests and concluded I would never be able to get pregnant again with that tube. He suggested I do the GIFT (Gamete In-tra-Fallopian Transfer) procedure. I needed a loving husband and a lot of money for that, and I had neither.

Back then, I had no one to talk to about work, my marriage, or my life. I cried every morning as I drove to work at children services. I asked God to hold my hand and help me through this as I walked into that building every day. Foster kids were in and out of our home and never knew anything was wrong with my job or marriage. I told no one about anything. I never mattered. I just wanted to save the world. The task given to me was too great. I couldn't even save my own unborn children.

Todd withdrew further and further. Finally, he asked me to go for a drive to talk. I knew what was coming, and I was ready. Todd told me he wanted a divorce. He said I could have the house and kids if I reduced the amount of child support. He wanted to keep his retirement. I agreed. I only had one request, that he not discuss it with his family and it be over as soon as possible. He agreed. On the way to the divorce hearing, we stopped at a nice little place for lunch. I told Todd that he had worked hard building the house, and I would understand if he didn't want to walk away from it. We didn't even have to get divorced.

He quietly said no, this is what he wanted. Todd took me home and dropped me off, and then he took the boys for a visit. It was official now, not on paper, but in our hearts. This was the first time I didn't go on a visit with the boys to Todd's trailer. I went to the bathroom and shut the door. I was no longer allowed in my own family. The house had never felt so empty and quiet. I sat down and let the tears flow, and I prayed. God was the only one I had to confide in. I was all alone in the world. I still had my sons to care for, but without Todd, I was empty.

I sat there and poured my whole heart out to God. I asked God why. Why hadn't my parents loved me? Why hadn't my siblings loved me? Why hadn't my own husband of sixteen years loved me? People just hated me. My family, Todd's family, people at work. I sobbed and released thirty-four years of built-up hurt. I surrendered once again to defeat.

I cried and cried, doubled over in agony, searching for an answer, knowing there was none, feeling so very alone in the world. A world that didn't care about anyone or anything but themselves. The quiet and stillness in the house seemed so loud that it hurt to listen to it.

Suddenly, to my right, I heard a male voice say, "My child."

I stopped and sat up in amazement. God had spoken to me. ME!

"That's right!" I said as I began laughing tears of joy. God was my Father. He was all the family I needed. I was so overcome with joy from God calling me "His child" so sweetly and lovingly, to ease my pain. I wiped away the cold tears of joy from my face hot from tears of sorrow just a second before. Of all the miracles I'd seen, this was the first one I didn't quickly dismiss. I celebrated it with my whole heart and soul. I clutched onto it like it was a bag of gold. It was mine!

I got up, laughing and dancing around the house, praising God for that miracle of hearing His voice. I never cried one more tear over any of those people again. God's love filled my heart fully and completely and healed me of all of my sorrow.

Todd called and asked me to go to a party on the river bank. There was a band playing. He wanted me to go with him in his boat and wouldn't take no for an answer. I once feared he would kill me on that boat, and now he'd just asked me for a divorce. He was unpredictable. I couldn't trust him, yet I wanted to go to the party. I was in the mood to celebrate. Todd had no idea where my heart was at now, and I wasn't about to tell anyone. This was my special secret. I wasn't ruining it with the dumb opinions of others.

I went with him to the river party, but I didn't get in his boat, no matter how he pouted and coaxed. I danced all night barefoot by myself to the music in the summer breeze. I was free. I was strong. I had survived! I didn't recall the talk with that Wildflower yet— that would come much later. But my soul must have remembered, because that whole night I danced in the wind rejoicing, and could not stop. I didn't care what people said or thought, my soul had been set free! I knew God was smiling down on me. I was full of hope for the future. The sky was the limit in what I could do with my life now. I was "in the spirit"! I felt like I had just been born.

The divorce hearing lasted about five minutes. We sat close beside each other, smiled and agreed on everything. We left there, walked to the court house, and Todd signed the deed over to me. We went to a bar to celebrate, then we went home and made love. We promised to remain friends. We wished each other all the best in life. It was bittersweet. For me it stung like a knife, but a hot knife that was closing a wound. Healing could now begin.

After the divorce, Todd and I tried dating other people, but always ended up back in bed. I still went to the boys' visitations with them. I spent every other weekend with them at their dad's. I knew I had to cut the cord, but I didn't trust Todd to watch our boys because of all the drinking there. This was my family—Todd and the boys.

One night a doctor took me out to dinner. I had him drop me

off at Todd's, because it was his birthday. Chuck was there, and seemed angry, fearing we would get back together. I just missed Todd sometimes. I missed the good times and our friendship. Chuck and his wife left, and after talking awhile, I asked Todd to drive me home.

Apparently, Todd got the wrong idea, and assumed I was going to invite him in for sex. He became furious when I told him he couldn't come in. I had let him come and go as he pleased before, but if I refused sex, he begged and I couldn't get away from him. He never took *no* as *no* the whole time we were married, but he had to learn it now.

I went inside and locked the doors. I looked outside and saw Todd backing up. He parked over the hill so I couldn't see he was still there. I went downstairs and told the boys to turn up the music and pretend they didn't hear their dad if he knocked on the basement door. We had one window in our living room that didn't have a lock, and he knew which one.

I was sure he was going to try to force sex again. He wanted his freedom, but refused to let me have mine. I worried how far he would go to gain control of me. I worried he would sneak in and kill me. I had no idea what he was up to. I just knew he was furious.

I went upstairs to my bedroom and grabbed the phone and hid in my closet. I called Chuck and told him he better come get Todd out of my house. Chuck snapped at me, saying we were getting along fine at Todd's trailer when he'd left, so what was the problem? I said the problem was that I just wanted to be friends. I didn't want to have sex with him, and he was breaking into my house.

Chuck accused me of lying and said Todd wasn't there. I said if he didn't come get Todd, I would call the police. If the police came, it would be a second domestic violence charge, which meant six months in jail and he would lose his job.

I heard Todd walking around downstairs looking for me. I sat quietly, knowing he would find me. I heard him walk into my bedroom and stand there. I opened the closet door.

I smiled and acted friendly, hoping he wouldn't get angry because I had hidden from him and had called someone. As my eyes scanned him for a weapon, he said, "We are sick. This has to end." He turned and walked out. He must have thought I had called the police. He had planned to catch me off guard and alone. I have no idea what he had planned to do after breaking in.

Todd changed after that. We became friends. He dated and called me for relationship advice. I never let on that his questions hurt—I just needed him to stay sexually separate from me and for us to move forward as friends in order to end the violence.

The boys were now fifteen, fourteen, and thirteen. I worried they would become alcoholics and get hurt, and learn to be cruel to women too. Yet, Todd was who I chose for their father, and I couldn't change that now. I wouldn't want to, either. Todd and his family loved my boys. I would never take that away from them, even if I could.

Their aunts told me they kept an eye on them when the boys were with Todd. They promised me they would be fine, so I started staying home. There was no way I could keep them from their dad or his family. That wasn't an option. They would resent me and move in with him.

I had resigned from doing foster care when we first separated. The agency refused to accept my resignation, so I had put my license on hold. The quiet was unbearable, so I tried dating again. I didn't like anyone I met. Men had changed a lot since 1979. I had no idea what I wanted. So, I started going out with a friend of Tonya's, a DJ, because he was fun. I was dating just to get out of the house again.

I enjoyed being on stage with him and helping people have a great time. I loved little kids at school dances. I bought a box of party hats, crowns and hula necklaces, and watched the kid's imaginations and freedom soar. I loved being creative on the spot. Sometimes we dressed up and had little random dance routines. I loved getting out in the audience and enjoying everyone. I felt free in those moments. People who knew me when I was married to Todd couldn't get over how I had changed. They said, "You used to be so shy."

Yet, when it was just us, I didn't click with this guy. I knew I had to break it off. He wasn't someone I wanted to marry, and he wanted me to marry him. Plus, he was an older brother to Jerry and Joel. He told me he knew his brothers had raped me, "because everyone was talking about it back then." That, and other things about him, made me uncomfortable.

I sat in the passenger seat of his car, headed back to his house to get my car. I was planning my exit, the breakup. I felt dull and hollow inside. I now knew being alone and miserable was better than being stuck in a car with someone you couldn't stand to be alone with. Suddenly something flew straight at me, coming towards the windshield. It was a bluish spirit. It yelled, "There's a guy down that road who has two girls and he needs you!"

What was I supposed to do? Go knocking door to door? I knew this was really happening, but I also knew it couldn't be happening. We were passing the road that led to Warren High School that we moved from in 1977.

That thing just came through the windshield yelling at me right in front of my face. I knew my guy friend didn't notice anything. This was only happening to me. I had to just shake that off. I thought if it happened again, I would get in to see a doctor. I broke up with him and went home.

Soon it was the holidays and I couldn't even afford a Christmas tree or many presents for the boys. I was a newly divorced working mother of three teenage boys. Chuck brought us a Christmas tree one night, and I was humbled by his gesture. On Christmas Eve, Todd called, drunk, and demanded that I take him back or he was going to get a Christmas tree with his girlfriend and her son. He promised to stop drinking, take it or leave it. I said I passed and hung up.

Christmas morning, Todd brought gifts for the boys, and I was grateful. I gave him back his wedding ring, thinking that would make him and the boys happy.

It didn't. They all looked at me like it was pointless. By evening Christmas Day, Todd demanded that I put his name back on the deed to the house. He said he would give up whiskey but not beer. I told him that wasn't the deal.

He was back to drinking in no time and back to not coming home after work. He would go straight to the bars again and not bother to call. He also had his own place, so who knew where he'd end up each day.

A few weeks later, it was a Friday night at 8:30 and I hadn't heard from him. I was working on a marriage that didn't exist.

I went to the bathroom and looked deep into the mirror. I recalled the day I heard God's voice calling me, "My child." I began to talk directly to God from the spot where I'd heard him last. I said, "Okay, God, you are my Father. I want an arranged marriage. Apparently, I can't pick 'em." I asked God to pick a husband for me. I gave in to His will.

I then had a tiny vision in the top right hand corner of the mirror. I saw a leaf blowing in the wind. It reminded me of the Forest Gump movie, when the feather floats in the wind. Forest wonders if life is destiny or just an accident, or a little bit of both. I then understood: Trust God and follow Him. He was like a leaf blowing in the wind. Follow God like the leaf follows the wind, and I would be led to my husband. He had heard my offer, and all I had to do was trust and follow. I agreed.

My mom had been bugging me to go "man hunting" with her at the Eagles Club. I think she was looking for husband number five. I always refused to stoop that low. But now I called her and accepted her invitation.

I sat at the bar, and after a while, I told Mom, "He isn't here," so we went to a few other nice places. Rich men in suits kept asking me to slow dance. I would, but it didn't feel right. I realized I wasn't looking for a rich man. I had nothing in common with them. I sat there sad for a while. I was being led, but didn't know where to go.

I realized I wanted a man in blue jeans and work boots, not rich, but a working man. I felt the need to go to a carry-out close to where we lived when I was little.

"What do you want to go to that dump for?" Mom asked. "All these rich men asking you to dance, you have your pick, and you want to go there?"

Mom had met a guy friend that night, so he drove us in my

car to the carry-out. As I walked towards the door and heard the loud juke box, I wondered what was wrong with me. Was I crazy, following a hunch, looking for a husband, and following the wind? I thought about turning around and going home.

Then I heard a voice. "Don't look left, don't look right, look straight ahead."

I walked in and only looked straight ahead. And there he was. A man with dark-brown, curly hair in a mullet style. I had never walked into a bar, sat beside a man, and started a conversation before in my life. Until then.

This felt holy, even though I knew it appeared slutty. I had to trust where I'd been led. Besides, he *was* really cute.

My mom and her man sat on my right, as this man was on my left. We talked a little, but he didn't seem that interested. He drank coffee and kept over-tipping the waitress.

Mom asked him if he was going to ask me to dance or not. I wasn't sure if he was shy or if he didn't like me. I was about to give up.

Then he asked me to dance. I could tell his heart wasn't in it. I let him know it was okay, he didn't have to feel forced to do so. He explained that he hadn't danced with anyone since his wife, who'd left him a year ago. Today was his daughter's birthday. He had visited her at his ex-wife's boyfriend's house, where he was told his daughter was sick.

I looked into those baby-blue puppy-dog eyes and felt his heart ache. I knew I had a keeper. His heart was still loyal after the marriage was over, just like mine.

I wanted to protect that big heart from ever being broken again. It felt like my mission in life was to care for this great big heart in this man's chest. I could feel the size of it—it was a huge circle that spaced clear out to his shoulders. I wasn't sent to him just for me a husband, I was sent to protect him from being hurt again. At that very moment, I promised the spirit guiding me I would accept that responsibility. I would honor his heart. I felt this was important to God.

We sat down and talked awhile. He had an innocence about him. His name was Jim, and he wasn't the drinking and picking-up women type, so he didn't know how to act. He hadn't planned on being there that night. He was supposed to meet friends somewhere else. They hadn't shown up, so he stopped at the carry-out for coffee before heading back home. He said he'd never been much of a drinker. After talking a while, I left. He didn't ask for my number. Once we got in the car, I panicked. We would never meet again if I didn't give him my number. He was too shy to ask for it, and I was too shy to offer it. I wrote it down and gave it to mom's guy friend. I told him to go back in and give it to Jim.

When I got home about one a.m., I asked the boys if their dad had called. They said he'd called around 8:30 to say he was at a bar.

The next afternoon, I walked into the kitchen by the phone and sat down. I knew Jim was about to call, and I hoped he called before Todd did. About that time, Jim called and asked me out. I accepted. He would pick me up after he got off work. He was a construction worker.

It was destiny. I felt God's hand in it. I knew this was going to work out.

Only a few minutes after I hung up, Todd called and asked me out. "No, I have a date."

He was furious. "We were supposed to be getting back together!"

I politely told him I had to go. "Goodbye."

Todd was pointless.

CHAPTER 16

MY SOUL MATE

Jim picked me up and asked me where I wanted to go. We stopped at a bar five miles from my house, had a drink and talked. He was such a proud father. He beamed as he showed me pictures of his kids.

Some of Todd's friends were there, and I was getting a lot of dirty looks from them.

Jim said we could do anything I wanted. I felt so at ease with him. He wasn't controlling at all. He didn't make moves. I felt safe. I felt free to be me with him.

I said what I really wanted was to go home and go sledding in my backyard with my boys and their friends.

"Let's do it then," Jim said.

We went home and joined my sons and their friends sledding off the hill behind our house. Then we went inside and made snow ice cream.

Jim looked at a Polaroid picture on my fridge. "I know everyone in that picture," He said.

"You do not!" I insisted.

He named them all.

I went over and took it from him and looked at the back. There was no writing to tell the names. I was confused. It was a photo of us kids with Dad before he died of cancer, taken about a year earlier. There hadn't been another family photo since we were little. We had just gotten together this one time because he was dying.

Jim said his ex was best friends with Tonya. She and Tonya worked together at the hospital, and they were at Tonya's house all the time. He had spent more time with my family than I had during the last few years. He didn't like them—his ex-wife made him go. We now felt familiar.

The next day I called Tonya and told her I met a guy at a bar and we were dating. She thought that was terrible. She was upset with me because she knew Todd and I were trying to get back together. That was, until I told her his name.

"Jimmy! You're dating Jimmy?" She went on about how nice he was and how the divorce was all his ex's fault, and said she had cheated on Jim a lot.

A few weeks later, Jim asked me to come to his house and meet his two daughters. As I drove there following the directions he wrote down, it suddenly hit me. I had to pull over and catch my breath.

I was turning onto the road that led to Warren High School to meet this guy's two daughters! Just a month earlier, that blue spirit/ voice screamed at me through the windshield that there was a guy down this road with two girls who needed me! How could that be? How could what seemed so crazy, be so real?

I sat there in my car trying to comprehend it all. There was no way I could understand it.

A few months after that, it dawned on me that I had gone to school with Jim when I had gone to Warren. He was the guy a voice told me I would meet again someday, but I had to go become a better person first!

Was Jim and I being together planned by God all along? Was I sent to Todd's family in order to become a better person? I had tried to be good and do everything by the book, to please Todd and his family for sixteen years. I thought it had gotten me nowhere. Todd had told me he would've divorced me a long time ago, but I'd never done anything wrong.

I now saw that all those years of trying to be good enough for Todd, was actually meant for me to become worthy of Jim!

I told Jim about these things much later. I didn't want to sound like a mental person right off the bat.

One night we were watching country music videos. Faith Hill's "Hey, Baby, Let's Go to Vegas" was on. When it was over, I asked Jim if he wanted to go to Vegas and take a gamble.

He said, "Sure."

A few days later we were at The Little Chapel of Flowers in Vegas saying, "I do," and entering my perfectly-arranged marriage.

We met in January 1996 and were married in November 1997. We fostered kids while we waited for a call about adoption. A sibling group of five were matched with us in 1998, and we adopted them in 1999. The youngest, Zach, was born in November 1994 near Thanksgiving. That was when Jim's wife left him, and when Todd and I were scheduled to be divorced the first time. Three unrelated lives seemed to have been meant to be together. Zach had twin sisters, Hope and Faith, and sisters Nicole and Lora. When I heard there were twin girls in the sibling group, I knew they were all hand-picked by God just for us. Every wound was healed.

We continued to foster, and in 2000 a sibling group of four sisters, Tina, Maggy, Heather and Miranda, whom we'd been fostering for a year, were eligible for adoption.

I was working at Marietta Memorial Hospital while finishing my Bachelor's degree. I had been accepted at law school in Michigan, which I'd applied for before we got the last four kids. I still wanted to fight for children's rights. I wanted to be a juvenile judge. When I got the letter that I was accepted to Cooley Law School in Michigan, I was so excited. I could continue my mission helping abused children. When I ran in to workers from Human Services, I would tell them to put the word out that once I graduated from law school, I'd be offering free legal services to anyone wanting to sue the director.

Jim said he could get a job in Detroit. We didn't have the heart to tell the four foster girls we couldn't adopt them, so we adopted them anyway. We moved in the fall so the kids could start school at the beginning of the school year. I was to start law school classes in January.

Our five biological kids were grown and our nine adopted children seemed well-adjusted. I finally had the big, happy family

I'd always wanted, complete with the man of my dreams.

After we were settled in Lansing, 9-11 happened. After Cameron had graduated from high school, he'd enlisted in the Army for three years. He got out on Mother's Day, and he and Ty were working and living in our house in Ohio. He reenlisted immediately after 9-11.

The following November, we had to return home for the final adoption hearing of the last four. I didn't know it at the time, but their biological mother gave the oldest child, Tina, her phone number in the bathroom, and told her to call. All I knew was Tina and Maggy started acting up every night while Jim worked night shift.

Then one morning Maggy refused to eat breakfast. She refused to take her lunch bucket to school, then she refused to stop screaming outside our bedroom door where her dad was sleeping. Then she refused to get on the bus. She ran down the street as the other kids were loading onto the bus. I ran after her, fearing she would be hit by a car or kidnapped.

We were country people. Our kids had played in caves, cow fields and the woods, but now we lived in downtown Lansing. There were drug dealers on the street corners and a lot of crime. I took Maggy by the shoulder of her jacket and walked her back to the house. We had a one-year lease, and we couldn't get out of it. I regretted not checking out the area better. I didn't know it at the time, but their biological mom told Tina to misbehave and Tina had told her younger siblings to as well.

Tina didn't like rules, and she was jealous of the oldest girl of the sibling group of five, Nicole.

I gave Nicole extra attention because she had mental health issues. Nicole would pretend she heard voices or would make up allegations on her biological mom or would throw fits for attention. Tina and Nicole were either very close or worse enemies at any given moment.

I tried to talk to Maggy about her behavior, and she just blew me off. I woke up Jim and told him to whip her butt. He had recently made a paddle as a joke. He carved "The Boss" on one side and "The Big Boss" on the other. We had been surprised when he walked up from the basement carrying it a few nights before. I asked him why he'd made it, and he said it was the only thing he learned to make in wood shop in school, and he wanted to make something. We all laughed and the kids lined up for a little tap. We never thought we would ever actually use it.

Now I was I handing Jim the paddle. He was half asleep and didn't want to whip Maggy, but I insisted. He said "I don't know how." He had never spanked a child before. He gave her one light tap.

Maggy looked at me, her expression serious. I had her attention now. I asked her if she was ready to behave. She agreed she was. As we drove her to school, I talked to her and explained she had to go to bed early again tonight. This was her last night of early bedtime. If she was good, she would be able to join us for movie night the next night, Friday.

She then started to cry and said she was sorry. We both cried and hugged and then laughed because she had me crying too. We had never used corporal punishment before. I used private heart-to-heart talks instead. They worked the majority of the time.

Maggy was the type that when she cried, she rubbed her eyes hard and they turned red quickly. I knew the school could tell she had been crying, but thought they would just tease her a little and tell her she'd better behave, and they would laugh it off. Even though the kids had only been going to school there a few months, the school knew me. They had "go to school with your child day" for a month. I went one day with each child. I had been at the school for week. (We had twins in the same class, Tina and Nicole were in the same class, and Maggy and Heather were in the same class.)

After we dropped off Maggy at school, Jim and I went to the mall and started getting ideas for Christmas. I was very happy that day, because I'd finally received my book list for law school. Jim was up early for a change so we had some alone time together. I couldn't wait to get my books. I had taken a pre-law class online with the law school, and felt confident I was going to love it. We saved the kids' adoption subsidies for their college. We were financially stable and loved our big happy family. Jim supported me in everything.

We were both forty years old now, but we looked and acted thirty. We were both high energy and full of life. We were just big kids ourselves. We didn't have a care in the world.

I was putting supper on the table when the kids got home from school. I noticed Tina and Maggy weren't in the dining room. The kids always rushed in to tell me about their day. I knew something was up with those two girls—likely boys. We'd had an issue recently with Tina letting boys feel her up under her sweatshirt on the school bus.

Yet, all day under the surface, I had felt something strange was about to happen. At the mall, I briefly panicked about the cost of law school, and wanted to change my mind and go home. I secretly wished something would happen so I could save face and not go. It was a tiny bit of the jitters, I thought. Everything was going too well. Then I heard a voice say, "Remember, you asked for this." I wondered, "What had I asked for? To not go to law school?" That feeling stayed with me as the kids got home from school, like a doom hanging over us that I tried hard to ignore.

Just as I headed upstairs to tell the kids supper was ready, there was a knock at the front door. I thought it was the neighbor kids. They knew what time we ate. I taught them to come to the window by my cook stove if they were hungry. I passed food out that window like we were running a fast food shop. I was sure someone forgot they needed to go to the window.

I opened the door, and two women stood there. They said, "We are with the Family Independence Agency." I knew that meant Children Services, because I had to report a toddler who kept running down our street unsupervised after we moved in. They said they were there because Maggy had been spanked.

I said yes, she had been. I had told my husband to spank her, but it was just a tap. I figured this was just a formality.

They said she had bruises.

I laughed. "Maggy does not have bruises."

"She does," they said with stone faces.

I told them to have a seat, I would be right back. I ran upstairs and asked Maggy if I could look. There was a gray splotchy rash all over her butt. I gasped, and asked her how that had happened.

Maggy said she didn't know. The school nurse had asked her why her eyes were red. She told her she'd been crying, and made a joke about being spanked. She said she was fine, but the nurse called case workers.

Maggy was told to sit on a hot heating pad all day in the bathroom while she waited for them to come talk to her. They didn't come until late in the afternoon. She said she kept wanting to get up and complained it was too hot, but the nurse wouldn't let her get up. She said Tina stayed in the bathroom with her and talked to the workers when they came.

She said Tina was mad and telling everyone lies about what had happened. Tina immediately started an argument with Maggy in the bedroom. For some reason, Tina was making a bigger deal out of it. She acted like we were abusers, and it was clear she wasn't on our side.

I knew how this looked—it looked bad for us. But anyone could see this was not from a paddle, but we had no way of proving it. I didn't think a heating pad could cause a gray rash, although later we discovered the rash was from the heating pad.

I walked back down the stairs in a total disbelief and terror to the point I felt outside myself. I went back in the living room where they were still seated, in total shame because I knew what they thought. I told them the marks were not from the paddle—he barely tapped her. But I did see marks. I told them I was shocked and confused. They said they had already called for foster homes for all of the kids before they'd come, and the kids would be in foster care immediately if they had found homes for them all.

This was a nightmare. This was not happening.

Then they said the adoption of the last four wasn't legal, and they were therefore terminating those adoptions. (There is a clause that an adoption can be terminated up to six months after it is final.) I told her we waived that right at the hearing because they had been in our home for over a year. I told them the adoptions were so legal, they were done by county children service agencies.

They said if we didn't agree to no corporal punishment, they would remove the children.

I handed her the paddle and told her to just take it.

They acted like I had handed over a smoking gun after being accused of murder. The workers looked at the paddle like it was a torture device, and was mad about the "Boss" and "Big Boss," making out like we beat our kids all the time with it. They had us all figured out in their minds, and it was only getting worse by the minute.

They said we had to either sign all our kids over to them, or agree to live in Lansing until the youngest turned eighteen. They said a worker for each child would live in our home. Our little boy Zach was only seven years old! We only came for one year of law school, and then I planned to transfer to Columbus, Ohio.

I told them I had been a child abuse investigator for seven years and a therapeutic foster parent for sixteen years for sixty kids, and I had never heard of anything like this. We had never had even one indicated or substantiated case against us. There are never services that long, or that many case workers on a case. In Ohio, teachers still use a paddle in the classrooms. They said in Michigan, it is child abuse to paddle your child using any object.

They said they had already called our former county, which advised many reports had been made against us. My former coworkers at Children Services told them that they suspected abuse, but could never prove it. They said I only became a worker so I could learn how to abuse kids and get by with it.

I told them that was not true! The last four girls' biological mom made a false allegation, but Tina tape-recorded her mother telling them to lie or she would beat them all the way down the Children's Home hill. It was investigated, and she was charged and given a restraining order to stay away from us and our home. The kids denied their biological mother's allegations. Jim's ex made a couple of reports out of jealousy, once she found out Jim and I were dating and where I worked. They also were unfounded. They weren't even enough to make a report, but since I was a worker, the prosecutor's office had to handle it. The second time she did it, we filed false report charges on his ex. She was found guilty of trespassing on our property and also given a restraining order to stay away from our home.

They ignored me and looked at us like they hated us. I felt all my enemies had joined forces and followed us to Michigan. I was being punished for taking better care of everyone's kids than they had.

I felt three ex-parents had come back to haunt me. Jim's daughter's mother, the second adopted kid's mother, and my boys' dad. I was sure Todd and his family were behind this somehow too. I had raised those people's kids because they had better things to do than be a full-time parent. But now the trouble they caused me in Ohio had followed me to Michigan. It was so unfair.

After Jim and I got married and adopted the nine kids, Todd was jealous and didn't want to pay child support anymore for Ty. He told everyone we were supposed to be getting back together, and Jim was living in his house. His attorney demanded to know how much we received in adoption assistance, even though it can't be used to adjust child support. The judge went along with it. Todd used the fact that I let Ty visit him whenever Ty wanted, because Cole stayed at Todd's a lot after he graduated. Therefore, Todd got $2,000 back in child support. He owed me $2,500 in medical bills. He paid his attorney $4000 to take me to court. So, Todd only won $500 out of the deal. The fighting ruined Ty's senior year. Todd made Ty file income tax as an independent so I couldn't claim him as a dependent. Todd was doing anything to get back at me. Therefore, Ty couldn't use our family size to get grants for college. Who was making my Ohio county attack me like this? These were out-right lies coming from Ohio to Michigan, at the worst possible time.

The Child Support supervisor had apologized to me after Todd "won," saying he had never seen a custodial parent have to pay a non-custodial parent in all of his years there. He said the director forced him to file the claim, telling him to "get that bitch."

Before I left town, Todd made threats about getting ahold of Jim's ex to conspire against us. She requested joint custody of their girls until he moved in with me. Then she fought him tooth and nail. It was clear my former co-workers used this opportunity to get back at me by lying. Everything was unsubstantiated, and the reports came from parents of kids I was raising.

I hate the saying "If everyone is saying it, it must be true." I never based my case decisions on hearsay. I did full blown through investigations until I was satisfied I knew the truth about a family. I also suspected the supportive worker was directly responsible for this lie. She was caught lying to my foster agency about me when I started working at the agency. The foster agency went to the director and wanted her disciplined. They had my back 100%. The director just told us to "get along." I thought I had left past enemies in Ohio, but here it all was, in one unified force. I suddenly regretted boasting about free legal services against the director.

The workers said a family moved from Ohio to Michigan and killed an adopted child and buried him in the backyard. They said we would do the same.

It was getting more ridiculous by the minute. They talked about termination of parental rights after they had been in our home for only five minutes. They planned it before they'd even gotten there! It was insane. These people were trying to scare us into signing our kids over. They said we could go to prison. The police were coming and maybe they would arrest us. It would all go away if we signed our kids over to them right now. Had they done this to everyone, or were we just that unlucky? My PTSD was in full swing.

My mind swirled around in paranoia and fear trying to un-derstand this. I was terrified because it made no sense. The world makes sense if you do something wrong and you deserve it, but we had never harmed a child. We spanked a tiny tap one time, and got all of this because of it? I was excited about going to law school and having a happy family, now I had to prepare to go to prison and lose all of our children, and my husband? I would never recover from this identity crisis. But that wasn't the worst part. The worst part was the fear of what my kids would go through. These beautiful sweet children had been through hell before we got them. They had security and love now, and someone wanted to rip them to shreds to get back at me. This reeked of my former county.

We had just put our lives back together, making a wonderful new life for us all, and now the rug was yanked out from under us. I couldn't comprehend. The workers left, saying they would be back the next day at noon when the kids got home from school. Their school let out early on Fridays.

Jim went to work. Our eleven-year-old twins, Hope and Faith, were scared and asked to sleep with me. They told me Tina was saying we beat Maggy with a belt. They were confused and scared, just like I was. They were afraid they would be taken from us, and so was I. I felt incapable of making anyone believe me. The workers said they would remove our kids if we discussed the case with them. I couldn't even get to the bottom of what was going on with Tina. I couldn't comfort the twins with any rational explanation. I was under a gag order.

I wondered if this was punishment for all the children I had removed. I had never came to a conclusion before I completed an investigation. I questioned every removal I'd ever made and every door I'd ever knocked on. Is this how people felt? Did I do this to people? Had I caused them to be this scared? I wanted to "fight for children's rights" without ever knowing what it did to the family. I was praised in the newspaper once for my fairness. Still, I didn't know this. Nobody could ever know this—unless it happened to them.

I had been an abused child, then a foster mother, then a therapeutic foster parent, then a children services investigator, and then an adoptive parent. Now I was an alleged perpetrator and I feared soon I would be a client, a parent whose children were taken away, possibly forever. I had experienced the system full circle. No law school or college could have ever given me this insight. As horrific as it was, I almost felt blessed to have had my eyes opened before going to law school to "save the world."

What was that nagging whisper I felt all day leading up to this? Was this what I had asked for? If so, when? Was I given this to help abused kids somehow? There had to be a reason somewhere for this. God was about to give me the biggest task on earth I feared.

I couldn't fix the child welfare system in my county, was I now supposed to fix it for the whole country? I would certainly try. I was not giving up my kids without the biggest fight Michigan ever saw. Would it take a mother's love like mine to make a difference?

The next morning, Maggy refused to go to school again, refused to eat breakfast, and refused to get dressed, and I was afraid to make her. The other kids went to school. I went upstairs and talked to Maggy. Once the kids were on the bus, she was fine and acted like she had some sense. She still wouldn't say why she did it. I checked her bottom and the rash was completely gone. She told me the school nurse accused us of putting bleach in her eyes, and said that is why they were so red. The nurse told her she was adopting all of our kids. I was shocked.

The nurse said we had adopted them for the money, and if she adopted them, she would quit work. I thought this was crazy. We would file a complaint against this nurse, and this would get cleared up. I would get ahold of the county case workers, where we adopted our kids, and they would stand up for us.

Maggy insisted that the heating pad caused the rash. She said it was very hot, and she kept asking the nurse if she could get off, but she wouldn't let her. I told Maggy not to worry, we were going to talk to the workers about going home. I didn't feel the kids were safe here now. For some reason, these workers wanted nine beautiful blond kids at Christmas time.

Noon came and went. The kids didn't come home from school. Workers showed up and said they kept them there. I didn't understand how they had the authority to do that without custody. This was interference with custody, if not kidnapping. I would have been fired and had charges on me if I had done that as a worker in Ohio.

They wanted to know why Maggy wasn't at school. I told them she had refused to go, and I couldn't make her. I was afraid to even yell at her now. They said when Maggy wasn't at school, the nurse called in another report and said we had killed Maggy because she told on us.

"You can see she isn't dead—or harmed in any way," I said. "The marks are gone as well. They were caused because the school nurse tried to make her look abused so she could get adoption subsidy for nine kids and quit her job."

They got mad because I said that. She was a friend of theirs.

They said if I agreed to put our kids in Catholic school, they wouldn't remove them. It was against our constitutional rights for them to even say that. I told them I would have been fired if I'd dishonored a parent's religion like that.

They just blew me off and continued advocating for the Catholic religion. I told them my ex was Catholic, and my sons are Catholic, and I was, but we hadn't decided about these kids. They had been baptized and attended a Protestant church in Ohio before moving.

The worker kept wanting to discuss religion. I told her my ex was in the process of having our marriage annulled in the Catholic church. A church in town had received the paperwork. This was now a nightmare from which I couldn't awake. I was full blown paranoid. I wondered if the Catholic church was now involved in this conspiracy! I needed to get my kids and go home, and never return to Michigan.

I told her she had given us an option of going home and doing supportive services there instead of staying until our youngest was eighteen and having all those case workers in our home. She agreed. She said just have a doctor see Maggy when we got home, send them a report, and get the services set up when we got there. She said they just needed to talk to our kids at school before we left. They were being interviewed at the school now.

They said, "Go pick them up, and go back to Ohio."

Jim objected. He didn't want me giving up on going to law school. I told him the kids came first. Jim was heartbroken for me.

The workers said they didn't want me not to go to law school. I explained I couldn't focus on school with all this going on. I was traumatized and I wasn't going to recover any time soon.

Jim and I took our fifteen-passenger van to pick up our kids. They were all in our eight-year-old Lora's classroom. She was in her new red velvet Christmas dress, chugging down juice boxes and devouring snacks. (She had food hoarding issues.) I had lunch at home on the table waiting on them to get off the bus when the workers had arrived. The workers had questioned why I didn't send the kids to school with a lunch that day, as if I withheld food as a punishment for Maggy telling. These people had no business doing investigations. They were drama queens.

I had to explain that this school didn't serve meals, they served Lunchables. I didn't let my kids eat those. That was why I packed healthy foods for them every day but Friday. They ate lunch on Fridays as soon as they got home. I was the type who made sure our kids got all their food groups every day.

I was tired of the stupidity, but I remained polite. They had seen the wonderful homemade meal on my table, waiting for the kids.

They kept calling the kids in the office one at a time to question them. We were there for hours. Then I noticed the kids' coats and book bags were in the other office.

"They're waiting for a judge to call back," I said to Jim. "They're removing them."

Jim protested, saying they promised we could take them home. "They lied."

We walked back into the classroom, and Lora was swinging her beautiful red Christmas dress to show how proud she was of herself. "I told them Daddy spanked my butt," she said with a big toothless smile from bottle rot.

"You see?" I said to Jim. I knew she'd been coaxed and bribed. The workers finally got one to lie. We were screwed.

I watched our kids playing games on the computers, something the teachers didn't allow before. I watched our happy kids, knowing they had no idea what was about to happen. The workers had no idea how this would destroy them, nor did they care. They thought they were the child saviors. I remembered that feeling. This had to be karma.

I recalled a client calling me one day, asking, "How do you sleep at night?" because I had interviewed his children. I scoffed at him, saying, "I sleep just fine." I had rolled my self-righteous eyes and hung up.

I had seen all sides of the child welfare system now. It was an education I couldn't obtain any other way. This was the most gut-wrenching event of my life. Not rape, neglect, abuse, divorce, miscarriage, or assault could compare to this trauma.

My poor husband didn't believe me. I knew he was about to find out too. I was seeing the future, while my family was still living in the past. I knew the bomb was about to go off, and I knew what the aftermath would look like, and there wasn't anything I could do about it.

Another hour passed, and the workers called Jim and me into the office. I told Jim this was it, get ready. Our hearts were about to be executed. I felt horrible for my innocent husband. He didn't even know what Children Services was before he'd met me. I woke him up to whip Maggy. I knew he didn't hurt her. She didn't even cry until we were in the truck. The heart-to-heart I had with her had made her cry. The tap on her bottom was just to get her attention. This was so undeserved. But I knew they had us over a barrel. They didn't want the truth—they just wanted our kids.

We walked into the office, where two police officers waited. I told my husband they were just there in case we got upset. If we got upset, they would arrest us. They told us they had been waiting to get the judge's approval, and it had just arrived. They removed our kids. There would be a hearing the next morning to see if we could get them back.

My husband protested, saying we were told we could take them home.

They responded that they told us not to whip them, and Lora said he whipped her last night.

He said he wasn't even home, he was at work.

I explained to Jim that they didn't care. They had already removed them without asking us if we had done anything or not. It was done.

I insisted we had to leave because we needed a lawyer with us in the morning.

The workers insisted they provided attorneys. I refused their "help." I told Jim everything would close soon, so we needed to go immediately.

I had to lead him out of there. He wouldn't accept it. I knew I had to take care of him right now, and hold myself together and not feel anything. They watched us.

When Jim and I got in the van, Jim wanted to go back in and get our kids. He said he wasn't leaving them. I told him to just drive, or he'd get arrested. I needed him with me right now.

We found a lawyer late on a Friday night, that could meet with us and be available for a hearing the next day, a Saturday morning. As we explained our situation to the lawyer in his conference room that night, I knew how it sounded. I wouldn't have believed me. My life had become one big conspiracy theory that no one would believe. Again, guilt over having been a worker myself for seven years consumed me. As we were leaving, I saw my reflection in the elevator. I saw what those workers thought, and what my lawyer suspected: "Child Abuser." I had lost my identity. Once again, I let the world tell me who I was.

The next morning, as we waited in the lobby of a small building to see the judge, we overheard the worker talking to the judge about us. Back home, this was not done. Parties could not talk about the case to the judge until we were in court. Then we heard her tell the judge, "They are like military—they beat all the kids for the slightest infraction!" I stopped the guilt right then. I knew that was bullshit! Then we heard her tell the Judge that Maggy has bruises all up and down her back and down her legs. She said she had pictures. I told our lawyer, I want to see those right now. That was a lie I could prove!

Our lawyer went to the case worker and came back with Polaroid pictures. I looked at the pictures and wanted to vomit. This girl looked like Maggy. You could see the side of her face and her back. This child had been severely beaten by someone. *That's not Maggy! She doesn't have those marks!* Someone had altered this picture. It was fake!

Our lawyer looked at the pictures, then looked at us like we were monsters. "I thought you said there were no marks?" He threw the photos down on the table.

Now our own lawyer didn't believe us. If he had, we could've had Maggy examined right then. My guilt for things I'd never done came back. I knew that wasn't Maggy, but people don't care about the truth. I was reduced to sixteen again. I couldn't help myself any more now than I could then. I was too traumatized to help my family.

We went in the court room in front of the judge. We found out this was not a real judge, but a "court worker." This was to see if the kids stayed in custody. With this fake Polaroid, I thought we were going to jail. I told my husband to not say a word. I wanted to wait until we got in front of a real judge before we provided our evidence. We were playing with corruption at a whole new level here.

The judge was continuing custody. We were now in Russia, not the USA. My son was risking his life fighting for Hitler and didn't know it.

I thought about Cameron dying for the United States of America when we had no rights here in Michigan. After the hearing, right in front of the court worker, the case worker urged me to put the kids in Catholic school again. She said I could see my kids every day for lunch if I agreed they could go to her kids' Catholic school. I refused.

The "judge" just watched me. I knew I couldn't fight this alone if my husband were in jail. I felt that was their strategy—either scare us so we go home without our kids, or put us in jail so we couldn't fight to get them back. One way or another, they were getting our kids.

I asked why the twins were separated. She said they asked to be. I told her that was a lie. She said all the kids were still in the school district, so they could see each other after lunch every day. I found out that was a lie too. Several were placed out of district with people who told her they couldn't drive them to their school, so they couldn't go to school. She put two of our kids in Catholic school. They wore uniforms, and had strict fasting for lent. Tina and Zach were sent to a house with broken glass and dog poop everywhere. Tina was taken to the Emergency Room for anxiety, and they were removed from that foster home for neglect.

They were not fed until late Friday night, and after all the junk food they were given, they ate at McDonald's. Several of the kids were placed with the workers' friends, who were teachers at their school and not licensed foster parents. Hope kept calling me, crying. She was placed with Heather in a home with three black families who weren't supposed to be living there. Heather was acting like a gangster all of a sudden and bullying Hope. I had to convince her to not run away.

At the real hearing, a few days later, the worker told us they had a statement from a doctor who examined Maggy on Friday, saying Maggy had those marks, and was prepared to say it was child abuse. The lies and intimidation made me feel like I was losing my mind. I had barely eaten or slept since the first night the workers came. All I did was send complaints to every governmental agency I could think of. Maggy told us later nobody ever took her to a doctor, and she knew there was nothing on her the next day, and she knew Dad never hurt her or left marks. All of the kids were upset about being removed and denied all allegations—except Tina.

The workers lied in reports, saying we had visits that we did not, and that the kids said things they never said. The worker said if we agreed to everything they said, we would get our kids back that day. I agreed. Christmas was coming up, and I wanted my kid s back immediately. Somebody had to end this insanity. I didn't care what they wrote down on paper. Jim told me not to, he wasn't agreeing to lies.

As we waited for our hearing, we watched drug addicts and alcoholics agree that their kids could stay in custody while they got help. As they called our case, deputies stormed in with arms folded, like we were dangerous criminals. The worker asked to keep our kids until they got psychological evaluations on everyone in our family. The judge ordered our kids to be returned to us immediately.

Every day I called to see when they were bringing the kids home. We were not even allowed to attend their Christmas program. The nurse and workers continued to tell our kids that the adoptions were not legal and would be terminated, and the nurse was adopting them all. Our psychological exams were not scheduled by the workers until after Christmas. They claimed we couldn't get our kids until they were done, even though that isn't what the order said. Charities donated bikes and things for our kids as if we were poor, and they were not allowed to call us. Two of the foster parents snuck and let them, because they said they could tell our kids came from a good home and feared their adopted kids could easily be taken too, because they spank.

After visits at the agency, the workers had to pry our kids' fingers loose from our waists. The workers blamed us, saying we had to learn to make this easier for our kids. I told them this was all their doing—they weren't putting this on me. They told us how difficult the trips back to the foster homes were. I said they should send them home, then. Tina usually stayed in another room, insisting I talk with her alone with her foster parent present. I told her we have other kids to visit, after I saw she just wanted to upset me and accuse us of things. She claimed we lined the kids up and beat them from head to toe every day. Her foster parent told me she knew Tina was lying, and Tina was drinking with her husband, who was a former alcoholic.

Nicole said she was beat in the head by her female police officer foster parent. I knew Nicole lied about abuse before for attention. Before we moved to Michigan, she had claimed her biological mother allowed men to rape her. This came about after the last four we adopted revealed to me sex abuse by their biological family members. I had to take the last four to a lot of appointments because of those allegations, so they missed a few days of school. Abuse stories got my blood boiling, and the kids knew it. So, I had to be careful not to feed into it. Yet at the same time, I was very concerned. We had been meeting Nicole and her worker at the hospital for brain MRI appointments that I already had scheduled for her before the removal. Nicole started going cross-eyed during stress before we moved. The eye specialist said it was lazy eye, but I wasn't buying it. The MRI results showed a tumor in the back of her head. According to Nicole's adoption history papers, brain tumors ran in her biological family. The possibility that someone was hitting our sensitive, unstable daughter was frightening enough, but her medical issues made my concerns even worse. I was closest to Nicole, because she was so fragile. She was emotionally dependent on me.

Meanwhile, allegations against foster parents poured in during visits. The workers heard them at the same time we did. Older foster kids forced Faith and Miranda to drink Kool-Aid with alcohol in it, then forced Miranda to molest a younger child. Heather molested a child in her foster home. I told the worker not to place Heather in a foster home with younger children for that very reason. They didn't listen to me. I was livid that a child was molested due to their inability to take me seriously. I was never a smart person, but one thing I knew was kids.

Everything that happened to our kids and the other kids was all their fault. We were assigned new workers. They finally admitted we hadn't done anything wrong. They said our kids had lied and couldn't be believed about anything after they told things about foster homes. They said our kids were the talk of the agency. I was in full bitch mode at this point. I found the fighter in me again. I stopped taking it personal, and fought for my kids.

The kids were returned two months after they were removed. They said I should be happy—nobody gets their kids back that fast. I said they should never have been taken in the first place! We were given one case worker and two court workers—one who had been the first "judge." They came frequently, but certainly didn't move in. The new case worker said she "would've gotten a lot worse than Maggy got, if she would've done was Maggy did." The court workers said the problem was Tina. I could never get a straight answer about the fake Polaroid or the fake doctor who said he would testify. Maggy was never taken to a doctor. I asked why we had to do services when they now know we never abused Maggy. They said we might as well accept the help since they were there. I always said we want to go home, we don't need help. They had "jurisdiction" over our kids—we were not allowed to leave the state with them. This also meant that one more allegation and they would be removed from us again, possibly for good.

The worker who had removed said she would make sure we

never fostered or adopted again, and that I never worked with kids again. The first two workers were mental nut jobs, possibly on drugs. No one is that stupid. I called to speak with supervisors on a regular basis and was always denied.

Ever since the removal, I spent most of my time on the computer, writing to Senators, Governors and even the President of the United States. The kids' adoption workers from Ohio supported us one hundred percent, and one was ready to come to Michigan and talk on the radio about this. She said the prosecutor in our hometown told her "Peggy has taken our hardest children and turned their lives around." She said if she came to Michigan, he was coming with her. I was glad to know that even though he and I had our differences, he knew I was not capable of child abuse.

After the kids were all home, the movie *I am Sam* came out. It was about a mentally challenged father having his daughter removed by social workers. I made the kids T-shirts that each said "I am," then I put their name. They proudly wore them to the movie. This was a sign of protest about being removed. The first five that we adopted clung even tighter to us after they returned home. The last four we adopted had changed. They seemed to distrust us now. We had lost authority over them.

CHAPTER 17

FAMILY TRAGEDY

They sent Jim and me to parenting groups separately. We weren't allowed to go together. The kids also went to a group after school with kids who'd been in a lot of trouble. Tina and her sisters were trying to act like tough inner-city kids now. The first family of five we had adopted were terrified that the other four would lie and get them taken away again.

The psychological report stated the only recommendation he had was that we may want to un-adopt the last four, because they were dead set on destroying our family. Everyone lumped Miranda, the youngest in this. She was acting out, but she was just copying her three older biological sisters. Our family was now divided in conversations as," the first five" and "the last four." There was now two opposing teams at our house. The last four now terrorized and threatened our family.

The psychologists said even though our adopted kids had various extensive mental, emotional and behavioral problems, we were well equipped to handle all of them. While waiting for the results of the first report, I went to another mental health agency. They said the same thing, and rated us "zero" in needs, meaning we didn't need any services provided to our family.

We still didn't know about the biological mother orchestrating Tina's actions until the mother's brother called me one day. He told me what his sister was doing. He said he put his foot down when he overheard his sister and Tina bragging about who had sex with more men. He said he knew the kids were better off with us than with his sister, and he loved his sister. Tina had plenty of opportunity to be sexually active in Michigan's foster care system than she ever had while at home. I ran a pretty tight ship at my house.

The guardian ad litem said he couldn't recommend that we be allowed to go back home to Ohio, because he feared he would be on *60 Minutes* someday, having to explain why he allowed that.

This was some bad dream—it was completely insane. It made no sense. It wasn't possible. Nobody would ever believe this all happened. I knew people would assume I was lying if I told our story. People think social workers are angels or something.

The new workers all came to see we had not done anything wrong. Yet they still wouldn't allow our family to return home to Ohio after the kids were returned to us. I told them this was like being sent to prison and being told, "Yeah, we know you didn't do it, but since you're here, attend theses classes we know you don't need." They would just look at me, confused. I felt like I was living in a world where everyone had lost their brain but Jim and me.

The group meetings we were forced to attend were full of drug addicts that praised the agency for keeping their kids in care. I kept telling our story. My group leader finally told me one day that he checked into my story, and I was right, I shouldn't be there. He said I should be teaching the class. He said we were done wrong. Jim and I didn't have to go to groups anymore. I was so glad that one person in that agency had a brain.

I reported the agency to the ombudsman for not investigating our kids' allegations of abuse at the foster homes. Investigations were then conducted. We were never told the dispositions. The ombudsman's office said the Family Independence Agency violated rules by placing our kids in unlicensed foster homes and not investigating allegations of child abuse in foster homes. They were given a warning that their doors would be closed if they didn't send a letter listing what steps would be made so this wouldn't happen again.

I never liked to appear weak or ask for help, but I was begging for it now. The kids' Ohio adoption workers both said even if we had done what they accused us of, it wasn't reason to remove. We had never harmed a child and just wanted to go to our home in Ohio and try to recover from this. The last four just kept getting worse.

I recalled substantiating abuse by a teacher who paddled and left horrible bruises. He still taught. He went from a junior high to an elementary school. I was shocked at the time. He hated me because I dared to find fault with a teacher. I was targeted for being against abuse, by being made to look like an abuser, and it destroyed my family. I knew my former county was still behind this, working against us behind the scenes.

The adoption worker who gave us the last four had told us once to whip them—they were the most-unruly kids they'd ever had in care. We wouldn't hear of it. Now here we were living this hell on earth because we weren't like most people, we cared about kids, not just our kids, but everyone's kids.

Meanwhile, back home, my mom had conned an old man that she met at the Eagles Club. When he died, she got close to half a million dollars. She threw herself a big party at a restaurant. I asked God why. Here I was busting my butt trying to save the world. I fostered sixty kids, was an excellent child abuse investigator for seven years, adopted nine kids, and left all the comforts of home to go to law school, trying to change the child welfare system, and this is what I get in return? That is what my mom gets in return for what she had done?

Tonya and Jack hadn't spoken to mom since their kids were little, but they went to that party—probably to see what they could get. Sam and Kyle were the only ones who got anything. I felt she should be in jail for what she did to that man. She forced him to put CDs in her name when he was very ill. I told her I didn't want one cent of that dirty money. She had sided with Todd against me in the child support hearing that had nothing to do with her. She had disowned me because she said I owed her twenty dollars for pizza she had ordered while watching my kids for one night. Yet there she was, and here I was. This was my reward, and that was hers. We drained all of our accounts to pay for our attorney. Life was flat out not fair.

Finally, in Michigan Juvenile Court one day, I spoke up. I'd had enough. I told my lawyer I wanted to take the stand. He always advised us not to. I told them I lied when I signed the papers agreeing to anything the workers said, because she said if I did, our kids would go home *that* day. I had wanted my kids home by Christmas. I said none of what the workers said was true. I said I would rather they take me out and give me a public whipping than see what our kids were going through in foster care. The prosecutor never took his eyes off me. He then recommended we be allowed to take our kids and go home to Ohio. He said, "All this mother has asked for is to be allowed to go home."

The judge ordered that we be allowed to go home.

Our lawyer had to file contempt of court on the workers for not obeying orders, for not returning the kids to us, and now for still not allowing us to go home. Our former county refused to do supportive services when we got home, so therefore we couldn't go. Finally, our juvenile judge in Ohio had his probation officer do a home visit to our house in Ohio to verify it was suitable for us to return to. The Ohio Court agreed to do Children Services' job and provide the supportive service they refused to do. I didn't understand how our county human services director was getting by with refusing to offer a family in its county children services. This was proof of the harassment I received by him when I worked there. But I knew it never did any good to complain.

Meanwhile, the last four girls terrorized me while Jim was at work. I was now afraid of my children. They jumped on the bed at night and laughed, saying they were going to school the next day and say we starved them. They cussed and threatened the other kids. I kept the five who were adopted first in a bedroom with me with the door shut. They would cry and say they didn't want to go back to foster care, they didn't want to leave us. I couldn't promise that wouldn't happen. I wasn't allowed to discipline the kids in any way.

No one would believe any of this happened. I wouldn't. The kids often asked me why the workers only believed one lying kid and not the other eight. I had no answers.

One night I videotaped the kids' threats and jumping on the bed, then showed it to the workers who visited our home. They acted like I was terrible for recording it. They refused to watch it. They said to call 911 if I had a problem with the kids that I couldn't handle. They didn't care about the five kids that were being harmed by all this, they only focused on trying to get one of the mean girls to lie about us so they could remove again. They were mad that my lawyer filed contempt of court on them. I asked, what did they think I was going to do, sit back and take it?

One day Tina pulled a knife on her youngest sister Miranda. She held it to her throat and said she would kill us all. I called 911. They asked to talk to Tina, then they said she was fine now. I asked them to take her for a psychological evaluation. She had behaved this way at her foster home too. They refused. I told them that was what we would do in Ohio Children Services. They said, "We don't do that here."

The kids' teachers had told me that a lot of kids drop out of school because nobody is allowed to tell them what to do. Our lawyer told us the workers in this state were like Nazis. He said the judges are run by Children Services—if not, they don't get elected. He said there was no way to sue them, and all the lawyers in town were afraid of them. He said lawyers sit around and tell horror stories about what has been done to their clients.

I took this as a challenge I was sent to fix. I tried, but nobody would do anything. I couldn't have asked for a better education—or a more expensive one. Not just the financial costs, but the personal toll was the worst I had ever experienced in my life.

Finally, we were given a court date. We were allowed to go home as soon as we had a hearing. The judge in Michigan would transfer the case to Ohio, and then we could go home.

Jim moved our things home for us. He also had to show the probation officer our home. I had been a Therapeutic Foster Parent for years. Everyone could verify we had a nice home in the country, and there was no abuse or neglect indicated or substantiated. There was never a report until our exes got jealous because we were so happy. Now this report was unfounded as well, yet we still had to suffer.

Jim left for Ohio, and I withdrew the kids from school. It was the last day of the semester, so report cards were ready. The teacher knew we were all excited to go home. They acted like we were escaping their grip, like we beat them. We went to Applebee's for super that night to celebrate. Heather was acting up the way Maggy had that started this nightmare. I knew Tina was behind it, so I tolerated it. I was holding my breath until we got back to Ohio, and then we would get the kids in counseling. We had all been through hell. The kids were confused.

We got to our Michigan home and the kids' friends came to our porch to say goodbye. I told them to not leave the porch. Tina said her friends wanted to speak to me. I went out on the porch. The boys asked if Tina could go to the park. I said no. I started to walk back inside, but the boys pulled out knives on me. I told my kids to get inside and told all the other kids to go home. Tina ran down the street with the boys towards the park. I couldn't call the police—it would just make things worse. We were not living in the real world here. This was some distorted version of reality. It felt like we lived in a strange foreign country. This wasn't the United States I knew. People didn't have rights anymore.

Soon a mother of one of the boys called me. She said she had run Tina off because her son was on probation and Tina had gotten him in trouble in the past. She said, "Tina is nothing but trouble."

Then another mother called me saying Tina was at her house and was going to live with her. I told her Tina was not going to live with her. She was to get home right now. She asked why not. I hung up. Finally, the mother brought Tina to my porch. She yelled at me, saying, "Where is the love?" She grabbed Tina and left.

Finally, I called the police and they brought Tina home. They said if there were any more problems tonight, they would place her where she ran away to. I couldn't believe this town. I just wanted to go home in the morning after court. I felt like Dorothy in *The Wizard of Oz*. I wanted to click the heels of my ruby red slippers three times and say, "There is no place like home," and be back home. I wanted to wake up from this nightmare.

I told the kids to go to bed, as we had a big day tomorrow. We had court in the morning—the judge was signing the order for us to go home, since the judge in Ohio had agreed to do our services there. Dad was at home unpacking our things and couldn't wait for us to arrive. I had our van packed in the driveway, and all we had to do was go to sleep and this would be all over in the morning. I couldn't wait to see the "Ohio Welcomes You" sign as we drove away after court.

About one a.m. there was a knock at the door. It was two police officers and the case worker who had removed our kids and started all this. She had found out we had withdrawn the kids from school. She said we weren't allowed to leave the state. She claimed there was a report saying we didn't have food and we had a mouse in our basement. She said I had to let her in or all the kids would be removed, because they still had jurisdiction.

I opened the door. The police used their flashlights, like they were performing a raid. I turned on the lights, but they told me not to. The kids were all camped out on the living room floor because their dad had taken their beds home to Ohio that morning. The kids started to wake up and were scared to see police shining a flashlight in their faces and moving around our house.

I turned on the lights. This was ludicrous. They were not scaring my kids anymore. They had been through enough of this bullshit. I made them hot chocolate and pretended I wasn't afraid so they wouldn't be.

Luckily, I had left all the food in the house for Jim. He had to return to Michigan after we were settled in Ohio to work in Detroit and pay off our lease. The police took pictures of the food in our pantry and in our refrigerator.

They checked our basement and saw there were no mice. I showed the receipt where the kids all ate at Applebee's that night as well. The police said they had never seen a house so clean when someone was moving out. They said usually they leave it a mess.

I said I wouldn't know—we owned our home in Ohio; we had never rented before.

Even though everything checked out fine, the worker still said, "If anyone wants to leave, they can."

Tina said she was going.

I asked her please not to leave. If she ever cared for us, please don't do this.

She walked out behind the worker, and Heather, her second to youngest sister, followed her. Maggy said she had already told Tina, "I learned my lesson," and she would never do that again.

I was up worrying all night. The next morning, I was on the phone with Jim and our lawyer. Miranda, Tina's youngest little sister was pinching everyone. I put her in the corner, so she started pinching herself! That was all I needed—a child with bruises on her face before court! I knew Miranda was just trying to be a pain in the butt because her sisters were. I assumed she was trying to get me mad so she could be with her sisters.

Recently I had put Heather in the corner, and she threw cans of food at me from the pantry. She kept running outside. Their biological mom had run off a year before I got them, and they were raised by alcoholic relatives who let them run the streets, smoke pot, drink, and watch porn, instead of cartoons. They had been so good and loving before we moved.

I kept thinking, *if I hadn't wanted to go to law school, this never would've happened.* They were happy and settled in Ohio. We went to court and Tina and Heather were in a room with the worker. When they saw Miranda, Tina yelled, "Oh, Baby, what did they do to you?"

The worker told the judge that apparently I had the older kids abuse the younger ones now because I couldn't do it myself! I couldn't help but recall my own childhood of real abuse, and the fact that I never had any help, and compare it to this overkill of concern.

I had remained strong in front of workers all through this. I never let see anyone see me cry, but that was all I did when they weren't looking. My face had been puffy for months. I barely recognized myself when I did look in the mirror—which I had avoided since that Friday night in our lawyer's elevator. I still hadn't found my identity. It was stolen from me the night the workers first knocked on our door.

Our two court workers and our case worker were there. The court workers were scheduled to be there, and were to recommend we be allowed to go home. This was supposed to be a simple procedure. All parties had agreed (after our lawyer filed contempt of court on the workers). The case worker who had been coming to our house regularly had become a friend, as the court workers had. She showed up, and said she just heard about the removal last night when she got to work this morning, and came to see what was going on. The three of them sat with the kids while I went to a conference room to talk to my lawyer before court.

I walked in, and he showed me what the worker who had removed the kids last night had filed. It was a petition to the court for permanent custody of all nine children. She claimed I called Tina a name as she ran down the street with those boys.

My lawyer said, "Someone in Ohio hates you and keeps calling the judge. So the judge hates you." My conspiracy theory was confirmed.

I walked out of the conference room and into the hall. The three workers looked at me. I asked, "Do you know what she did?"

I thought they were all behind it and had been stabbing me in the back all along.

They looked serious, and said, "No, what?"

"She filed for permanency of all nine!" My lawyer was mad at me. He believed the lies against me. He felt I ruined his case. I felt myself start to collapse to the floor. I felt my soul disappearing into thin air from the pressure on me.

CHAPTER 18

LIFE GOES ON

I fell apart. My knees went weak and tears erupted.

The three of them jumped up and helped me sit. If they hadn't, I likely would have fallen on the floor in front of my kids. I felt like a rag doll.

They assured me they'd had no idea. "Well, guess what? There is three of us and one of her!" one of them said. They marched off like soldiers heading into battle for a cause they firmly believed in.

I'd never had anyone stick up for me before. I had never fallen apart in public before. I was grateful for their mercy, despite the agony and hell I was going through.

I had felt myself starting to separate. I wondered if I would resort to suicide if they took my kids. I couldn't bear this. They went in and talked to the judge, and then I was called into the courtroom.

I feared it wouldn't do any good. I saw my little boy run into the men's room and hide so nobody could take him again. The world was moving without me able to do anything about it. I wasn't able to help my kids. I didn't have my husband there. I knew I couldn't drive back to Ohio without my kids, not if they told me I'd never see them again. I also couldn't stay in that house alone after losing them for good. Seven of my kids were hugging me and crying.

I had let my kids down. I'd lost my will. What would become of them? Would they lose their will?

"Ha! Ha! You're all getting adopted out to separate foster homes," Tina yelled. "Say goodbye to Mom and Dad!"

The kids looked at me to do something. I couldn't. I was defeated. I went into the courtroom, feeling like a pin cushion without room for one more needle.

The judge sided with the three workers. We were sticking with the plan. All nine kids were to go home with me. I held my breath.

They took a break. My lawyer said a friend of his saw the worker who had removed the kids last night and who wrote up the removal petition in the ladies' room. She was stomping her feet, screaming, and slamming things because she'd lost.

That worker came back into the courtroom and said Brittney and Heather wanted her to drive them home to Ohio for fear the other kids would be mean to them. The judge said she didn't care, and asked the prosecutor if he cared. Nobody asked me. I was afraid to blink wrong. The prosecutor shrugged his shoulders and gathered his things to leave. He acted like "Why are you asking me? This case is over."

So, I took our seven remaining kids, went to the van, and drove out of Lansing. When we saw the "Ohio Welcomes You" sign they all cheered. I laughed, cried tears of relief and started to breathe.

Once we were home and settling in, Jim told me I had to come see something. I walked through our living room. Our little boy Zach was lying on the carpet, smiling. He had written "OHIO" with popsicle sticks on the floor and lay down beside it, smiling. The girls gathered in to see what was going on. Everyone laughed and hugged and said, "I love you," and "I love you too." We were finally a family again.

We took his picture. It signified to us all that we were finally home, we'd made it, and we were going to heal.

The worker didn't show up with Tina and Heather. Nobody could be reached on a weekend. Monday morning, I called her and asked where my kids were. She said she'd tried putting them in a foster home in another county. She then said she couldn't bring them because she couldn't cross state lines. She'd have to go through Interstate Compact, and that would take months of red tape. Interstate Compact is a bunch of paperwork that needs filed to transport a foster child from one state to another state.

Again, I made calls, but no one helped.

Meanwhile, I got a letter there was an investigation into allegations of abuse that were substantiated. We were not even there! They just made up stuff. I called the worker.

She said she had to write something down to justify why they still had the two girls.

I said, "So you just lie and make up that there was a report of something, anything?"

She said yes.

"Why not sexual abuse? If you're just going to make up stuff, why not come up with something new?"

She said she didn't know what my problem was. She had helped my family.

She couldn't comprehend that it was wrong for her to fill out a report with a fake reporter, fake allegations, a fake investigation, and a fake conclusion—a conclusion that would ruin my career for life. She'd done it to justify Michigan keeping two kids who were given back to their parents.

Her supervisor would never return my calls.

Later, they called me and told me to come get Heather. She had gotten kicked out of day care, school, and foster homes. Nobody could handle her.

Suddenly, there was no need for Interstate Compact or red tape. We left right then and drove seven hours to get her. I was given the hardest kids for a reason. I was the only one who could handle them. They were brats, but they were my brats, and they belonged at home.

Nicole began acting out like Tina. Our insurance maxed out after half a million, so we could no longer afford her mental health care. It would all be out-of-pocket. Her doctors all recommended "Locked Long Term Residential" treatment. Our school district refused to allow her to attend, even though she had never acted out there. They had a class for kids with mental health issues, but said she was too bad for it. They were all mad at me now because it was the "in" thing, so they wouldn't help our daughter. They were friends with people at Children Services and Todd's family—and the director provided funding to them for programs. I was the witch in a backwoods witch hunt.

I obtained a Legal Rights Services Attorney for Nicole to guarantee her the least restrictive environment. I scheduled a cluster meeting to find funding for her treatment. Our own county removed her from my home because I didn't return one phone call immediately about Voluntary Respite Care. They filed for permanent custody of Nicole within a month of removal. My former coworkers were behind what happened in Michigan, and then used what Michigan did as an excuse to do this. They had a stack of documents—Michigan's lies—to back them up if needed. They didn't let the judge know these allegations were all recanted.

I had obtained a federally protected educational plan for Nicole, and they put her in Adult GED at age thirteen. I reported them to the Ohio Department of Education. The school then refused to allow my kids to ride the bus, because they claimed they all had lice. Lora had one nit after a break-out in her class, and I had her checked at the Health Department and presented a note saying she was clear.

The close "nit" community was the only danger to my family. My nightmare continued.

They also refused to provide adequate speech services for Lora. I had to transport her out of the county for speech services.

Maggy was molested on the bus after her Special Ed teacher showed *American Pie, The Naked Mile* to the class for Christmas. Then the Special Ed teacher called Maggy a slut for the way she dressed and said she deserved it. No one would do anything. The school superintendent refused to enforce his policy of reporting to Children Services when it was one of his teachers at fault.

I complained to the Ohio Department of Education and got an anti-bully policy adopted. I complained that our County Children Services didn't have a complaint procedure in place, and got a complaint form adopted.

All we accomplished was fighting Children Services and the school.

After Tina heard Nicole was gone, she decided to come home.

Her case worker said she wasn't worried about Tina—she was worried about us. She knew Tina would make false reports as soon as she got home and put the other kids at risk.

I brought her back for Miranda, Tina's youngest sister. I know how badly I had missed Tonya. I wanted to spare Miranda that.

Tina claimed she was raped at a school dance in the locker room. Maggy saw the guy drag Tina in, so Maggy beat on the door, but the boy had locked it. Just like in Michigan, our county wouldn't investigate it unless it was against me and my husband, so we called the newspaper. The investigator at the prosecutor's office shamed us for that, and said girls just needed to forget it when raped. Everyone now knew they could abuse us and get by with it.

Within a few months, Tina's drug dealer boyfriend was asking her to steal from us so he could buy and sell drugs at the junior high. Tina showed me the letter he wrote to her asking her to do this. She knew I had been trying to get him help. We even took him for an emergency psychological evaluation one night on the Fourth of July when he was suicidal.

But later when she wanted to date him again and we refused to allow her to do so, she tried to get one of the other girls to run away with her again. This time her sisters told on her and said they all had learned their lesson. Tina was on her own.

Tina complained about us at school, saying she "didn't know where her home was." They called Children Services, who were happy to remove her because she "might run away." Jim came home from the school with a small piece of notebook paper saying she was removed by my former co-worker. They had permanent custody of her in just a few months. They broke every law and rule just to hurt my family—out of revenge because they hadn't liked me when I worked with them. It was one year after they took Nicole.

Children Services is required to show proof that they worked to reunite kids for eleven months. They never tried. This was a "get the bitch" game. Pure and simple.

When we returned home, I worked as correctional counselor in a maximum security prison for a year. The school used to call me there, harassing me to let Tina date her abusive boyfriend who was threatening to kill us in letters. I quit my job to home-school the kids because they were afraid if they went to school, they would be removed from home.

I brought them from below grade level to above in a few months. I put them back in school, and I started working as a child protection case worker for West Virginia. I was honest with them about what happened to our family, and let them know I would never remove any children. A former guidance counselor from my hometown now worked there, and told them what a good children services worker I was when I handled his school's reports. He made me sound like a superhero. In one case I recall, he had called me because a teenage boy returned to school with a note from his doctor. He had been diagnosed with an ear infection. The boy was unsteady on his feet, so the guidance counselor called the doctor, who assured him he was fine, yet the counselor wasn't convinced.

He said there was nothing to make a report, he was just concerned. I told him I would stop in and check on him. I was also very concerned after observing him walk. I called the doctor, who blew me off as well. I went back to the office and discussed it with the staff, who all said, "You did all you can do. You can't do anything." I said I could call the parents and let them make that call. They all said not to, the doctor said he was fine. I went to my desk and thought about it for a minute, and then called the parents. I said we don't have a complaint or anything, and we checked with his doctor, he says he's okay, but he doesn't seem okay.

The parents thanked me and said they felt the same way I did, that something was wrong. They said they were headed to the school now. Later that afternoon my supervisor got a call from the parents praising our department. They said we saved their son's life. Due to the worker who called, they took their son to the emergency department, and he had a brain aneurysm. If they hadn't taken him when they had, he wouldn't be alive. They caught it just in time. This is why I went back to working for child protection—I knew I had a gift. Yet six months later, in my wonderful supervisor's absence, I was ordered to remove children, and I knew they did not need removed. I had been working with the mother, and she did everything I asked her to do. I quit.

Later on, I worked as a social worker in a mental hospital. One day, my boss told me I had a call from a case worker.

It was Nicole's adoption worker from her former county. Our county had dumped Nicole off at the home where she'd been removed from before coming to us. Nicole ended up attempting suicide and was in the hospital. Our county never got her the help she needed.

Furthermore, our county lied and told that county's Children Services that *we* still had custody! That we had done this to Nicole! I guess they had gotten by with so much already, why not? That county said we were being prosecuted for non-support to Nicole. I told them our county removed her and had taken permanent custody a long time ago. She said they denied that—even the juvenile court denied it.

I told her I had a copy of the order. She asked me to fax it. If I hadn't saved that piece of paper, my county would have succeeded in having us blamed for the neglect they had done.

I could never get anyone to investigate the deputies trying to have me killed or the workers who abused or neglected clients when I worked there. I had contacted everyone I could think of, and here I was, with all of this that they continued to do, and still, there was no lawyer who would touch the case and no place to report them to.

If God had given me the job to correct this system, he had given it to the weakest link. I was barely hanging on.

Heather asked to spend the night with a friend, so I let the mother know she was not to be around any boys or drinking. The mother promised me. The next day when Heather came home, she was sulking, and I overheard her conversation on the phone. She had gotten drunk and boys took advantage of her while she was away from me for one night. The sheriff's department blamed her. They sided with that low-life family who watched our daughter being assaulted.

One day the assistant principal called and told me to come in. He said they had a very serious situation. I thought the worst—a school shooting. He then said one of my kids had been caught with a piece of candy on the bus.

In the background, I could hear crying. "Is that my kids I hear crying?"

"Yes," he said. "It's a serious matter."

"Over a piece of candy?" I told him I would be right there. A teacher had given one piece of candy to one of my kids for good behavior, and I was furious that all my kids were in tears over being interrogated over a piece of candy that was eaten on the bus.

The bus driver was there and said we had so many kids that he couldn't keep them all straight. He asked me what I intended to do about that.

I told my kids they were coming home—they were too upset to be at school right then. As we were leaving, I overheard the assistant principal make fun of me. I told the kids to go on and get in the van.

I went back in and let him know I had heard him, and he needed to behave in a professional manner when dealing with people.

It was one thing after another. When the school reported Tina didn't know where her home was, the school principal and the guidance counselor were at the custody hearing. The judge said it must be serious—no one from the school had ever come to a hearing before. I asked the school representatives if this case was the most serious thing they had ever reported.

They said, "No," and looked confused.

"Why are you here, then?" I asked.

They couldn't answer.

"Did you feel she was abused?"

Again, they appeared confused and said, "No." They pretended they didn't know what I was talking about.

I knew they had come to show support of Children Services removing our daughter for a report they had made. Tina told someone she didn't know where her home was, she was fourteen years old—it was pathetic. This circus needed to stop. This was a game of cat and mouse.

This began the first of several times I had to contact the school district, who agreed with me every time—the school had no right to interfere. The district superintendent said I was a good mother trying to protect her children and his staff would be disciplined.

We had five quiet years until Lora was a teenager and decided to pull what her oldest sisters had. I found out she and a boy were having sex, so I told her she couldn't see that boy. So, she accused her dad of sexual abuse. Later she said because I had made them break up, she wanted us to break up. She admitted she lied.

Then she kept running away, saying I hit her. Then she would admit that I never touched her. Zach tried to stop her from going one day, and she yelled rape.

He apologized for not catching her. I wasn't home. I was at the sheriff's office, taking her off the missing list. Yet, I was supposedly home hitting her at the same time.

I told Zach he did the right thing. Nobody was to lay a finger on her. She wanted an excuse to get someone in trouble. She wanted a home with no rules, and she would do whatever required to get it. She knew, as everyone did, how bad the department and the school hated me, and that they would do anything to get revenge on me. Nicole had told me they'd had a party at the office when they took custody of her from me. Her new county wanted to give me back custody of her. We tried visits at home with Nicole, but it was clear she needed to stay in the mental hospital.

I went from loving kids and bending over backwards doing flips to help them, to fearing them more than I ever feared men. A former case worker started her own foster care agency. She hired me to do case management for a group of teen foster kids. As soon as I was alone in the room with them, I ran out the door. I told her I was sorry. I was afraid they would lie about me.

She understood, she knew my situation well. Everyone did. Everyone knew my county was out to get me. It was not paranoia. Every job I looked into, I knew Child Welfare lies would follow me. I became disabled with PTSD and anxiety, and I still struggled to find my identity.

One day I got a call. My mother was at my county Children Services with Lora. My enemies wanted me to come and talk to them. I had an anxiety attack right then. I couldn't do this again. I couldn't add my mother to the list of enemies using CPS to hurt me. They said they didn't have a report of abuse or anything, and didn't want custody of Lora. They just wanted me to go there and talk to them. It was a set-up. They would lie and have me arrested for who-knows-what. They would have a field day with this. They used our exes, our kids, the school, and now my mom against us. I could smell danger a mile away now.

I asked if they could come to my house to talk. My mom could bring Lora home. I said workers could come, even bring deputies if they wanted, but I couldn't drive right then due to the anxiety this was causing. The worker said he would ask the supervisor. I knew who that was, the supportive worker's husband. My old supervisor had retired due to liver issues.

Five minutes later, they called back and said, "We just removed her from your custody because you won't come in."

I said, "I have a disability and requested accommodation, and you removed my child because of that request." I immediately filed a complaint with them and with Ohio Civil Rights.

Ohio Civil Rights had the case bumped up to the United States Health and Human Services—who had it open for investigation for five years, and then closed it when I complained nothing was done.

They said a worker said it was West Virginia that removed, not Ohio, which wasn't true. They also said there was a rule that children services didn't have to go by the rules. They adopted her out to a family that she ran away from all the time, but they just sent her back. The family kicked her out when she was eighteen. They removed her from us because she "might run away" and I wouldn't come in when there wasn't even a report.

The day we had court over this stupidity with Lora, my mom sat in court laughing at me. She yawned and giggled when I cried and poured my heart out to the judge. I let him know this was corruption and revenge. The judge said nothing had ever come across his desk about us abusing anyone, but said he had to do what Children Services said.

As I drove away, I passed my mom getting in her car. It took everything I had not to ram my car into her. Three times in my life I felt homicidal for a split second. One was when I came to after Jack knocked me out. Two was when Todd had me pinned against the wall in my kitchen. And three was now. All three times I had been treated less than human and felt there was no way out. All three times I was hated by someone who could never get enough revenge on me. I thank God for my strong will.

Nicole went through a foster home a month for twelve months before they put her back in the county she had come from. Then she was finally institutionalized. Tina was adopted, but her new parents divorced and they gave her to a relative, who gave her to her biological mother. They didn't get along, so she moved in with a boyfriend.

We got the remaining six raised, but most went back to their biological parents as soon as they turned eighteen. If we would've had support instead of stabs in the back from our government, maybe things could've turned out differently. Their growth was stunted for a while like mine was from the tragedy of removals. I don't blame the kids as much as I do our county, Michigan, and anyone else who had a hand in the travesty.

I researched Michigan Family Independence Agency one day. I was shocked to learn that the worker gets a bonus check for each child she removes. The agency gets a fat check when the worker gets permanent custody. A Child Advocacy Group from New York was suing the state of Michigan for its neglect of children in foster care. One county in Michigan had removed fifty percent of the children.

Complaints against the state said kids were removed because a parent was single or because the kids were latchkey, or because of any other minor situation a worker deemed as unfit. To me, it was clear we were not the only victims of this state-wide child trafficking. Yet, I never saw it on the news or any talk show.

What our county in Ohio did to us once we finally got home was nothing but pure abuse of authority in order to seek revenge on me personally. They used our kids as weapons against me. Our kids knew it, and used the county power to get back at us as well, whenever they didn't like a rule.

CHAPTER 19

SHELL SHOCK

Jim and I got pregnant several times naturally, but I miscarried at six to seven weeks each time. The specialist said he believed the fetuses all dissolved naturally in my tube. When I was 43, we tried IVF. I had twenty eggs, and nineteen fertilized. They put five in my uterus and told me to stay in bed and avoid stress.

Cameron came home from the Army for a visit, and when it was time for him to return, I couldn't see him off at the airport due to bedrest. As I hugged him goodbye in our driveway as his dad came to pick him up, I lost it. I felt I would never see him again. I was sure he would die in the war.

Cameron assured me he would be fine, but I just knew I wouldn't be one of the lucky ones. I feared all I would get would be a triangular box with a flag in it, and not my son. That was not a trade I was willing to make for my country or for anything in this world. My husband felt like I was not being patriotic, but I told him to send his girls there, and then tell me about being patriotic. My hormones were out of control from all of the infertility drugs.

None of our embryos made it. I was failing fast emotionally. PTSD was starting to take over, and I'm sure hormones didn't help. I developed a cyst in my right ovary that grew rapidly. My GYN said it was from IVF. In addition, I was on a lot of steroids to help me breathe due to a lady bug allergy. I was putting on weight from them. I am the most allergic person on record to Asian lady beetles, which our government dumped to get rid of fruit bugs.

Every time I heard the song "Simple Man," I prayed for Cameron more than ever. My prayer was that he live long enough to know what it was like to marry and have a child. The song was about a mother encouraging her son to seek love and not gold. I wanted my kids to know that blissful love of being a parent more than anything else in this world.

Cameron didn't talk much about the war, but one day he told me this story: They were all riding in back of a truck, talking and joking around. The radio was on and there was a lot of noise. The song "Simple Man" came on, and everyone stopped talking so they could listen to it.

Suddenly, they were ambushed out of nowhere. Because it was quiet, they heard them approach. They were able to quickly respond with gunfire. When it was over, they looked around and couldn't believe it. Not one of them had been injured, but they had killed the enemy.

He said there had been many attacks like that before, and none of them ended in their favor. If they would've been attacked a moment sooner, before "Simple Man" came on, it would've been bad for them, because they would've been caught unprepared. The stillness they felt during the song gave them a chance to respond quickly. I believe mothers' prayers saved them. A preacher in the waiting room of the hospital where I had worked, told me this once. He said he had no doubt we were all saved more than we know, due to our mother's prayers.

Cameron was later injured and sent home. He married and had a baby. I was thrilled to be her babysitter while they worked. She was like the baby girl I never had. One morning, I knocked on his door to babysit, but nobody was home. His wife, a native of New York, had fired me as their free babysitter because I allowed the eleven-month old baby to have a chocolate "flavored" Popsicle once. She had lectured me the night before because I gave the baby "chocolate" before twelve months of age. Apparently, this was not recommended by doctors. Cameron's Aunt Lucy, who lived next door, was now the babysitter because I couldn't be trusted. I had laughed when his wife was upset with me over a Popsicle, and this was my punishment.

This was the straw that broke the camel's back. It was now confirmed—I must be a "child abuser." My own son now thought so. My own granddaughter was removed from my care. Nobody trusted me around children. I was tired of trying to hang on to my identity. I went completely numb. I had been taking Ambien at night to help me sleep. The doctors believe that attributed to my inability to reason on this morning. I dropped my kids off at Catholic school and waved goodbye, knowing I would never see them again.

I parked the van and called Jim, apologized, and said my goodbyes to him. I called Joann, Cole's beautiful, kind, intelligent wife. I asked her if she remembered that we had appointed her and Cole to keep our kids if anything happened to me. She immediately became angry and demanded to know what was going on. I told her where my will was and said goodbye.

I drove to where Joann was working and left my van unlocked in the parking lot with the keys in it. I wanted her to have it to pick up the kids after school. She would make a better mother than me. She and Cole were young and kind. I was used up and completely broken.

Originally, I had planned to go to our County Human Services, where I had worked, after I dropped the kids off at school that morning. I had an appointment with the Ohio Bureau of Vocational Rehabilitation (BVR) to help me find work. I had recently been found disabled with PTSD by social security. This was the first step to admitting I was crazy like everyone always said I was. But the worst part was, the BVR. waiting room was shared with Children Services. I was about to be totally humiliated by everyone I once worked with, the people who had taken my kids from me, by being seen there. But now it looked like they were all right. I must be a child abuser because my own son didn't trust me to take care of my grandbaby and I was now disabled with PTSD and anxiety, so they were right—I was crazy. I gave up. Everyone would be better off without me.

I couldn't take one step further in this life. It was just too hard now. I knew it was the end of the road for me. I loved my grandbaby and my son so much. Losing them was more than I could bear.

I got out of the van and walked across the bridge to Belpre. I went in Rite Aid and got all of my prescriptions refilled. I was on stuff for anxiety. I had been trying to get into counseling for depression the last few weeks, but they kept calling and changing the appointment.

I walked out with my prescriptions. I wondered if I should confess my intentions to the pharmacy. But I didn't know how to ask for help for myself. So, I told myself this was for me. I told myself I deserved this peace, and God would understand. I had the right to do what I had to do.

God was waiting for me, and soon I would hold the babies I'd lost. All of them. Nobody would take them away from me. God would forgive me. He had seen what I'd gone through my whole life.

These thoughts kept me walking. I found myself walking down the train tracks to our old house on Constitution Hill. I had bought that old shack a few years earlier. It had been our childhood home near the pond where I had drowned. I had gutted it. I tore out everything inside—walls, ceiling and floor. I didn't want anyone else living in our house again. The adopted kids and I had worked on it in our spare time. We were going to fix it up but we never had the extra money.

I finally arrived at the house. I sat outside and took pills with coffee. I scratched a fuzzy note on a receipt. I lay down to die. But just like in high school, I just woke up. I was refreshed, but embarrassed and ready to make amends to Jim and Joann. I hoped they didn't call the cops, and I hoped I could sneak back quickly before school was out. If I hadn't had problems before, I had them now. I tried to think up lame excuses. My thoughts were clear—it was like I had just needed a good nap.

Just as I sat up, Sam and his daughter pulled in. They looked mean as hell. I had just confronted Sam about his sexual assaults in front of our mother a week or so prior. At first Sam had denied it, but then he admitted it. Once Sam admitted it, he walked outside to pout. Mom followed him and babied him. This too, had been weighing heavily on my mind lately. I was tired of a world that rarely offered compassion to me. I saw other people get it, I always gave it, but it was just not in the cards for me it seemed. Now, here I was during a suicide attempt, getting a lecture on how badly I treat my mother by my niece, and my brother kept his back to me. My niece snarled at me that I was terrible worrying my mother like this. She said the police went to my mom's and asked if she knew where I was. They didn't know my mother like I did, she never worried about anyone but herself.

The next time I went to mom's house, after she babied Sam and not me, for his sexual abuse to me, she showed me a picture of Sam and me slow dancing at a party where everyone was slow dancing with family at Christmas. I only danced with him because Todd was complaining at the time that I needed to learn to get along with my family. Mom was now claiming this was proof that I was always hanging on Sam, and that was why he sexually abused me. The only people I ever hanged on was my husbands.

Now Sam was getting his revenge on me like everyone else. Everyone was winning by my suicide attempt. Sam was the hero because he found me.

As Sam walked up the steps to the top of the hill where I was sitting, he was already on the phone with someone, reporting me. I got up and walked down the steps to the road. I wanted nowhere near Sam. I also had to walk back to get my van, and let the police know I was okay, and do some serious apologizing to Jim and Joann, and my kids. Hopefully I could fix this before they found out I was "missing."

"Get back here!" Sam demanded.

I didn't have to listen to him. He chased me, so I ran from him. There were people fishing at Catfish Paradise, where I had drowned when I was little. I hoped someone would stop this man from chasing me. Nobody did anything.

As I got to the highway to turn right towards town, Sam caught me. He yanked me backwards really hard. The next thing I remembered was waking up in a gazebo. I was sitting up, had wet myself, and an emergency squad was there. A really good-looking EMT was talking to me. He looked like an angel—like Michael Landen.

I was confused as to why I was okay earlier, but now I felt drugged.

The EMT asked if they could take me to the hospital. I said I didn't want to go to Memorial. He said okay. I asked if he would keep Sam away from me.

Sam and his daughter stood next to the squad glaring at me. He looked back at them and agreed. I went in the ambulance, and they took me to a hospital in Parkersburg WV. I now was hallucinating. I was drugged, and I assumed it was from what I had taken earlier.

My kids were all there, and Jim came from work in Philadelphia. I couldn't understand how Jim got there so fast. He made a seven-hour trip in five-and-a-half hours. I felt horribly guilty for causing everyone to worry. I was so embarrassed. I wanted to die because I worried that I was a bad mother—but I hadn't been a bad mother until now.

A nurse handed me charcoal to drink. I gulped it down and said, "I deserve it."

The nurse's eyes looked at me in disbelief. I had worked in an emergency room before, and I knew nobody drank charcoal like that.

Protocol was to have me admitted to the psych ward, but they made an exception in my case because I had an appointment for counseling that I had made myself, and because Jim was now home and very supportive. I was in no danger of attempting this again because of my remorse. They also believed my mental state was due to Ambien. So they made an exception for me.

I sat in a hot bubble bath for hours and talked to Jim. He listened intently. I felt the effects of the medication for several days. I kept stressing that I was shown there was nothing to be afraid of, nobody should ever fear anything, not even death. God has our back, and we should never fear anyone or ever be afraid. This was a message I felt I had learned—to not fear life nor death. I am not sure when or how I learned it, but it was there playing in my mind for days like a melody. I felt I was being cradled by a warm loving spirit.

But that peacefulness was soon gone.

Jim had to go back to work eventually. Just like being raped when I was sixteen, and the removal of my kids from my home, I couldn't talk about this with anyone. I was too ashamed. But at least I had done something to deserve the shame this time.

As the meds wore off, so did the bliss. My neck and back hurt quite a bit. When I complained, I didn't know why I was hurting all over.

Our youngest child Zach said, "That's because your brother Sam had to beat you up." I sat up and looked at Zach in disbelief.

I called Jim and asked about being beat up. He said Sam had to knock me out to keep me from killing myself. I had tried to run into the highway.

I was livid that Sam took the opportunity to beat the hell out of me and be seen as a hero in the process! I wondered if Sam forced the rest of my medication into my mouth after he knocked me out. I know I was fine before he knocked me out. I went from running from Sam, fully aware, to sitting in a gazebo, wet pants and hallucinating in back of a squad. I saw Cole and his wife standing at the opposite side of the squad, but I learned later they were never there. They went to the hospital when I was found. Then I remembered the hospital saying I hadn't taken very much medicine when my labs came back. I was confused. How much did Sam hit me in the head? What had he done to me?

I went to the hospital and got a copy of my report, and then I went to the police station. They made me wait so long to see them, I lost my nerve to discuss it. I had wanted to see if it could be investigated and if any witnesses had come forward—and report his trespassing and abuse. I had fought so long and always lost, I was tired and gave up. The truth never wins. Sam's daughter would protect him. I was sure Sam bragged to mom about what he did. But she always loved it when I got knocked out cold. She would never help me.

I talked to my shrink about it, and he said Sam raped me. I said he did not—his grown daughter was there. He said it didn't matter, my whole family was sick and I needed to stay away from them. He said I shouldn't have put myself in that situation. Otherwise, it would never have happened. Justice and compassion are lies. They do not exist, I thought.

Every time I went to my doctor's office for my prescriptions, my doctor made me repeat after him that I would be on medication for MS symptoms the rest of my life. I didn't have any psychological issue, I just had physical symptoms from stress, similar to MS symptoms. The medication was increased to a high amount, until I no longer had pins and needles sensations. It also was supposed to help with generalized anxiety. There is no cure for PTSD.

My counselor would fall asleep as soon as I started talking. She said I was "monstrous" when I first started coming. My husband was with me then, and I was feeling great because I was still medicated, or so I thought at the time. Later, I remembered the hospital said my labs showed only a small amount of medication in my system when the squad brought me in. I am not sure what caused my bliss state for a week.

I had no faith in my doctors. I found faith in myself then. I think the counselor must have had a nightmare. Jim's daughter had her as a teacher in college, and said she fell asleep while teaching too. I weened myself off the medications after a year.

I haven't been on any meds since 2009. I had no mental disorder, stress doesn't cause psychological symptoms in me—it causes physical symptoms like I have MS. My will is apparently too strong to allow me to go crazy.

I know I will never play God and try to take my own life again. I had lived in fear like the Jews in the Holocaust. I knew at any moment my government could come take my children away from me forever for no reason at all. They could try to kill me again. They could try to forge documents and lie and try to have me prosecuted again. There was nothing I could do to protect myself or my children. I had no control over my life. I believe the labels had caused an identity issue. In counseling, I ran through my abuses like a grocery list. I didn't feel any of it. I had memory of them, they were always there, but I avoided it.

Before my "incident," our Priest had asked me to be a teacher at the kids' school. I completed the training, but I knew when they did a background check, it would be full of damning lies and they too would see me as a monster. Children Services can write down anything they want, and mark the substantiated box on a whim. They don't know how those records will affect one's employment, nor can anyone dispute them.

Everyone knew about my "incident." I had lost what little credibility I had left, because I broke.

I know no one believes me, but I am telling my story anyway. I have learned the importance of believing in yourself.

I started having myself tested by psychiatrists when I was thinking about marrying Jim and wanting to adopt children. I wanted to be sure I was all right. Everything that was happening at work at Children Services at that time had me confused. The shrink told me at that time to not quit my job—the system needed more fair case workers like me. He said he dealt with clients and families damaged by the system all the time. He said I could make a real difference. All those hopes are gone now. I can't help anyone. We don't have a system that allows it, as far as I can tell. If you make waves, they will destroy you one way or another. There is no lawyer, court or agency to help you.

When I went back to work as a child protection worker in West Virginia. They wanted to make me a supervisor. I was naïve in thinking I could help families without being told to break them apart.

When I quit the first Children Services in Ohio, my supervisor kept calling me, begging me to come back. When I left WV CPS, my former supervisor got out of the hospital and asked me to come have lunch with her. She wanted me to come back. I have never been fired or had a bad evaluation from any job. I felt I was kept from my mission by evil forces who always won. I finally accepted it, and got on with my life. I was tired of fighting the system.

I would cringe when I heard a worker laugh and say, "I'm going to take that bitch's kids!" The other workers would laugh. They did things for revenge—it wasn't about caring for the kids. The prison system was no better. Corruption is everywhere. If you can't tolerate it, you can't work. While at the Corrections Academy, I reported an incident. As a result, a paper with cut-out letters saying "Snitches get Stiches" was slipped under my door during the night.

They had to put a bodyguard on me. I objected to mistreatment of others everywhere, and I always was the only one that paid the price. The person that tells will always be a target in this system of sticking together. There is no checks and balances.

The Ohio Bureau of Vocational Rehabilitation (BVR) allowed me to see a BVR counselor outside my county, at my request. They concluded that I could not do any job that I did not believe in. The first time I heard the phrase "high moral compass" was when they described me.

That makes me sound like I have delusions of grandeur. I also know this entire book sounds made up and paranoid. Yet, I am telling the truth. Jim and I had wanted to adopt again, so we went through the training in different counties. We were honest about what was done to us, and hoped to find a resolution somehow. Even though our psychological, physical, home and finances were in perfect condition, the lies and the damning letters were sent to the agencies, preventing us from adopting again. We asked for copies of these letters and a chance to dispute. We were denied any rights to confront any of our accusers or even see the evidence against us.

We knew with 100% certainty we could disprove every allegation and action against us. But there was no recourse. I had withdrawn my retirement funds from my previous employers to help make ends meet. I thought if I applied for disability through my former work at Ohio Children Services, the director would simply deny it. He had denied my workman's comp, my educational reimbursement, and my adoption assistance out of hate for me. I had to fight to get the last two. He told my supervisor and his secretary he wasn't giving "that bitch" anything.

Social Security found me to be disabled (PTSD/Anxiety), but due to Jim's income, I couldn't receive any benefits. They said I shouldn't have withdrawn my county retirement. They are the ones who informed me the director had no control over it. So, my being intimidated by him cost me my disability benefits.

Jim and I celebrated our tenth wedding anniversary by getting married in the Catholic church. Jim became Catholic, as had our adopted kids after Cole got married there. I went back to the church because Cole asked me to.

Once while I was in church kneeling after communion, I saw before me Gods hands opened like a cup, and a tiny body of Jesus hovered above them, with blood dripping off his side onto God's cupped hands. I watched this as I continued to hear our priest tell people the bread and wine were the body and blood of Christ.

One night, someone contacted me with information about our county and why I was targeted. He said it was because I had a sex abuse case on the biggest drug dealer in the county. He said everyone knew the drug dealer sexually abused his kids, because he always laughed about it. He just didn't like me talking to them.

He also went into great length, and named names about payoff's and corruption in our county. This included attorneys and judges—and it included unsolved murders. It involved custody cases being bought, the cost to make charges go away, and setting people up while avoiding evidence on others. A lot of this I had heard rumors of, like everyone who lived there had. He explained the KKK and Masons were in charge. He said the Beueau of Criminal Investigation (BCI) was corrupt, and gave names and situations.

This was all talked about on Facebook messaging. I took notes from it, and asked him if I could forward this information to the FBI. He agreed as long as I left his name out. He said I was like a mother to him when he was growing up, and this was his way of repaying me.

I forwarded it to the FBI and to The United States Health and Human Services. I never heard a reply. As one last effort, I contacted our new governor and explained what happened to us. His reply was for us to get an attorney.

Years before I made complaints to the Ohio Department of Human Services. I wanted them to investigate my concerns with our county children services agency regarding involvement with our family. The regional investigator said, "The directors in these counties are like gods, and the county is their kingdom. They can do whatever they want."

CHAPTER 20

FINDING MY WILL

For Christmas one year, Jim and I surprised our seven adopted daughters by turning the basement living room into one big bedroom for them. We painted the walls and added boarder trim. We bought them canopy beds and lined them all up along the wall. I stood back and admired how cute it looked. I recalled being five years old and gazing into the nursery rhyme book at the story "The Old Woman Who Lived in a Shoe." This bedroom reminded me of that page as I gazed at it. The beds were all lined up neatly in a row along the wall. Then my mind went back in time to Todd always saying how our property was shaped like a boot. I chuckled to myself. Maybe fairy tales do come true after all.

Once all our kids were raised and moved out with their own kids to raise, I had more time to think about everything that had happened in my life. I was traveling with Jim for his work—he was a union pipefitter/welder. We frequently left our home and traveled in our camper for months at a time. I had plenty of time to think while he worked. I felt safer being out of our county.

We have a new sheriff now, one that my family and everyone in our county trusts, yet I know the backwoods Mafia still runs deep. I was called for jury duty, and the prosecutor made sure she humiliated me in front of everyone before dismissing me. She tried to prove I was mad at Children Services in Colorado—we had stayed there for a year for Jim's work. She failed. The sheriff at the time was called in because I wasn't admitting I had been mad. I think they wanted to arrest me for lying as a jury member. The cat and mouse game continues. I wondered if I was going to jail as the sheriff whispered something to the judge, as he kept his eye on me.

I knew I wasn't lying, therefore I knew they couldn't prove it. I believe there was a payment or favor for anyone who could successfully get me put in jail for any reason. The judge didn't go along with it. He just dismissed me and told me to not forget my check on the way out. I knew and trusted this judge. I had trusted he would not fall into their petty trap, and he hadn't. That sheriff was the one who tried to get me killed in that boxing ring that night. He still wanted revenge on me. He was friends with Todd's family. This was a game to them. One that they played with people every day. I just learned to stay home, or out of the county as much as I could. Still, after all those years, whenever I thought I heard a car pull up in the driveway, I panicked for a moment. I always feared it was the police coming to get me for something I hadn't done.

One day Cole overheard me telling the story about the day he almost drowned in our creek. This was the first time I'd ever talked about it. Cole said, "I remember that. I heard you praying." He said it happened as I had imagined it—he had panicked and tried to swim out instead of walking out. He heard me praying, telling him to calm down, put his feet down and walk out of there. I stood there with my mouth open in shock. His friend yelled, "That's a mother's love right there!"

I ran into Todd's cousin several years ago. We were talking about old family reunions, and I mentioned the little boy drowning in the ditch.

He sat back and stared at me. "That was you?"

He said they had always wondered who that was—that little boy was his little brother! He explained that his brother still swears that an angel saved him from drowning that day.

He couldn't wait to tell his mom that they now knew who the rescuer was. They thought his brother might have dreamed it or something.

I found it so odd that the one person I told the story to twenty-four years later just happened to be the boy's brother. It felt like I was meant to be given proof these things were real. But why?

In the last several years, there has been a few times that angels have appeared to me. It happens before a family member dies.

One day I was busy working in the backyard when two angels flew over and came right down to where I was. They were clear outlines of movement. They hovered over me and asked if I were still praying for Todd's dad.

I was confused and answered *no*. They sped off. Why would they ask me that? To be shown the power of prayer?

There is a raw honesty when angels come. I couldn't lie to them if I tried.

I was married to Jim now. I didn't see Todd's dad very often. I had visited Todd's parents a few times. When I was still married to Todd, I once forced his dad to go to the hospital because he was having heart attack symptoms. He refused to go, saying his father never went to the hospital until he died. I promised to not leave his side and I wouldn't leave the hospital until he did. He agreed to go.

Turned out he *was* having a heart attack and needed heart surgery. I had slept on the waiting room floor a few nights before Todd's dad told his wife to tell me to go home, he would be fine. I prayed for him a lot back then. I no longer did.

The night after those angels came to the field, I got a call that Todd's dad had another heart attack, and he died. I knew I wasn't crazy, but I only talked to Jim about it. I knew what Todd and his family would say about me. I still didn't understand it, though.

A few years later, I heard Todd's mom was in the hospital. She had fallen and broken her hip, and then had a massive heart attack in the nursing home. The last time I saw her, our adopted kids were volunteering at the nursing home. We stopped in her room to say "Hi." She always enjoyed seeing me and the kids.

Someone asked me what my last name was now. She answered for me with that sweet smile of hers and said, "You know what I still think of you as."

I knew she and Pappy loved me like a daughter. I wanted to go see her in the hospital now, but I didn't want to upset Todd or his family. Cole called and said she was doing better, to go see her.

Our youngest daughter Miranda and I went to Kroger's to pick up flowers and a card for her.

As I looked at the flowers, I couldn't decide. Then I felt something—someone was there telling me not to go yet. I got the flowers and card, went to a store across the street to get a vase, and then I sat in my car. Miranda didn't understand why I just sat there. I told her what I was hearing and I knew it was odd. Usually you are urged to go before it's too late, but I felt the urge to wait. It wasn't time for me to go there. It was too real to dismiss.

Then I was told to go. I started driving down the street and Cole called. "Grandma just died," he said.

I continued driving. I learned the whole family was at the hospital. I was afraid of this family. I always had been, but even more so now that Todd and I were divorced. The way Todd told it, I got the house and kids and refused to take him back. I was now remarried, had all these kids, and clearly had moved on.

Several of Todd's siblings had lied about me to the Catholic church when Todd wanted our marriage annulled. I did not want to go to the hospital with Todd and his family all there just after their mom had died. But something was telling me to go. It wouldn't take *no* for an answer. I felt it was Pappy, Todd's dad. I could never tell Todd's parents no. I never disrespected my mom, dad or grandparents, and I felt the same way about Todd's parents. I may have not had the best upbringing, but I was taught that.

As the elevator opened to her floor, I wanted to run the other direction. But now I knew for sure who was leading me—Pappy had a hold of me. All of Todd's siblings stood in the hallway with their backs against the wall. I could tell they had just been informed their mother had died and didn't know what to do. The first one I came to was Donald. I went up to him, gave him a hug, and told him how lucky he was to have had such a good Christian mother.

He agreed with that and hugged me back. I went on down the line, hugging them. They all burst into tears as we embraced. I knew Todd's dad was living inside me during the hugs to his children. I reached Todd, who stood in the middle of the hall watching me. He'd had several girlfriends since the one he almost married, and his new one stood looking at me. Todd reached out his arms and offered to hug me. After we hugged, he said all twelve kids had been with his mom singing hymns and saying prayers. She couldn't speak, but she mouthed every word. Then she passed quietly. We talked about what a beautiful death that was for her.

Todd said they were cleaning Mom up now, and when they were done the family would go in to see her. He said that if I wanted to go see her, to wait there until they were finished. I agreed. Kent, Lucy, and Ryan looked upset that I was there, so I didn't hug anyone else.

Finally, Todd told me I could go in now. I took Cole's wife by the hand to go with me. As soon as I touched Todd's mom's arm, as if to say *hello* to her, it felt like she was there. She was refusing to go on to the next life and told me she wanted to come back.

I saw her eyelash flicker, and reminded myself they say that it's just a nerve, but I wasn't so sure. I felt her struggling to come back, and she was desperate. We had a full mental telepathic conversation right then and there. I told her to go. She'd had a wonderful death and she didn't need to be afraid. She refused. I told her she'd fallen and broken her hip, and then had a massive heart attack. There was nothing here for her but pain. She kept refusing. I told her to go find her husband, her siblings, her parents, someone must be there waiting for her.

It was no use, she was determined. She wanted me to help her come back.

Nobody else knew about this debate going on between us. Todd's oldest sister, and a brother and his wife sat on the other side of her bed. I looked up at them, and his sister said she didn't know why we were all so upset. Mom was having a good time with Dad right now.

I said she was right, knowing she wasn't, and knowing she couldn't deal with what was going on in this moment. If I would've told them, they would've thrown me out of there. I pulled my hand off her arm to end that conversation and get out of there as fast as I could.

I went to her viewing and the funeral. At the funeral, I sobbed as I looked at her twelve kids sitting in the front rows. I sat in the back with Ty. I felt overwhelming gratitude, because even though "Mommy" and "Pappy" had twelve kids, they had enough love in their hearts left over for me. I was filled with appreciation for the love they gave me.

After that, Todd's mother started appearing at the foot of my bed. I got up one night and told her to come in the living room and tell me what she had to say, and I would write it down in my Bible.

As I held the pen to listen, I knew Pappy was with her. She was doing the communicating, though. They stood close in front of me as I sat in my recliner, pen in hand, ready to write in blank pages in the back of my bible. They showed me a vison—this seems to be how things are communicated on the other side for me.

They showed me an afternoon many years ago, a memory that I had forgotten. It was before we moved from our trailer, and I had walked down to visit them. She was doing dishes and he was standing in front of the phone on the wall, looking very serious.

Pappy said, "You are our Loretta." I was stunned. Loretta was their stillborn daughter. I believe she died a few months after I was born. "You look like you could be one of our kids," Pappy said. "We love you like a daughter. Me and Mommy talked about it, and you are our Loretta."

I looked at Todd's mom standing at the kitchen sink doing dishes to see what she had to say about all of this. Pappy asked her. She nodded and said, "Yes," very seriously. I knew he wasn't drunk and I knew she wasn't off her medication. These two didn't always agree on everything, but I saw they did on this.

I scoffed at them and walked out the door. I thought they were nuts. How was I a dead girl? They weren't saying I replaced her, they said I was her.

Now here I was, remembering this for the first time in twenty-five years. I was in my living room at night, and they have reminded me of this by showing me this vision, this memory.

As crazy as this was, it made perfect sense that a vision of the past would be used now instead of words to explain a concept to me. I didn't put all of that together then, but I do now. It took years for me to finally get it. I wasted so much time denying the existence of miracles in my life. On the other side, visions of the past and future can be used to help us understand.

Todd's mom appeared to me another day. I couldn't see her, but I felt her beside me in the hall outside my bedroom. I told her if she was real to appear, because this popping in and out was making me crazy. I said, "If you are real, go to my closet. I will open the door, and if you're not there, I'll know I'm crazy."

I went to the closet and took a deep breath, sure there would be nothing there and I could put this all to rest. I swung open the door and said, "See? There is nothing there!"

Then I saw it.

There was a deep purple tube of light about three feet tall hovering in front of my mirror in my closet! It rolled up and down like a lava lamp. I screamed and slammed the door, then jumped on top of my bed, freaking out. I thought I was ready, but I was far from ready. I was ready to prove myself crazy, not to prove that she was communicating with me this way.

Later, in our camper, I felt she wanted me to tell her kids about our communication so they would know they were watching over the kids. I refused. I was not that crazy. I knew they would rip me to shreds.

After Cole was married, he had some health concerns. He had surgery to determine the cause. The doctor told us he had cancer. Cole didn't believe it, and neither did I. A few days later it sunk in, so I prayed hard. This could not be.

The next day while at church, a friend approached me and said she'd heard the news and asked if it were true. She said she was asking the church to pray for him, so I thanked her. Our priest then approached me, saying he noticed Cole was on the prayer list. I explained the situation. He was heartsick because he knew Cole and his wife well. They had completed the classes needed to marry in his church.

Cole was sent to Cleveland Clinic to have surgery. His wife and her family took him, and we joined them there. After Cole was examined in Cleveland, we were told there was no sign of cancer, and no need to do the surgery. Later, our priest approached me again in church and said he'd heard the news. With a big-hearted smile, he said, "That is a miracle."

"I know," I answered. What do you do with a miracle? Life just goes on like nothing happened. There isn't a newspaper or TV show, or book somewhere to list them in. It seems wrong to dismiss such wonderful gifts. It was out of character for our priest to say something like that. Our kids and I had helped him out a lot with dinners, grounds upkeep and Summer Bible Camp. He was pretty down to earth.

The anxiety slowly got better, but the PTSD seemed like it would be with me like an extra limb.

We traveled in our camper to many campgrounds and many towns. I kept mostly to myself while Jim was at work. I didn't get into socializing at campground very much. For a while, I kept myself busy sewing. I liked to make stuffed toys for our grandchildren. Finally, I got the hint that they had too many stuffed toys. Baking soon got old too, besides lack of exercise due to living in a camper was furthering my over- weight issue.

One day, I started writing my memories. I hoped I could trap the bad memories inside the pages. Then, I would trap them away in a drawer, and it would leave my mind forever. I wrote it all down as fast as I could. It took all day, and it filled several notebooks. I was exhausted when I finished and went to bed. As I fell asleep, I felt satisfied it was all out of me, and I would feel relieved of it all in the morning. PTSD was not going to own me anymore.

When I woke up the next day, I felt just as bad. I still had a heavy heart. I looked over at the notebooks on the shelf, and wondered what to do with them. I knew nobody would want to read these horrible stories of abuse, neglect, and despair. Besides, no one believed my stories. No one believed I was really abused. No one believed my stepfather, mother and siblings did those things. The rumor was that I was a crazy, lying, lazy, child-abusing whore. The people who did those things knew it was all true, but it was "in the past." I was supposed to forget about it all. Everyone was sick of hearing it. I was sick of telling it. Yet, none of it would stop playing through my mind like a broken record. I was annoying everyone with my "stories," including myself.

So, I gave in. I surrendered to my PTSD. I knew it now owned me. I accepted this would be my life now. I gave up.

I picked up the notebooks, telling them they'd won, and curled up on the couch and started to read what I had written the day before. I surrendered to its power. PTSD won. They all won. As I started to read, I was sad and felt helpless. I was sick that this was my life. I was the loser in every fight I had fought, and I fought hard and long. Inside, I waved the white flag of surrender. Knowing there is no such thing as justice.

As I read along, blah blah blah, I started to sit up, I felt confused. Something was happening. I started processing what I had written. I questioned it. I knew it was all true, but I wondered *how* it could be true. Not the abuse or neglect, or being unloved and mistreated, but how was all the other stuff, the good stuff, true. An angel? A wildflower? Feeling like I was about to sit on Jesus' lap? A ghost crawling out of my side? Seeing ghosts by my bed?

I had been so focused on the bad, I had overlooked the spiritual. I had pushed the past away my whole life, not realizing that I had swept the good under the rug as well.

Now the spiritual events were glowing and the bad was dimming. I was astonished that I had spent my whole life avoiding the good as well as the bad.

My life had been all about pushing things away, not on enjoying a memory or processing it. I always told my stories in a flat tone, like reading a grocery list. It was like I was in a dark lonely forest, wading through a disgusting, slimy swamp, but now I was finding bits of light along the way. I actually saw that image in my imagination. The vision of it was alive and real and I gained insight inside it.

Before I knew it, my world became magical. I paced the floor, laughing, crying and praying. I took a deep breath and saw my life in a new way. I spent the next several months praying, praising God and researching Near Death Experiences, After Effects, Spiritual Experiences, and After Death Communication and Shared Near

Death Experiences. I learned I was not crazy. I learned I was not alone. Other people had similar experiences. I let go, and found myself.

Every time I had a question, the information seemed to present itself. I now understood how kids are changed after a NDE, even though they can't process any of it. They have gifts they don't know they have until they use them. I realized when I drowned, I brought it all back with me. This explained my entire life. The ways of the other side—feeling conversations, leaving the body, seeing spirits, communicating with spirits, having a high moral compass with an ability to follow where it led, having insight. It all came back with me. That was why I was so good at investigations—so good, in fact, I was too good. I ended up discovering corruption everywhere I went. I couldn't turn it off.

Once the line is crossed, the line isn't there anymore. Once you've been to Heaven, earth is never the same. Once we lose the fear of stigma, miracles await. The more I tell about my NDE, the light and energy grows, sometimes to the point others feel it too.

In 2011, I searched the internet for anything I could find about Near Death Experiences. I came across a website that asked for story submissions. I was so excited. I pounded my story into the laptop while I sat on the floor. I didn't even proofread it. I couldn't wait to click the submit button. I was so excited to find a place to finally tell it.

Later on, I found the website again, and was thrilled to see my story was placed in the "Exceptional NDE" section. Later, while we were at the laundromat in Wheeling, I got an email from the webmaster, asking if she could include my NDE in her book. I was overjoyed. Now that I was finally opening up and allowing me to be me, the world was opening up to me. I found out there was a support group for people with NDEs two hours from my home, but I was too shy to attend. Finally, after months of stressing over it, I contacted the coordinator. She invited me to come and tell the group about my NDEs at the following meeting.

I went to the group and heard a speaker tell his NDE in preparation for telling mine at the following meeting. I felt so energized by this group, I couldn't wait to give my talk. Finally, when it was my turn two months later, my shyness and reservations were replaced with full throttle anticipation. I couldn't stop thinking about sobbing on Heaven's floor, asking, "Who else will teach them about you?" This was my chance to pay God and Jesus back for allowing me to return to raise my sons.

I started out by talking about the drowning. As I gazed in the circle of chairs around the room, the floor at their feet became the pond. As I told them about hovering over the pond, I was hovering in the room. As I told about the twins and going through the tunnel, then suspended in the bright white light, I was suspended in the bright white light again!

After I was done, I could hardly answer questions. I feared negativity would steal this from me. I just wanted to hold onto it as long as I could. I remember a lady saying my story touched everyone there in a way meant for just them. People were in line to hug me— they wanted to touch the light. Everyone could feel the light in the room too.

We had to go to Walmart afterwards to pick up a bike for our granddaughter's birthday party. I could hardly feel my feet on the ground—I was still walking on air. I felt the glow all day. I was high from the light and reliving the spiritual experiences. It was so much better than having PTSD! I couldn't believe I'd hid this from myself all these years!

Later, at a party one night, standing near a bonfire, I started telling people about my NDEs. As we walked back to the house, I felt spirits walking with us. As we went in the kitchen, I noticed the room glowed of white light. As we sat in the kitchen around the table, the light stayed as we continued sharing spiritual experiences. I never told anyone what I felt, but months later someone described what they felt and saw that night, and it was exactly as I experienced it. It should've been me talking, not them, because it was identical to what I had seen and felt. It once again confirmed the reality of these events.

People are often closed to these experiences. I was too, and they happened to me. Once we open up, we're drawn in. Sometimes I feel it so strongly, I feel like I'm levitating. It builds and grows, and I'm walking on air again.

Christian music has the same effect on me too. The more I allow the energy to flow through me, insights come and I channel something beautiful into the world.

I keep processing more all the time. You can tell an event without feeling it or understanding it. But when it all comes together and you allow yourself to experience it, you can see the magic of God so clearly. It is overwhelming joy.

For example, being in two places at once occurred during my NDEs—while being raped, when Cole was drowning, and in Sunday school when I was coloring, wishing I was with Jesus. It also happened when I recalled getting in trouble when I was five for knocking on the bathroom door.

During the summer of 2016, I started writing this book. I had written it for my grandkids, thinking my kids could give it to them after I was gone. I feared I would die before they were old enough for me to tell them about my horrible/wonderful life. I wanted the truth to be known. I wanted my family to know I wasn't making up stories. I wanted this to be left behind for generations to come. I wanted the truth to get out.

I wished I could send it to social work departments all over the country. After Michigan happened, I said I would never stop trying to find justice for my family. If they could do this to me, they could do it to anyone. We tell kids to keep telling until someone listens. We have to do the same.

When I turned eighteen, I swore I would never forget the abuse, and, somehow, I would help abused kids. I wanted to keep those promises. But now, what fueled me to continue writing was not the horrible, it was the wonderful. I don't think I could tell one without telling the other. I don't think anyone could understand one without the other. This all has happened for a reason. I feel God wouldn't allow it otherwise.

The morning I finished this book, Jim was rained out. I was excited because we were finally headed to the library to print out a hard copy. Suddenly, a sunbeam shined right on my book. We joked that God was showing His approval of my effort. For some strange reason, I took pictures of the sunbeam. I think I wanted to believe it was a sign. If that is crazy, so what. I will be as crazy as I want. Reality is overrated.

A few days later, I was looking at my pictures on my cell phone, and noticed there was an image of a wildflower around the sunbeam. Coincidence? How did that happen? Maybe cell phones always make a picture of a flower when you take a picture of a sunbeam, I don't know. I'd never tried it before. But I am accepting it as a wonderful gift, like a beautiful rainbow after a horrible storm.

I choose to see the magic in life now, and I don't bother with dwelling on the bad. Yes, I would love to see justice, I admit, but my life is about spirituality now. I received confirmation today that I was chosen to be a speaker at the 2017 International Association of Near Death Studies Conference in Colorado. After so much goes wrong for so long, it is so refreshing when everything starts to go right.

One morning I woke up, got on Facebook, and before I knew it, I was writing poems about my NDEs. I wrote them all in one sitting, like it wasn't coming from me, but it felt like it was coming from somewhere else. When the last one was done, it was over. The poems helped me process my NDEs at a rapid rate. They flowed out of me. I couldn't have described my experiences any better.

When I first got to Heaven, I hovered there alone in the bright white light. I knew earth was way down below, and I thought I was gone from earth forever. I knew people were still down there, moving around and living their lives. I felt I hadn't made much of an impact. I felt nobody would remember I was ever there, except for my boys. They would miss me terribly, and then I would become a distant memory.

As I get older, I recall that, and think I want to leave something behind to say I was here. This is what happened to me, and maybe someone can learn from my mistakes. Maybe someone can benefit from things that happened to me somehow. If I learned one important thing to pass on, it would be, know yourself, and never let anyone tell you who you are. Never let anyone steal your identity with labels, name-calling or abuse, and if a miracle happens, embrace it, shout it out and let people know God is here!

My mother is about to turn 83 and can barely walk now. She recently called and told me she saw a glimpse of her deceased parents and oldest brother in her kitchen. Wondering if this meant she was nearing death, I tenderly told her there was one thing that I wanted from her before she went. I needed to know if she had any regrets about the way she treated me.

She paused, then carefully said, "No. I know that isn't the answer you want to hear."

I said, "It's your honest answer. That's what I needed to know."

I asked her why she and Don hated me so much. She said she didn't hate me. She said someday maybe my kids will blame me for things I did. I asked her if she realized I had PTSD from my childhood. She said her mother used a switch on her. I then asked if she grew up believing her parents loved her. She immediately said yes, she knew her mom and dad both loved her. I said I never did.

I sat alone in the silence. The silence was my answer. I accepted she did not love me. Those three words—"I love you"—will never come from my mother. I closed my eyes and felt the familiar pain, and swallowed it once again. One last time, before telling it goodbye. At least I knew now I would never have love from her. I felt some comfort in that, at least. I had closure.

I then asked her very calmly, trying to understand, why did she and Don treat me the way they had? She said it was because I ran away, and Don hated black people. I then told her how I let them believe what they wanted, and told her the story once again, about how I was kidnapped and raped. I also recapped how Jerry and Joel tried to rape me at Tonya's before that. The phone was once again silent. No compassion. Nothing was there for me, as usual. I still wanted it. I still hoped for it. The silence filled the phone like a black void in my soul. A void that would forever remain a void.

I have waited my whole life to hear that she was sorry and to ask for my forgiveness, because I have it right here waiting to give. This wasn't the ending I wanted.

Months ago, I told her I thought it was odd that I never felt pain when Don and Jack hit me in the head, during or afterwards. She laughed and said, "Oh, you didn't?" There was a cruelty in her voice, like she had hoped I'd felt pain. She knows I am writing my memoir, and has made nasty comments like, "I will look for it in the fiction section" and "Even if it's published, it will never be a best seller." She also said, "I bet I sound like mother of the year."

So, this is my story. This is what happened during my life, the good that nobody believes, and the bad that nobody believes. I have come to believe if it wasn't for the Will of a Wildflower, I would not be here to tell it. I could spend eternity wondering why so much happened to me, and the only answer that comes is so I could write this book. God must have a reason for it beyond my understanding. I am just a messenger. The message each one reading it receives is up to them.

For me, writing this book has been the most rewarding part of my life. It helped me separate the light from the dark. I choose to stay in the light now. The light is amazing, full of love, miracles, and grace. My PTSD is still there, hiding somewhere in the shadows. It's in that dark forest, underneath the dry cracked mud, sticks, rotted logs and leaves. I have pushed my way out from it, sprouted and bloomed. I am dancing in the light now, feeling the warm breeze, and rejoicing because I made it. I have a strength inside of me that no one will ever take away again. No matter what happens, I will be fine, because I was given The Will of a Wildflower.

The Will of the Wildflower Poems

THE POND

I shouldn't have gone out to the deep
I'm sinking, but no one can hear a peep
Screaming under water does no good
It's too late to do what I know I should
The pain in my throat is more than I can bare
I can't get up to get some air
I have to stop and think what to do
I need to stop and stew
Suddenly I am fine, it is all right
I was splashing and putting up a fight
The water is shiny green now, and full of light.
The fish are bumping into me—what a beautiful sight
I know I've died, up, up I go
To the top of the trees as I look down below
I can see so far away
I don't think this is where I want to stay
There must be a lot to do, I bet
Then someone says, "Don't go yet."
I listen intently, but her voice is all I hear
I don't see her, but I know she is near
"If they find you soon, you might go back."
I don't see how—her wisdom I lack
Before I can decide which way to go
I am hanging over his shoulder with my head hanging low
Water pours from my mouth and out my nose
I am as sick as a dog but off he goes

The Will of a Wildflower

He runs in the house and leaves me alone
I want to go back. My life is my own
I can do what I want, and I want to do that
I was about to fly and never come back
I hear her voice again, but I see her now too
She tells me, "Someday love will be there for you"
I make her promise before she goes
I head on home and go to bed
If anyone was glad I was okay, they never said.

THE WILL OF A WILDFLOWER

Can a wildflower talk?
Because it did one day when I went for a walk.
I was just a poor plain little child
Alone, until I saw it growing wild.
It grew out from under a rock in a dry ugly place
It's joy and beauty I couldn't erase.
It danced and clapped with the wind
Somehow that flower became my friend.
It didn't speak or shout
But somehow it let me know what life is all about.
It held a secret that helped it grow
If I listened quietly it would let me know.
It showed me a vision, that's what it did
Of women discussing flowers that grow bright and big.
Then I saw girls in ribbons and bows
They were loved and given a lot of clothes.
Those girls were like the big fancy flowers
All dolled up and needing showered.
But they weren't like this wildflower, you see
It had a strong will just to be free.
I thanked the flower as I went on my way
Yet it had one more insight to say.
Someday too I would dance in the wind,
Gifts of beauty and strength God will send.
Neither riches nor pampered would my fortune be
But the will of a Wildflower grows inside of me.

CATCHING A RIDE

All I wanted was to escape the abuse
I tried to be good but it was no use.
He said he would take me to my dad's
But he won't let me out, and he's making me mad.
I try to get away but he wants a date
I need to get to Dad's—I can't go late.
He takes me out in the woods and to a shed
I crawl up against the wall in a tiny bed.
I have a skill that blocks out the pain
I try to use it now but it ain't the same.
I prayed so hard and so tight
I find myself in the sky in the middle of the night.
I float among the twinkling stars in the deep black sky
I feel so good I don't care why.
I know I am safe and was able to escape
He thinks he won and got his date.
I look down at earth and what a view
So weightless, and so blue.
The wind blows my hair all around
Nothing but me in space, not a sound.
Then I am back and he doesn't know
He thinks I was here, he didn't see me go.
Was it a wish or a trick, how can it be?
I avoided it all, it couldn't touch me.
Unaffected, so easy it was to leave after all.
God heard my cries and he didn't stall.

I prayed and God came and lifted His cup
High above the world so I wouldn't give up.
How do I repay Him, I'm not sure I can
All I can do is love Him with all that I am.

MY HILL

I walked through the woods
Alone but not afraid
The world was dark
I thought what a mess I have made.
Troubles followed me
Wherever I went
God seemed so far away
So, this is the prayer I sent.
God, help me, I'm just a teen
I just want to be loved
Why is everyone so mean?
What can I do?
I never know what to say
God, I just wish you
Weren't so far away.
I love you, and I need you
I am so lost and alone
Things haven't been good
Inside of my home.
I will be eighteen soon,
I will have no help
God Almighty,
I prayed as I knelt.
Please help me know what to do
The world is about to get scary
And new.

My Hill

Help me make a plan
For my future, you see
I am so scared
I am down on my knees.
I got up and along
A path I walked
I saw a hill
I climbed it and talked.
God, here I am
with pain in my heart
This is as close as I can get,
But we are still far apart.
A warm wind blew my hair all around
Everything got quiet
There was not even a sound.
His voice didn't speak
But somehow I knew
He was right beside me saying "I love you."
Hope filled my doubts
And security replaced my fears
It was nearly forty years ago,
But that love
Doesn't change with years.
God was right by my side
And I have never been alone
I only thought I was
Because of the hate in my home.

THE TWINS

The pain is starting to fade.
I think I AM going to be sick.
I can't seem to move my hands.
My head drops to my chest.
I AM about to pass out.
I AM shooting up to space.
I AM traveling so far away.
I AM so sorry, my children, I don't want to leave you.
I AM afraid, I know there's no turning back.
I AM in Heaven, I think I AM alone.
I AM still me, but I can't see me.
I AM seeing someone, who are they?
I know who you are, sitting up front and center.
I won't go.
You can't make me. I have kids to raise.
I AM not the boss here, I must humble myself before you.
If they will be better off, I will stay;
If not, I beg you to return.
I see now, it's not your fault that
I AM here

It's all mine.
Deep sorrow overwhelms me.
"Who else will teach them about you?"
I AM back. I feel my hands. I feel my body, then my feet.
I hear the nurse speak.
"What the hell was that?" I ask.
How can it be?
I was dead.
Now I AM me.

www.ingramcontent.com/pod-product-compliance
Lightning Source LLC
Chambersburg PA
CBHW031242090426
42742CB00007B/279